Lecture Notes in Business Information Processing 240

More information about this series at http://www.springer.com/series/7911

Andrey Maglyas · Anna-Lena Lamprecht (Eds.)

Software Business

7th International Conference, ICSOB 2016
Ljubljana, Slovenia, June 13–14, 2016
Proceedings

Springer

Editors
Andrey Maglyas
Lappeenranta University of Technology
Lappeenranta
Finland

Anna-Lena Lamprecht
University of Limerick
Lero-The Irish Software Research Centre
Limerick
Ireland

ISSN 1865-1348 ISSN 1865-1356 (electronic)
Lecture Notes in Business Information Processing
ISBN 978-3-319-40514-8 ISBN 978-3-319-40515-5 (eBook)
DOI 10.1007/978-3-319-40515-5

Library of Congress Control Number: 2016940883

Printed on acid-free paper

This Springer imprint is published by Springer Nature
The registered company is Springer International Publishing AG Switzerland

Preface

Welcome to the proceedings of the 7th International Conference on Software Business (ICSOB)!

The ICSOB conference is intended for researchers and practitioners who are involved in software business in different ways, including large organizations and start-ups with a focus on different types of software products and services. This year, we selected as the conference theme "Software as a New Way of Providing Cutting-Edge Solutions" to focus on the innovative solutions that we see around us and that are attempting to engage in our life. Advancements in the software industry have had a substantial impact on productivity and GDP growth globally. There is a noticeable spillover within other industries (e.g., manufacturing) enabling new business models. Software business refers to commercial activities in and around the software industry aimed at generating income from the delivery of software products and services.

Although the business of software shares common features with other international knowledge-intensive businesses, it carries many inherent features. It is making it a challenging domain for research. The examples of many successful companies show that software provides unique benefit to its users. Moreover, software has spread all over the world and has permeated in many industries, which are not usual for software. In particular, software companies have to depend on one another to deliver a unique value proposition to their customers or a unique experience to their users.

Cross-functional use of software is a challenge for industry and academia, studying not only the use of software but also software business, software production, and other surrounding themes. This year the conference attracted practitioners and researchers who are concerned with software business in different ways as well as its introduction to new areas of research and practice.

For this 7th International Conference on Software Business, we received 38 research paper submissions from all over the world. The papers went through a thorough review process by at least two, typically three, knowledgeable reviewers for each paper. The Program Committee deliberated over all the reviews and accepted 10 full and five short submissions, yielding an acceptance rate of less than 40 %. The accepted papers follow various methodologies and represent the diversity in our research community. The papers span a wide range of issues related to contemporary software business – from strategic aspects to operational challenges. The strong presence of software ecosystem papers confirms the importance of this topic and its influence on software business.

This year the 7th International Conference on Software Business was co-located with the 28th International Conference on Advanced Information System Engineering (CAiSE). We extend our heartfelt thanks to everyone from the CAiSE Organizing Committee and Marko Bajec, the general chair.

April 2016

Andrey Maglyas
Anna-Lena Lamprecht

Organization

Program Chairs

Andrey Maglyas	Lappeenranta University of Technology, Finland
Anna-Lena Lamprecht	University of Limerick & Lero, Ireland and University of Potsdam, Germany

Program Committee

Sergey Avdoshin	National Research University Higher School of Economics, Russia
Jan Bosch	Chalmers University of Technology, Sweden
Sjaak Brinkkemper	Utrecht University, The Netherlands
David Callele	University of Saskatchewan, Canada
João M. Fernandes	University of Minho, Portugal
Samuel A. Fricker	University of Applied Sciences and Arts Northwestern Switzerland FHNW, Switzerland
Thomas Hess	Munich School of Management, Germany
Georg Herzwurm	University of Stuttgart, Germany
Slinger Jansen	Utrecht University, The Netherlands
Thomas Kude	University of Mannheim, Germany
Stig Larsson	Effectve Change AB, Sweden
Casper Lassenius	Aalto University, Finland
Ulrike Lechner	Universität der Bundeswehr München, Germany
Ricardo J. Machado	Universidade do Minho, Portugal
Konstantinos Manikas	University of Copenhagen, Denmark
John McFregor	Clemson University, USA
Rory O'Connor	Dublin City University, Ireland
Efi Papatheocharous	SICS, Sweden
Samuli Pekkola	Tampere University of Technology, Finland
Wolfram Pietsch	Aachen University of Applied Sciences, Germany
Karl Michael Popp	SAP AG, Germany
Björn Regnell	Lund University, Sweden
Dirk Riehle	Friedrich-Alexander University of Erlangen-Nürnberg, Germany
Matti Rossi	Aalto University, Finland
Kari Smolander	Aalto University, Finland
Richard Berntsson Sventsson	Blekinge Institute of Technology, Sweden
Tobias Tauterat	University of Stuttgart, Germany

Pasi Tyrväinen	University of Jyväskylä, Finland
Krzysztof Wnuk	Blekinge Institute of Technology, Sweden

Steering Committee

Jan Bosch	Chalmers University of Technology, Sweden
Sjaak Brinkkemper	Utrecht University, The Netherlands
João M. Fernandes	University of Minho, Portugal
Georg Herzwurm	University of Stuttgart, Germany
Slinger Jansen	Utrecht University, The Netherlands (chair)
Casper Lassenius	Aalto University, Finland
Eetu Luoma	University of Jyväskylä, Finland (chair)
Ricardo J. Machado	University of Minho, Portugal
Tiziana Margaria	University of Limerick & Lero, Ireland
Björn Regnell	Lund University, Sweden
Kari Smolander	Aalto University, Finland
Pasi Tyrväinen	University of Jyväskylä, Finland
Krzysztof Wnuk	Blekinge Institute of Technology, Sweden

Software Product Categories in the Automotive Industry and How to Manage Them (Keynote)

[1] Peter Lick and [2] Hans-Bernd Kittlaus

[1] AVL List GmbH
Hans-List-Platz 1, 8020 Graz, Austria
peter.lick@avl.com
[2] InnoTivum Consulting
Im Sand 86, 53619 Rheinbreitbach, Germany
hbk@innotivum.com

Abstract. AVL List GmbH is the world market leader for powertrain development and test systems in the automotive industry. Software plays an ever more important role in this industry, not only as the backbone of manufacturing and administration, but increasingly as the main driver of customer value creation. Important categories are embedded software, pure standalone software products, or software products with a tight hardware-software system integration. In this talk we look at these categories in more detail, and analyze the consequences for product management.

Keywords: Software product management • Software product categories • Automotive industry

Peter Lick is the process and skills manager for product management at AVL List GmbH. He has been reporting to the executive vice presidents of AVL since 2007. Before that, Peter worked for several years as a product manager for process software and testing software. Peter's professional experiences are in the field of portfolio and innovation management, marketing, product and process management, and he also managed software development cooperations and software projects. Peter holds an academic degree in electrical engineering and automation from the Technical University of Graz and additional degrees in coaching, marketing and management.

Hans-Bernd Kittlaus is the owner and CEO of InnoTivum Consulting (www.innotivum.com) which he founded in 2001. Before he was Director of SIZ GmbH (Computing Center of the German Savings Banks Organization, Germany) and Head of Software Product Management and Development units of IBM. His main focus area is software product management. Hans-Bernd has been working as a trainer, coach and consultant for both corporate IT organizations and companies in the IT industry. He has published numerous books and articles, his latest being "Software Product Management and Pricing" [1]. He is Diplom-Informatiker (corresponds to M.S. in Computer Science) and certified as ISPMA Certified Software Product Manager, Certified Scrum

Product Owner (CSPO), and PRINCE2 Practitioner. He is a member of ACM (Association for Computing Machinery, USA), GI (Gesellschaft für Informatik, Germany) and board member of ISPMA (International Software Product Management Association).

Reference

1. Kittlaus, H.-B., Clough, P.N. (eds.): Software Product Management and Pricing. In: Key Success Factors for Software Organizations. Springer, Heidelberg (2009)

Contents

Supporting Strategic Decision-Making for Selection of Software Assets

Claes Wohlin[1], Krzysztof Wnuk[1(✉)], Darja Smite[1], Ulrik Franke[2], Deepika Badampudi[1], and Antonio Cicchetti[3]

[1] Blekinge Institute of Technology, 371 79 Karlskrona, Sweden
{claes.wohlin, krzysztof.wnuk, darja.smite, deepika.badampudi}@bth.se

[2] Swedish Institute of Computer Science (SICS), Box 1263, 164 29 Kista, Sweden
ulrik.franke@sics.se

[3] Mälardalen University, Box 883, 721 23 Västerås, Sweden
antonio.cicchetti@mdh.se

Abstract. Companies developing software are constantly striving to gain or keep their competitive advantage on the market. To do so, they should balance what to develop themselves and what to get from elsewhere, which may be software components or software services. These strategic decisions need to be aligned with business objectives and the capabilities and constraints of possible options. These sourcing options include: in-house, COTS, open source and outsourcing. The objective of this paper is to present an approach to support decision-makers in selecting appropriate types of origins in a specific case that maximizes the benefits of the selected business strategy. The approach consists of three descriptive models, as well as a decision process and a knowledge repository. The three models are a decision model that comprises three cornerstones (stakeholders, origins and criteria) and is based on a taxonomy for formulating decision models in this context, and two supporting models (property models and context models).

Keywords: Component-based software engineering · Service-oriented software engineering · Decision-making

1 Introduction

In the advent of software development, companies developed their own operating systems using proprietary programming languages and compilers (e.g. AXE10 developed by Ericsson). Later, companies moved away from this approach to focus their software development efforts on their core business (e.g. telecommunication systems and features). This maturing software business has spawned two significant trends: specialization and commoditization [11]. Specialization became a direct result of commoditization as companies discovered that to stay competitive they needed to specialize and optimize the costs of developing the commodity parts of their products. At the same time, the increasing popularity of Open Source Software (OSS) accelerated

A. Maglyas and A.-L. Lamprecht (Eds.): ICSOB 2016, LNBIP 240, pp. 1–15, 2016.
DOI: 10.1007/978-3-319-40515-5_1

the commoditization process and forced many software companies to look for alternative or multiple revenue streams and new sources of novelty and value. As a result, the primary focus is now on developing software that provides a competitive advantage (e.g. killer apps).

Thus, it is very important for companies to decide what to develop themselves and what to get from elsewhere. On the strategic (executive) level, the strategy of mergers and acquisitions becomes a relevant option of obtaining software and organizations that develop it [31]. However, acquisitions may not always be feasible or possible, e.g. for open source communities that may not be "for sale". Thus, decision-making efficiency also becomes critical for software components that can be realized using internal development resources (in-house), buying COTS, subcontracting or utilizing OSS software. Each of these four sourcing alternatives provides different benefits, consequences and impacts or shapes the business models. For example, obtaining OSS software is often related to joining and participating in a software ecosystem [16] that entails changes in ways of working and potential challenges. Moreover, the selection of one of the four strategies directs the company towards one of the four business model archetypes: creator, distributor, lessor and broker [26]. For many software companies, the time when they could only focus on being creators and thus solving technical challenges is history.

Component-based software engineering has been an important area of research for almost three decades [34, 35]. As a complement to components, the concept of service-oriented software engineering has emerged [14]. An attempt to bring the two paradigms closer and to use them in a complementary way has been presented in [6]. Here, we use the term "software asset" to denote any type of software, including components and services that can be used for achieving the business objective for a specific system, product or service being developed. Software assets may be divided into four main types when it comes to the source or origin of the asset (henceforth denoted asset origin): in-house, COTS, open source and outsourcing. Within each of these asset origins different assets may fulfill the identified needs, for example, several different COTS may provide the same functionality to the user. In-house refers to assets developed or reused internally within an organization. Thus, in-house includes software having been developed within the same organization, independent of location (e.g. sites in another country), subsidiaries or organizational structure (e.g. different business area). The other three types of asset origins are external, and hence outsourcing is here used as a sourcing option outside the organization that needs a software asset [32].

The key decision to make is what sourcing strategy is the most optimal for an asset. Should it be developed in-house or should we look elsewhere? To date, research has focused on comparing just a few of these asset origins, in particular, in-house versus COTS, and in-house versus outsourcing, and to the best of our knowledge no paper has addressed all four asset origins [2]. To be able to support these types of decisions in industry, a decision-making approach is outlined here that will form the basis for further research on the topic. The approach consists of three types of descriptive models: decision model, property model and context model, as well as a decision process and a knowledge repository. The main focus here is to look at decision-making between the four different types of asset origins (in-house, COTS, open source and outsourcing), although the models and process described in the paper are expected to be able to adapt to also selecting between different components or services of the same type of asset origin. We do not focus here on mergers or acquisitions as a sourcing strategy for software assets [31].

The remainder of the paper is outlined as follows. Section 2 presents related work from general decision-making theory, decision-making related to different asset origins, and a specific taxonomy intended to help formulating the three descriptive models for the purpose of making the types of decisions discussed in this paper. In Sect. 3, the proposed models are presented, and in particular their different parts are discussed. Section 4 introduces the concept of an evidence-based knowledge repository to support the decision-making process. A decision-making process outlining how the three descriptive models can be used is presented in Sect. 5. Section 6 provides a summary and pointers to further work.

2 Related Work

2.1 Decision-Making

Decision theory largely deals with actors making decisions (e.g. bring an umbrella or not) in the face of uncertain events (e.g. rainfall or not), leading to different outcomes (e.g. wet or dry) and pay-offs (e.g. dry and burdened by umbrella though there is no rain). There are many textbook introductions to the subject, e.g. [28], as well as extensive literature reviews on theories of decision-making under risk [33].

In the area of software engineering research, decision theory has been applied to diverse problems such as evaluating COTS [21], determining optimal intervals for testing and debugging [30], evaluating software designs [7] and assessing non-functional requirements [13]. Decision theory is also one of the cornerstones in the theory of value-based software engineering [4]. Empirical research includes studies on how people make decisions about service level agreements [11, 12].

The purpose of this paper is not to make a theoretical contribution to decision theory in software engineering and software business, but rather to *apply* it to a particular problem class: how to select an appropriate asset origin for a particular piece of software (component or service). In so doing, we use decision theory terminology and concepts to reason about the problem and present an approach that will make it possible to reuse previous experience and published results alike to make the best possible decision, given the knowledge available.

2.2 Deciding on Origin

The research related to selecting between different software asset origins is quite limited. In a recent systematic literature review [2], which is summarized here, no papers addressing all four types of asset origins were identified. However, some papers addressing two or in a few cases three origins were found.

The decision models for in-house vs. COTS are mainly based on optimization models. The optimization models proposed in [9, 10, 17, 18, 27, 34] help to decide which components should be developed in-house and which should be bought. Cost, delivery time, and reliability are the common objectives and constraints considered in all the proposed optimization models. The optimization models either consider single objective or multiple objectives in the decision model.

The objective in the optimization models proposed in [9, 10, 27, 34] is to minimize cost under reliability and delivery time constraints. The CODER framework proposed in [9] consists of a decision model based on optimization and accepts UML notations as an input. In [31, 34], the authors propose an architecture optimization approach based on a swarm intelligence algorithm. The CODER framework [9] is extended in [26, 27], allowing decision-making as early as requirements are available. Similarly, a general non-linear optimization model is proposed in [10] for the same objective and constraints i.e. minimizing cost under reliability and time constraints.

Multi-objective optimization models have been proposed in [17, 18]. A decision model for fault-tolerant systems is proposed in [15, 17] with two objectives – to maximize reliability and minimize cost under a time constraint. In addition, coupling and cohesion have been considered in the decision model proposed in [18]. The objectives in [18] are to maximize intra-modular coupling density and functionality under time, cost and reliability constraints.

Two papers focus on deciding between in-house and outsourcing [19, 20] were identified. The model in [19] provides tool support for requirements clustering to find a cohesive group of requirements using a graph-based model. In [20], the authors propose a decision model using decision tables. The input is the knowledge specificity (business, functional and technical), and interdependencies (priority between software components and communication intensity among developers).

2.3 GRADE Taxonomy

The work presented in this paper is grounded in the GRADE taxonomy [22, 24]. The GRADE taxonomy summarizes the relevant concepts and definitions for building models related to decision-making and supporting decision processes. On the highest level, the GRADE taxonomy combines five fundamental concepts of decision-making for software intensive systems: *Goals*, *Roles*, *Assets*, *Decision* and *Environment* (GRADE). These five fundamental concepts can be used as building blocks for creating models supporting decision-making.

Goals represent the starting point for a decision. They represent the internal business goals and customer goals, and have a broad impact on the entire product or even organization. The goals form an important input to the decision-making.

Roles in the GRADE taxonomy represent individuals involved in the decision-making. The roles are classified into types, functions, levels and perspectives.

The assets concept in the GRADE taxonomy describes the decision assets (often encapsulated in a software component or software service) characterized by: origin, attributes, type, usage and realization options.

The *decision* concept of GRADE contains the decision methods that can be used for estimating outcomes for a specific option among those evaluated in the decision-making process.

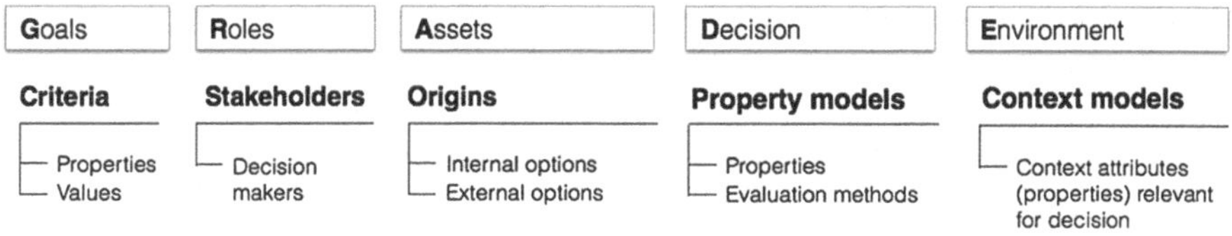

Fig. 1. Mapping of GRADE to concepts in the decision model and the supporting models.

The *environment* concept of the GRADE taxonomy describes the environment before the decision was analyzed or made. It includes the characteristics of organizations, products, stakeholders, markets and business prior to making a decision.

2.4 Decision-Making in Software Business

Running a software business requires making several decisions on multiple levels [1], ranging from strategic decisions about mergers, acquisition and take-overs [31], via tactical decisions on which ecosystem to join and support [16] to highly technical decisions on how to realize customer requirements in software. An increasing number of software companies evolve from the pure creator business archetype that implies code ownership but also development risk, high maintenance cost and full responsibility for delivering the required quality towards mixed or hybrid business models that imply taking on several business archetype roles [26]. At the same time, small and large companies take on outsourcing initiatives to reduce development costs and obtain valuable knowledge and inspiration. This shifts the center of gravity towards integration work and coordination of outsourced (often also offshored) sites into software products that deliver the value that customers expect. Finally, joining or creating an ecosystem entails a series of decisions regarding growing a healthy ecosystem [16], participating in ecosystem development and gaining importance and influence or disrupting markets by commoditization of ecosystem software. Each of the mentioned four asset origins thus has different implications both in the short term and in the long term. They come with different costs and prices and can bring different benefits. Decision-makers responsible for running their software businesses are faced with increased decision complexity and frequency that they need to cope with to succeed with their business endeavors. An example here is decision-making in cloud computing environments for selecting appropriate services from different providers [22].

3 Descriptive Models

Three descriptive models are built from the GRADE taxonomy to ensure that no decision-aspect is missed. Thus, the descriptive models become part of an instantiation of the taxonomy. The instantiation includes two main parts: description of the concepts based on GRADE (the three descriptive models) and the actual decision-making process.

The main objective of the decision approach presented is to enable a systematic way to select between different software asset origins, including potentially both software components and software services. The types considered represent four main asset origins: in-house, COTS, open source and outsourcing.

The three descriptive models correspond to the five fundamental concepts in GRADE, as described and mapped in Fig. 1. In particular, the five concepts comprise: (1) the three decision model cornerstones: stakeholders (roles), origins (assets) and criteria (goals); and (2) two supporting models – property models (decision) and context models (environment). The decision model with its three decision cornerstones are described in Sect. 3.1, the property models are discussed in Sect. 3.2 and the context models are further elaborated in Sect. 3.3.

In addition to experience of the involved stakeholders, it is beneficial to support the decision-making with related historical evidence and experiences. This can be captured in an evidence-based knowledge repository, which is elaborated in some more detail in Sect. 4.

3.1 Decision Model

The decision model consists of three main cornerstones:

Stakeholders – which stakeholders (and hence different perspectives) need to be involved? The stakeholders should be identified from the roles in GRADE that should be involved in the decision-making. The creator, distributor, lessor and broker business archetypes [26] help in identifying relevant stakeholders that influence the value creation and delivery processes. The current model involved both internal stakeholders as well as end customers and external stakeholders. As many software companies currently run hybrid business models with additional revenue streams originating from cross-selling and complementariness, the set of potential stakeholders is much broader than in the in-house scenario.

The stakeholders have different perspectives (as described through the *Roles* concept in GRADE) that should be taken into account in the decision-making process. This could be exemplified with the following five software engineering areas: (1) business and requirements engineering, (2) non-functional properties, (3) life-cycle perspective, (4) architecture, and (5) implementation and integration, including verification and validation. The business and requirements engineering perspective is responsible for capturing the customer value and translating it to the form that can be used for decision-making. Business analysts and requirements engineers play key roles in capturing and prioritizing customer needs. Other perspectives may also be relevant, for example the strategic management perspective.

Origins – which type of asset origins should be considered (in-house, open source, COTS and/or outsourcing)? In this case, the asset concept in GRADE is defined as potentially coming from four different asset origins. Thus, it is assumed that the main decision to be taken relates to where a software component or service needed in a product or system is developed, obtained or acquired. The actual choice of, for example, a specific COTS component is not considered, i.e. the selection between competing alternative assets of the same origin.

Criteria – which criteria should be evaluated to ensure an informed decision? The criteria are based on the *Goal* concept in GRADE. Since the goals may be quite general, some goals may not be relevant for a specific decision. It is important to acknowledge here that criteria can have at least three perspectives: customer perspective, internal-business perspective, and community (or ecosystem perspective). The goals and criteria should be identified and tagged by the relevant perspective and potential conflicts between perspectives should be identified and mitigated. The involved stakeholder roles should review the goals, mitigate potential conflicts and translate them into defined decision criteria to be used in the decision-making. Criteria should be more detailed than the goals and need to be measurable, i.e. contain a threshold for a certain property attribute (e.g. a specific attribute of software quality or gaining 1 000 000 users of a software service within 2 months after the service is launched). Thus, criteria should be possible to evaluate, for example, they could state that a certain property should be above a certain threshold, and each criterion should be evaluated for each viable asset origin. The chosen criteria should be evaluated, where business risk most likely is always one of the criteria. Risk is a criterion by itself in relation to a specific asset origin, e.g. the risk of a COTS supplier going bankrupt. However, risk is also related to the uncertainty in specific decisions, their criteria, and the data they are based on, e.g. uncertainty in historical cost or reliability figures.

The **stakeholders** contribute to the decision model as experts in their own area, for example, business, architecture or requirements. They are involved in evaluating possible asset **origins** viable for the specific case and formulating the **criteria** for the decision based on the goals. Furthermore, the experts provide input to the property models (see Sect. 3.2), they should describe the context of the decision (see Sect. 3.3) and they should help in identifying similar historical evidence and experiences using the evidence-based knowledge repository (see Sect. 4). The latter includes prioritizing among important factors to compare with historical evidence.

3.2 Property Model

The **decision** concept in GRADE includes both models to estimate specific properties and methods to, for example, weigh different criteria. The property models come into play in estimating outcomes of the criteria for different asset origins, i.e. there is a need to make the estimations wrt to different criteria for the relevant origins.

A property model is an estimation model with respect to a decision criterion. The property model consists of a well-defined property and an evaluation method. For example, the property can be the number of active users and the evaluation method can be to check how many of these users have used the service the last seven days. A property model may contain other property models. Examples of properties include coordination costs, IT service costs and maintenance costs for selecting cloud computing services [22]. The evaluation method may be quite simplistic, for example, expert opinion or based on a sophisticated formal mathematical decision model [1]. Property models can also be more advanced, e.g. for the reliability criterion using software reliability growth models (SRGM) based on historical data from similar situations. Furthermore, some evaluation methods use generic statistical methods such as regression analysis, while others are based on general methods but still are tailored for a specific purpose such as SRGMs. Properties can and should also be estimated for aspects relevant for communities, ecosystems and markets and not only for a company's internal or a project's internal aspects. A good example here could be the degree of influence on ecosystem members or the state of a company's reputation in a given ecosystem [16].

Property models provide estimates of values for the different criteria, and in most cases the property models only handle one or a few properties at the time. Thus, there is a need to decide the priorities of the different criteria and hence the weighing between them, for example is cost more or less important than security. The methods for managing the priorities between criteria, or for combining outcomes in different ways are referred to as decision methods. For this purpose, it would be possible to use, for example, methods such as AHP [29] and HCV [3].

As part of the decision-making, it should be decided, for example, whether the stakeholders should try to take different time perspectives into account "manually" or if the property models should instead be used more than once, for example, to make estimations both for a short-term and a long-term perspective.

3.3 Context Model

The context model is a representation of the environment in which the decision is taken. There are two main objectives of the context model. First, it helps in identifying relevant criteria, property models and solutions previously used by others. Second, it structures the decision at hand for future use in the evidence-based knowledge repository. An example of a context model representation is presented in [25]. It comprises six dimensions of the environment, four that capture the organizational characteristics (including practices and tools) and two that are external to the organization (business environment characteristics). The context model also extends the environment concept in GRADE as it helps to understand the context in the future and is integrated with the evidence-based knowledge repository described in Sect. 4.

The context model should capture the current situation within an organization with respect to (1) product before the decision, (2) people involved in relation to the decision, (3) processes as well as (4) practices, techniques and tools. Furthermore, (5) the organization as such should be captured, (6) the market should be described as a part of the context and other relevant aspects from the ecosystem that a company is involved in. We believe that for a comprehensive context description that includes business characteristics and can be effectively used for guiding business decisions, a possible future area of research is to expand the six dimensions described in [25] to better cover aspects such as the market, ecosystems and also business models.

4 Evidence-Based Knowledge Repository

Historical information should be structured so that it is possible to find relevant or similar cases, for example, similar context, prioritized similar criteria or an interest in the same asset origins. The stored information may facilitate decision-making, but also to provide what is generically known as traceability of a decision: what a decision was about, who made the decision, and why the decision was made. This is often referred to as the rationale for a decision. In this respect, any repository ought to record all relevant aspects of a decision-making scenario. Furthermore, a repository ought to contain other available information such as research articles on the topic, and in particular systematic literature reviews, as well as publically available data or data shared between trusted partners that can help support different steps of decision-making.

Former decision information can represent an important support in the decision-making process, at least to avoid errors made in the past. Therefore, if the repository was considered as a mere post-decision storage support, it is difficult to justify and motivate the effort of documenting decisions in detail. Furthermore, the repository would miss a lot of its potentials: (1) as mentioned before, recurring decisions might contain important lessons learned; and (2) multiple decisions could entail an agreement about a more general development vision (e.g., different properties derivable from the same goal by different stakeholders), thus requiring consistency. Thus, continuous and reliable data collection, as well as use of the data, should be performed to unlock the full potential that an evidence-based knowledge repository offers.

The repository should be able to smoothly manage large amounts of data and should offer meaningful mechanisms to retrieve decisions as filtered by their prominent characteristics (i.e., the cornerstones of the decision model), and pointers to relevant studies on the topic. Compatibility and interoperability are important quality attributes of a good decision knowledge repository and therefore we recommend using open data standards supported by reliable quality management measures, e.g. ISO/IEC 25012 SQuaRE [15], OGD eight principles [23] or Web Information Quality assessment [5].

5 Decision-Making Process

The decision-making process represents the actual conduct of decision-making, and it is illustrated in Fig. 2 using the numbering of the recommended steps below. Some steps may be perceived as more important than others. However, it has been chosen to present all steps as recommended steps, since the actual usefulness of the different steps and preferred order of the steps may vary from case to case. Thus, the order of the steps should be seen as one possible suitable order. Furthermore, an evidence-based knowledge repository may not be available in all cases, and hence those steps may not be applicable in all cases. It should also be noted that iterations are expected. They may appear between any steps depending on the specific decision, or the specific circumstances in relation to a decision. Thus, Fig. 2 only illustrates the expected iterations based on the evidence-based knowledge repository.

The recommended steps in the decision-making process are as follows:

(1) Identify stakeholders to be involved in the decision – It is important to ensure coverage of roles and persons to make sure that the decision made is possible to implement efficiently. Each stakeholder that is relevant for the decision and its consequences for the business should be identified here.

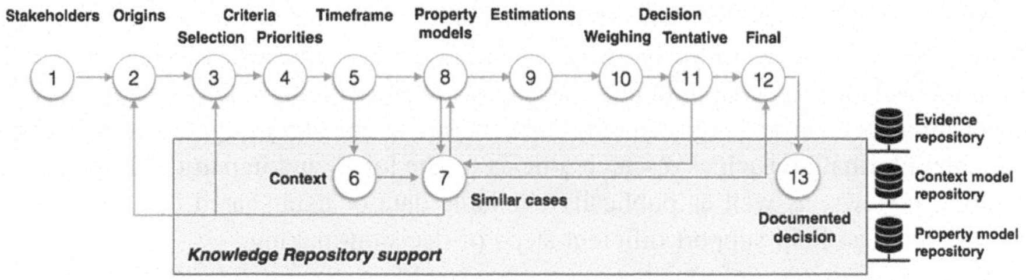

Fig. 2. The decision-making process including having a knowledge repository.

(2) Evaluate the suitability of the four asset origins – The possible origins for a software asset should be identified. This includes investigating the technical and business compatibilities and the short and long term costs of selecting each asset option. In certain cases, not all asset origins are allowed or suitable. In some cases, the main decision is whether to do development in-house or going externally. Sometimes, open source solutions are not an option. Thus, the possible asset origins need to be identified carefully.

(3) Decide criteria from goals – Based on the goals of the development, criteria (both business and technical) have to be decided and suitable targets have to be set. The latter should be done so that different asset origins can be evaluated and compared with each other. In most cases, risk needs to be considered as one criterion, since it may differ substantially for different asset origins (in-house, COTS, open source and outsourcing).

(4) Decide on priorities of criteria – In addition to deciding on targets for each criterion, it is also important to decide how they should be prioritized, e.g. using AHP [29] or HCV [3]. It may also be the case that certain stakeholders have more say in a decision, which has to be taken into account, i.e. different stakeholder roles may need to be weighed differently in the prioritization process.

(5) Decide on how to handle the time aspect – Certain solutions may be perceived better or worse in the short-term and long-term respectively. For example, a certain solution may be very good to get a product on the market, but it is not very good for the long-term architecture of the product. The time aspect is highly relevant for decisions that concern ecosystem participation or OSS involvement as in these two cases the competitive advantage created based on the ecosystem or OSS commodity layer comes with a long term maintenance cost. Thus, selective revealing should be considered and based on competitive advantage time estimates. The degree of commoditization or commoditization index should be projected onto the average sale time for new products. To cope with the time aspect, the decision-makers either have to take time aspects into account when prioritizing between different asset origins or evaluations have to be done separately for different time aspects, e.g. short-term and long-term, and the tradeoff between them has to be agreed upon.

(6) Describe the context – To enable comparison with previous cases internally and externally as well as with the research literature, the case has to be described. This should be done using the context model, where salient aspects have to be captured. This may include business model(s) used, application domain, system size and development method as well as a range of other aspects [25]. Independently, it is crucial to capture these aspects to enable identification of similar cases and hence relevant evidence and experiences.

(7) Look for similar cases in a knowledge repository – The identification of similar cases is done using the context model as well as the asset origins considered as suitable and the criteria. Thus, a similar case is defined as having some key aspects of the context in common (from Step 6) as well as a focus on similar criteria (from Steps 3 and 4) and similar suitable asset origins (Step 2). Similar cases are identified and studied to identify evidence and experience that are perceived important in the current case and to uncover potential alternative decision scenarios [8]. The knowledge repository could be solely based on internal cases or a more elaborate database containing both internal and external cases. The information in the knowledge repository may indicate that in other similar cases other asset origins, criteria, property models or decisions have been considered. Thus, it is important to be able to challenge the choices made in the other steps as illustrated in Fig. 2.

(8) Decide on property models to use – Once the criteria are decided, there is a need to decide how the criteria should be evaluated. If having a knowledge repository, this can be done by retrieving valuable information from the knowledge repository in terms of what others have used in similar cases (Step 7). If there is no knowledge repository, the property models for each criterion have to be decided without additional support, whether they are expert opinions or more advanced estimation models.

(9) Make estimations using the property models – Given the chosen property models, estimations need to be done for each criterion for the asset origins under consideration and potentially for different time aspects based on the approach decided in Step 5.

(10) Weigh the estimation results of the selected properties based on the priorities of criteria – Based on the priorities of the different criteria, the estimation results from the different property models should be weighed together. This is non-trivial given that the values as such cannot be combined easily in many cases. It is rather the estimation of each criterion and its distance from the targets that need to be weighed together.

(11) Make a tentative decision – Once the outcomes from the property models have been weighed together, it should be possible for the decision-makers to make a tentative decision. If a knowledge repository is available, it is recommended to browse previous decisions and review relevant tentative scenarios and compare the tentative decision with decisions from similar cases as described in Step 7. Relevant business context factors should be evaluated here based on similar cases. This should be done to make a final evaluation of the decision, and ensure that the reasoning done is as correct as possible and that no relevant available information is ignored.

(12) Make a final decision – This has been the objective of the decision-making process and hence it is a very important step for the development. It is important that the stakeholders are able to communicate both the actual decision and the rationale for the decision.

(13) Store the case in the knowledge repository – The case information, including the context model, the criteria used, the stakeholders involved and the asset origins considered should be carefully documented. This step is important as it allows for transparency if the case is properly documented (including the decision rationale) and helps to organically grow the evidence-base knowledge repository. It is important to add new cases given the speed of change and hence ensure that recent cases are available for decisions to come.

(14) At the end of the decision-making process, the objective is that the stakeholders should have come to either a consensus or at least that the involved stakeholders know why the decision was made, and are able to communicate it in the organization.

6 Summary and Further Work

The decision support models and process may seem complex, but they address a challenging area for companies. The development of today's software products, systems and services is a complex endeavor. The decisions of choosing software components (or services), whether being in-house development vs. external options such as COTS, open source and outsourcing, are most often strategic decisions and they heavily influence competitiveness. The approach presented in this paper provides a starting point for supporting such decisions and address the research gap identified in a recent systematic literature review [2].

The approach addresses several key questions to make a decision with respect to selecting the origin of software assets (components and services). However, before using the approach the actual decision needs (what) should be determined. The decision process as such illustrates ***how*** a decision may be made. Furthermore, ***who*** makes the decision is determined by the identification of the stakeholders. The main reasons for the decision, i.e. ***why*** a decision is made, are captured through the criteria in the decision model.

The focus of this work is on selecting between different types of asset origins, and not between different actual components or services of the same type. The objective is to integrate selection of competing specific alternatives into the models and process, including both the tradeoffs between components and services as well as between different components or services of the same asset origin. This is part of further work as well as to empirically evaluate the proposal through case studies.

The presented models and process is based on the assumption that the stakeholders involved into the decision-making process capture customer needs and values. Thus, the model can be applied for both B2B and B2C contexts as long as all relevant stakeholders are identified and involved in decision-making. For B2C contexts, end users and other external stakeholders need to be involved and accurately represented.

In future work, we plan to survey a number of business scenarios that involve diverse business models, asset origins, company characteristics and ecosystem participation models. We aim at characterizing these scenarios by identifying common and variable parts and clearly outlining short- and long-term consequences of each decision alternative. These should form guidelines that software business practitioners may use when considering various sourcing options. Moreover, we plan to expand our research on the evidence-based knowledge repository and create the first implementation of a repository that can support decision-makers. Finally, we plan to conduct an empirical study that will evaluate the presented decision-making approach and identify future work directions.

Acknowledgments. The work is supported by a research grant for the ORION project (reference number 20140218) from The Knowledge Foundation in Sweden. Furthermore, we would like to thank our colleagues in the ORION project for fruitful discussions and the external reviewers that have helped improving the paper.

References

1. Aurum, A., Wohlin, C.: The fundamental nature of requirements engineering activities as a decision-making process. Inf. Softw. Technol. **45**, 945–954 (2003)
2. Badampudi, D., Wohlin, C., Petersen, K.: Software Component Decision-Making: In-House, Open Source, COTS or Outsourcing - A Systematic Literature Review. In revision after review for journal publication (2016)
3. Berander, P., Jönsson, P.: Hierarchical Cumulative Voting (HCV) - prioritization of requirements in hierarchies. Int. J. Softw. Eng. Knowl. Eng. **16**, 819–849 (2006)
4. Biffl, S., Aurum, A., Boehm, B., Erdogmus, H., Grünbacher, P. (eds.): Value-Based Software Engineering. Springer, Heidelberg (2006)
5. Bizer, C., Cyganiak, R.: Quality-Driven Information Filtering Using the WIQA Policy Framework. Web Semant. Sci. Serv. Agents WWW **7**, 1–10 (2009)
6. Breivold, H.P., Larsson, M.: Component-based and service-oriented software engineering: key concepts and principles. In: Proceedings of the 33rd EUROMICRO Conference on Software Engineering and Advanced Applications, SEAA, pp. 13–20 (2007)
7. Cárdenas-Garcia, S., Zelkowitz, M.V.: A management tool for evaluation of software design. IEEE Trans. Softw. Eng. **17**, 961–971 (1991)
8. Cicchetti, A., Borg, M., Sentilles, S., Wnuk, K., Carlson, J., Papatheocharous, E.: Towards software assets origin selection supported by a knowledge repository. In: 1st MARCH Workshop at WICSA and CompArch 2016, April 5, Venice (Italy) (2016)
9. Cortellessa, V., Marinelli, F., Potena, P.: Automated selection of software components based on cost/reliability tradeoff. In: Gruhn, V., Oquendo, F. (eds.) EWSA 2006. LNCS, vol. 4344, pp. 66–81. Springer, Heidelberg (2006)
10. Cortellessa, V., Marinelli, F., Potena, P.: An optimization framework for "build-or-buy" decisions in software architecture. Comput. Oper. Res. **35**, 3090–3106 (2008)
11. Cusumano, M.A.: The Business of Software: What Every Manager, Programmer, and Entrepreneur Must Know to Thrive and Survive in Good Times and Bad. Simon and Schuster, New York (2004)
12. Franke, U., Buschle, M.: Experimental evidence on decision-making in availability service level agreements. IEEE Trans. Netw. Serv. Manage. **13**, 58–70 (2016)

13. Gregoriades, A., Sutcliffe, A.: Scenario-based assessment of nonfunctional requirements. IEEE Trans. Softw. Eng. **31**, 392–409 (2005)
14. Huhns, M., Singh, M.P.: Service-oriented computing: key concepts and principles. IEEE Internet Comput. **9**, 75–81 (2005)
15. ISO/IEC 25012: http://iso25000.com/index.php/en/iso-25000-standards/iso-25012
16. Jansen, S., Brinkkemper, S., Cusumano, M.A.: Software Ecosystems: Analyzing and Managing Business Networks in the Software Industry. Edward Elgar Publishing, Cheltenham (2013)
17. Jha, P.C., Bali, S., Kumar, U., Pham, H.: Fuzzy optimization approach to component selection of fault-tolerant software system. Memetic Comput. **6**, 49–59 (2014)
18. Jha, P.C., Bali, V., Narula, S., Kalra, M.: Optimal component selection based on cohesion & coupling for component based software system under build-or-buy scheme. J. Comput. Sci. **5**, 233–242 (2014)
19. Kramer, T., Eschweiler, M.: Outsourcing location selection with SODA: a requirements based decision support methodology and tool. In: Salinesi, C., Norrie, M.C., Pastor, Ó. (eds.) CAiSE 2013. LNCS, vol. 7908, pp. 530–545. Springer, Heidelberg (2013)
20. Kramer, T., Heinzl, A., Spohrer, K.: Should this software component be developed inside or outside our firm? - a design science perspective on the sourcing of application systems. In: Kotlarsky, J., Willcocks, L.P., Oshri, I. (eds.) Global Sourcing 2011. LNBIP, vol. 91, pp. 115–132. Springer, Heidelberg (2011)
21. Lawlis, P.K., Mark, K.E., Thomas, D.A., Courtheyn, T.: A formal process for evaluating COTS software products. Computer **34**, 58–63 (2001)
22. Martens, B., Teuteberg, F.: Decision-making in cloud computing environments: a cost and risk based approach. Inf. Syst. Front. **14**, 871–893 (2012)
23. Open Government Data (OGD). https://opengovdata.org/
24. Papatheocharous, E., Petersen, K., Cicchetti, A., Sentilles, S., Shah, S.M.A., Gorschek, T.: Decision support for choosing architectural assets in the development of software-intensive systems: the GRADE taxonomy. In: Proceedings of the 1st International Workshop on Software Architecture Asset Decision-making, Article No. 48 (2015)
25. Petersen, K., Wohlin, C.: Context in industrial software engineering research. In: Proceedings of the 2009 3rd International Symposium on Empirical Software Engineering and Measurement, pp. 401–404 (2009)
26. Popp, K.M.: Software industry business models. IEEE Softw. **28**, 26–30 (2011)
27. Potena, P.L.: Composition and tradeoff of non-functional attributes in software systems. In: European Software Engineering Conference and Symposium on the Foundations of Software Engineering, pp. 583–585 (2007)
28. Resnik, M.D.: Choices: An Introduction to Decision Theory. University of Minnesota Press, Minneapolis (1987)
29. Saaty, T.L.: Decision making with the analytic hierarchy process. Int. J. Serv. Sci. **1**, 1–83 (2008)
30. Singpurwalla, N.D.: Determining an optimal time interval for testing and debugging software. IEEE Trans. Soft. Eng. **17**, 313–319 (1991)
31. Schief, M., Buxmann, P., Schiereck, D.: Mergers and acquisitions in the software industry. Bus. Inf. Syst. Eng. **5**, 421–431 (2013)
32. Šmite, D., Wohlin, C., Galviņa, Z., Prikladnicki, R.: An empirically based terminology and taxonomy for global software engineering. Empirical Softw. Eng. **19**, 105–153 (2014)
33. Starmer, C.: Developments in non-expected utility theory: the hunt for a descriptive theory of choice under risk. J. Econ. Lit. **38**, 332–382 (2000)

34. Ssaed, A.A., Wan Kadir, W.M.N., Hashim, S.Z.M.: Metaheuristic search approach based on in-house/out-sourced strategy to solve redundancy allocation problem in component-based software systems. Int. J. Softw. Eng. Appl. **6**, 143–154 (2012)
35. Vale, T., Crnkovic, I., de Almeida, E.S., da Mota Silveira Neto, P.A., Cerqueira Cavalcantic, Y., de Lemos Meira, S.R.: Twenty-eight years of component-based software engineering. J. Syst. Softw. **111**, 128–148 (2016)

Software Analytics for Planning Product Evolution

Farnaz Fotrousi[1,2(✉)] and Samuel A. Fricker[1,2]

[1] SERL-Sweden, Blekinge Institute of Technology, 371 79 Karlskrona, Sweden
{farnaz.fotrousi, samuel.fricker}@bth.se
[2] i4Ds Centre for Requirements Engineering, FHNW, 5210 Windisch, Switzerland
{farnaz.fotrousi, samuel.fricker}@fhnw.ch

Abstract. Evolution of a software product is inevitable as product context changes and the product gradually becomes less useful if it is not adapted. Planning is a basis to evolve a software product. The product manager, who carries responsibilities of planning, requires but does not always have access to high-quality information for making the best possible planning decisions. The current study aims to understand whether and when analytics are valuable for product planning and how they can be interpreted to a software product plan. The study was designed with an interview-based survey methodology approach through 17 in-depth semi-structured interviews with product managers. Based on results from qualitative analysis of the interviews, we defined an analytics-based model. The model shows that analytics have potentials to support the interpretation of product goals while is constrained by both product characteristics and product goals. The model implies how to use analytics for a good support of product planning evolution.

1 Introduction

Software products are evolved throughout their life cycle through extension and adaptation of functionality and quality [1]. Such evolution is inevitable as product context changes and a software gradually becomes less useful if it is not adapted [2]. The flexibility of service-oriented approaches enables such evolution thinking [3]. Early release of a minimal viable product followed by evolution is beneficial for the product organization because it allows increasing return on investment when compared with a late release of a near-perfect product [4, 5]. Also, early release of a product allows learning about actual customer wants and needs; and the use of such market information in later product evolution is determinant for product success [6].

Mature companies plan how they intend to achieve their strategic objectives and satisfy market needs [7, 8]. Planning concerns the product portfolio, the long-term roadmap of each product, and the short-term release plans [9]. Portfolio management is about the strategic choice of which markets, products, and technologies the product organization addresses and, consequently, how it intends to spend its scarce resources on marketing, engineering, and research [10]. Roadmapping supports strategic and long-range planning for exploring evolving markets, products, and technologies and for

A. Maglyas and A.-L. Lamprecht (Eds.): ICSOB 2016, LNBIP 240, pp. 16–31, 2016.
DOI: 10.1007/978-3-319-40515-5_2

coordinating the actions of the product organization to address opportunities and threats [11]. Release planning, finally, addresses the short-term time horizon by selecting an optimum set of features to be delivered in a release so that competing stakeholder demands, benefits for the product organization, and available resources are balanced [12]. The impact of product planning, in comparison to the absence of such planning, are shorter projects, fewer delays, and improved quality [13].

Product plans are based on information about company goals, market trends, product requirements, and stakeholder priorities [9]. That information is collected and the resulting plans validated by consulting company-external stakeholders such as customers, partners, and consultants that monitor the market and company-internal stakeholders such as marketing, sales, research, development, support, sales, and company board representatives. Many techniques exist for such consultation of stakeholders, including workshops [14], focus groups [15], and surveys [16]. Stakeholder consultation is essential for achieving clarity, support, and stability of the product vision and the plans that refine it [17].

Even-though stakeholder consultation is widely established and considered good practice; the value of information obtained by this approach is limited, especially in a context with many users and customers. The consulted representatives are intermediaries to the real stakeholders. Non-probabilistic sampling, especially convenience sampling, tends to produce biased input [18]. Even if a representative set of stakeholders is identified, it is questionable whether their expressed opinion corresponds to the actual interest. An expressed customer wish does not necessarily translate to a buying decision [19]. Finally, dependency on stakeholders exposes the product manager to power and politics. Stakeholders exert their power by telling the product manager what to do and by creating a reality in which the product manager has to act according to these instructions [20]. The resulting political decisions risk benefiting the most powerful of these stakeholders, but not necessarily the product.

This paper proposes the use of software analytics [21] as a new source of information for product planning evolution. Analytics are the quantitative measures of an entity [22], which provide insight and actionable information [21] for a data-driven decision making [23, 24]. Analytics have the potential to become useful decision-support for software made available to customers and users, but still is undergoing evolution. In contrast to stakeholder consultation, measurement of product use and quality provides evidence that is representative, unbiased, and free from power and politics.

Based on a review of existing literature on software product planning and analytics, the paper introduces a conceptual model that connects measurements of the software product to product planning decisions. The study explores the connection by discussing it in interviews with 17 software product managers. The Inductive content analysis method [25] was used to identify how the measurements would be interpreted and used for product planning decision-support. The results provide insights for method and tool engineering [26] and for research targeted at simplifying product planning and improving the reliability product planning decisions.

This paper extends an earlier paper that presented the statistical analysis performed to understand product manager preferences for analytics [27]. The present paper gives an in-depth analysis whether and when analytics are valuable for product planning and how the interviewed product managers would use analytics for obtaining product planning decision-support for evolution.

The remainder of the paper is structured as follows. Section 2 reviews existing work in software analytics and introduces a conceptual model that describes how software analytics provide decision-support for product planning. Section 3 describes the research design used in the study. Section 4 presents the empirical results and analyze the collected data. Section 5 discusses the results and their implications on practice and research. Section 6 summarizes and concludes the paper.

2 Background

Software product analytics are the quantitative measures, collected during product use, giving actionable insight [21] for deciding about product evolution [23]. The actionable insight characteristics of analytics differentiate it from measures or metrics terms, which are used interchangeably in literature (e.g. ISO-9126 used the term *metrics* but replaced by *measures* in ISO 15393). Some literature refers to analytics as the process of developing actionable insight [28]. However, our definition emphasizes analytics as quantitative measures.

In product planning context, analytics measures a product, feature, or quality attribute. A product consists of features [29] and each feature is composed of a set of functional and non-functional requirements [30]. A product manager should deal with decision-making about creation, change, deletion, prioritization or allocation concerning product, features or requirements. Table 1 gives an overview of decisions that can be made during the planning of a software product. The decisions are distributed based on the practice areas including portfolio management, roadmapping, and release planning.

Table 1. Taxonomy of product planning decisions

Practice area	Decision object	Decision alternatives						
Portfolio Management	Products in the company's portfolio	Create	Enhance, Change	Prioritize	Remove	Allocate Resource	Allocate to Release	Confirm Technology
Product Roadmapping	Features of a product							
Release Planning	Requirement in a feature selected for release							

The decisions of product planning have a strong relationship with software product delivery. The trend of changing the software delivery from packaged product to SaaS (Software as a Service) delivery model [31] implies faster and smaller release of new features [4], ease of developing more features upon request [4] in addition to facilitating data collection to support planning decisions. SaaS delivery model enables monitoring of software use and provides first hand information about market, attractiveness of software and its features.

Table 2 illustrates a taxonomy of the measurement attributes in SasS based products. For such products, the measurement attributes belong to entities such as a product, feature/content or GUI requirement that can be mapped to entities of a website, page or GUI element in a general web application. Product managers conceptualize a web application as a product that consists of features instead of pages. Page is the definable unit of content. A feature can be one page, part of a page or distributed among pages. A request for the feature can be defined as a page request. Similar to a feature, a page can be conceptualized as a content, since it provides an additional information resource for the feature contributing to the end user knowledge. In a SaaS-based product, functional requirements may belong to graphical elements of a feature (i.e. page) measurable for a GUI requirement entity.

Table 2. Taxonomy of measurements for SaaS-based applications

Mapped entities to product	Entities	Attributes		
		Health	Usage	Context
Product	Website	Errors, Downtime, Response time, Throughput, Attacks	Use, Time between uses, Duration of use.	Users, New users, Returning users, Referrers, Location/ISP per use, Search engines and keywords, Campaigns, Browsers, Operating systems, Languages, Plugins, Screen resolutions.
Feature/content	Page	Errors, Response time	Use, Time between uses, Duration of use, Entrance, Click activity, Depth of use, Click stream/path, Exit, Bounce.	Users, Search engines and keywords, Campaigns
GUI Requirement	GUI Element	–	Use, Time between uses, Click activity, Click stream/path.	–

The second part of the taxonomy presented in Table 2 categorizes the corresponding measurement attributes based on the measurement purpose for products' *health*, *usage* and *context*. The attributes corresponding to *health* of entities inform technical quality of services [32]. The category of *usage* measurement attributes specifies the key data for understanding a traffic behavior of users [33] from the entity-use perspective. Context measurement attributes address the circumstances of users or sources in which entities' requests are issued from [34].

The taxonomy in Table 2 introduces the measurement attributes belong to web analytics context [35]. The taxonomy excludes other attributes such as those discussed in business analytics [36], which support broader aspect than customer centric application. Business analytics provide better insights particularly from operational data stored in transactional systems to inform sales, marketing, price optimization and workforce analysis [35]. The data are usually collected offline by the executive staff in a company [37] or an e-commerce platform [35].

This section confirms the usage of software analytics for product planning, but that it is yet to be understood how the measurements would be used for product planning evolution. These are the aims of the current study.

3 Research Design

To achieve the discussed aims, we designed an inductive study based on product managers' interpretations of analytics for product planning. We explored the following research question:

RQ: How are analytics used for planning product evolution?

To answer the research question, we conducted an interview-based survey with the purpose of identifying the relation between analytics and decisions of product planning. We performed data collection using semi-structured phone interviews. For the interviews, we initially designed the questionnaires, but we also asked the interviewees about their motivations for the provided answers. To avoid disadvantages of telephone survey related to lack of visual material and avoid complexity, the screen of the interviewer's computer that presents the questionnaire was shared with interviewees through web-based screen sharing applications.

Samples: We asked a well-established consultancy company in software product management to introduce experienced SaaS product managers in a wide variety of SaaS contexts. We selected 17 product managers from 3 micro, 4 small, 7 medium, and 3 large companies. The product managers managed 7 new respectively 10 already existing software products. All interviews were structured alike. The similarity of questions, homogeneity of interviewees and number of interviews could make the saturation of the interview results [38].

Designing the Instrument: We designed a questionnaire in which the taxonomy of measurement attributes discussed in Sect. 2 was a base for asking product managers how they would use analytics. The questionnaire was started with questions about context facets of the product, organization (company size and development team size) and people (role and experience). Questions about product planning formed the core of the interview, in two parts: "Planning Decisions" and "Analytics". In the first set of questions, the interviewees were asked to select a product that they have planned and are most satisfied with. Then questions were asked about the planning decisions that the interviewees usually take for the selected product. Later on, the interviewees were asked to rate the importance level of measurement-categories and measurement-attributes for taking the decisions and provide comments for their reasons behind the selections.

Interviews were piloted by two product managers and two students having product planning knowledge. After initial testing and several refinements, the interviews with the product managers were scheduled.

Selecting and Presenting the Results: We recorded the interviews by getting permissions from interviewees for the sake of future reference and transcribed for qualitative analysis of their argumentations. From the selected applications, 4 were "Business oriented", 7 were "Consumer-oriented" software and 5 were "information display and transaction entry". 41.2 % of the products were new products, and 58.8 % of the responses were evolutionary products. The distribution of interviews among different application magnifies the difference of product characteristics on interview results.

Analysis Method: We used inductive content analysis approach [25] for analyzing and coding the argumentations of the interviewees. In the first step of the analysis, we selected a unit of arguments, tagged with the headings describing the argumentations' concepts for the role of analytics, and repeated the process for all arguments. In the next steps, we grouped the headings in two rounds to reduce the number of similar categories in each round. The categorization provided a mean of interpreting the phenomenon, increasing understandability, and facilitating decision making ability [25]. At the end of the content analysis, we performed abstraction, which led to general descriptions and further discussions based on the categories. During the process, initial codes were gradually improved to form the final codes.

4 Analysis and Results

4.1 A Model for Analytics-Based Product Planning

By the analysis of interviewees' argumentations, we could conclude that product managers use *analytics to interpret the product goals while the analytics are constrained by both product characteristics and product goals.* This relation has been illustrated in Fig. 1.

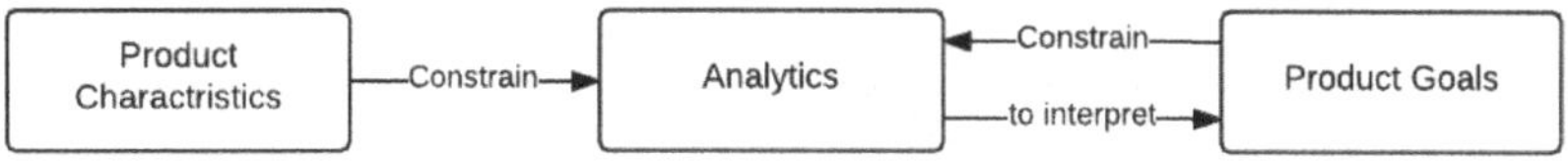

Fig. 1. A model for analytics-based product planning

For building and evolution of a product, product managers define product goals aligned with the companies' business goals. The essential goal of a product is to ensure that a product is built to deliver business values to a specific set of customers and meet important business goals of companies.

The analysis of interviewees' argumentations showed that product managers did not recognize some analytics useful for specific characteristics of a software product. In another word, product characteristics limit the scope of using analytics. Table 3 in Appendix provides a list of product characteristics and corresponding supportive quotes about constraining analytics. As an example, the application type filters and constrains the applicable measurements:

"For our specific product, error and response time could be used, but others healthiness measurements did not have a role in our intranet-based product."

Coding the argumentations clarified that analytics can be used to interpret products' goal in terms of assisting product manager to evaluate how far product goals are achieved. These products' goals might also constrain the analytics. Table 4 in Appendix outlines the interviewees' interpretation of analytics for product planning. The extracted codes for product goal characteristics (i.e. the left column of Table 4) reveal that product managers mostly addressed a dimension of product quality as a goal. "User satisfaction", "customer satisfaction", and "freedom from risk" are quality in use attributes in ISO/IEC 25010. The usability, functional suitability, maintainability, reliability, and performance efficiency codes are static and dynamic properties of software products in the quality model of ISO/IEC 25010. Such analytics support product evolution decisions from the technical perspectives.

Also, extracted code "market positioning" for product goal characteristics (i.e. the left column of Table 4), introduces a business goal [39], to be interpreted by analytics. Such goals complement the technical evaluation of the product to give 360-degree view to the product manager for taking decisions [40].

Product managers define product goals alongside with business goals considering inputs from stakeholders. So analytics can point out to the level that a product goal has been achieved. On the other hand, the product goals can constrain analytics and specify which measurements have more or less value to achieve the desired level of the goals:

"For referral source measures, if I can find out in what segment the user belongs to, and then it is very important. If from the measures, I can find out from which country they use it, it is mostly less important."

The example indicates that extracting statistics about user's segment from referral source attributes is valuable and can be interpreted toward a product goal, while other statistics of referral sources might not be valuable for this case. For all codes, although interviewees' argumentations were not available to support both interpretations and constraints, the logical relations between interpreting product goals and constraining analytics can cover the argumentation shortage:

"Click steam is important to see the sequence of clicking to track the usage and see do the users follow the pattern in a right way or not."

The example illustrates that high level of click streams might interpret a good level of user satisfaction for the feature and can strengthen the quality of the feature. Logically it is evident that achieving user satisfaction wishes to have information about click streams, which strengthen the constrained relations.

4.2 Validation of the Model

The model in Fig. 1 was validated by examples of product managers' experiences. We mapped argumentations of product managers (i.e. interviewees) for different groups of products to the model. The mapping helped us to check whether the chains of arguments can support the model. The products that interviewees selected during the interviews belonged to three product types: "Consumer-oriented software", "Business oriented" and "Information display and transaction entry". For each product type, one interview was selected to show how the shifting from constraining the analytics to interpretation of the product goal is performed. Table 5 in Appendix presents three examples of different products. The following example shows how argumentations of an interview (first row in Table 5) can support the proposed model.

Based on the characteristics of a mobile application, "*referral source is not important [analytics] because users are from all over the world*". "*Dos and worm attacks are not important [analytics] in an IPhone application*" but when the product is mature, the other "*product healthiness statistics are extremely important because having errors and bad usability makes it hard [for users] to understand a feature*". By collecting data about product healthiness "*The errors* [analytics] *can be seen very quickly and repaired in each month release*". So product manager will monitor analytics to find out error and take an action toward a healthy product. Having a healthy product will facilitate the customer benefit goal.

In this example "mobile application" is the product with specific characteristics, "referral source, Dos attacks and worm attacks" are analytics and "customer benefit goal" is the product goal. The relations between product characteristics, analytics, and product goals could confirm the relations defined in Fig. 1. Similarly, the other argumentations can also confirm the defined relations in the model.

5 Discussions

In this paper, we contribute to creating a model for understanding how analytics are used for planning of a software product. The study introduces a new perspective for product planning by applying analytics. Analytics are filtered based on product characteristics and product goals. The analytics are interpreted to evaluate the level of product goals' fulfillments. The evaluation enhances a product manager's intuitions to help to find out the rationales for his decisions. Deviation from the product goal requires an action that reflects a new decision in the product plan [8].

The results have implications for research on understanding the relations between product characteristics, analytics and product goals for supporting product evolution. The results have also implications for product managers of software vendors on interpreting analytics to use data science as a basis for decision supports of product planning. In Fig. 2, we propose a product manager to carry out a chain of activities to take planning decisions for product evolution by the supports of analytics.

In step 1, the product manager prepares a list of goals corresponding to the candidate product. The study showed in a SaaS-based product, most of the product managers set quality goals with the focus on quality-in-use (ISO/IEC 25010). In this

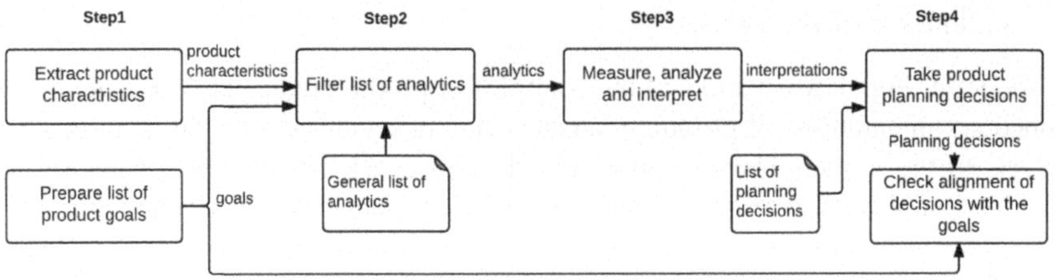

Fig. 2. Suggested activities for product managers to support planning decisions and product evolution by analytics

study product managers looked for acceptable perceived experience of use (efficiency), acceptable perceived results of use (effectiveness), acceptable perceived consequences of use (Freedom from risks) and the customer's satisfaction in a particular context of use [41]. Quality of services and marketing goals were also on the list of goals, with lower priority than the quality-in-use goals.

In step 2, from the general list of analytics (i.e. created using a general list of measurement attributes such as Table 2), the product manager excludes those with less importance based on the defined product characteristics and goals. The study showed some of the factors that constrain the analytics for product planning. Product characteristics such as product's context, features, users, platform, network type and maturity constrain the analytics for product planning. Also, product goals such as managing the quality of product, managing market positioning and organization grows can constrain the analytics. Although few goals were discussed by the interviewees, it is not a big deal to generalize to different goals such as growth and continuity of the organization, meeting financial, personal objectives, and etc. [39].

In step 3, the included analytics are measured, analyzed, and interpreted to provide required information and inform the product managers' decisions. The alignment of the decisions with the product goals is investigated in step 4. Argumentations of interviews showed, product managers usually benefit from analytics about product and feature usages, which supports goals corresponding to functional suitability and usability. Product healthiness analytics support performance efficiency, reliability and security goals. The result is in the same direction with the study that recognized feature use, product use, response time, users, error and downtime as the most preferred measurements for planning, despite planning decisions' types [27]. To create, remove, or enhance a feature, the data trends provide a broad view of requirements or feature desirability in the current or even future time and clarify how these changes can impact the product's goal. Comparing the corresponding measurements' impacts on the defined goals can prioritize features. This impact can support both reactive and proactive planning for an evolution of the product.

The chains of interrelated activities explained in step 3 are mapped to the measurement information model defined in ISO 15939. We propose to enhance the model by adding a box for product goals with two outgoing arrows: One to *constrain* measurement attributes and one to *support* the information needs. The enhancement would adapt the ISO 15939 to support product evolution using analytics.

The proposed model in Fig. 1 is not specific to product planning of a traditional software development, but the model may support planning of products using modern development approaches [42] such as an agile development, continuous integration, and continuous deployment. In such approaches instead of listing the product goals in the beginning (i.e. refer to step1), sub-goals of the corresponding iteration are identified instead. However, for the iterations that do not release a software product or prototype, analytics approach is not applicable. Because the prerequisite for using runtime analytics for product planning is to have a software prototype or product.

The study was limited to 17 answers of product managers experienced in SaaS-based products. However, the stratified sampling ensured the results are from the variety of product managers. Although the study focused on analytics of SaaS-based products, the model in Fig. 1 could be generalized to the other application domains, by considering that meaningful analytics may vary in different categories of products. For example, *Throughput* measurement does only make sense in networked-based applications. Furthermore, another limitation was due to the choice of product managers for focusing on roadmapping decisions. More detailed study of portfolio management and release planning decisions may reveal other constraints on analytics in future. It is also valuable for researchers to know which measurements support each product goal and how the product manager may prioritize the measures, which we propose as future work.

6 Conclusions

Products are the artifacts to satisfy the customers' needs, and hence product managers require bringing the voice of market and customer to the product planning processes, where this happens effectively through a data-driven endeavor of sensing and understanding the requirements. Different types of analytics assist a product manager in product planning, where each might be gathered through a different channel and process. SaaS-based product delivery facilitates gathering a new range of detailed, usable and real-time product-use data. Measuring and analyzing the data to support product-planning decisions are targeted by analytics.

This study introduced two taxonomies as inputs for the other parts of the study: A taxonomy of SaaS-based measurements in categories of two dimensions: "Product", "Feature/content", "GUI Elements" in the first dimension, and "healthiness", "usage", and "context" in the second dimension. The second taxonomy was related to planning decisions taken in portfolio management, roadmapping and release planning.

To present how analytics assist product managers and contribute to product planning, an interview-based survey was conducted with professionals in the product management area by focusing on roadmapping decisions since the interviewees were experienced more. Through the interview-based survey, the justifications of interviewees for assigning a value to a measurement show that both product characteristics and product goals constrain analytics, while it is interpreted to product goals. In the other word, product characteristics and product goals specify which analytics can assist product managers in achieving the product goals.

The findings helped us to propose an analytics-based model. Some parameters such as product maturity, users, network type, context, and technology change the scope of analytics usefulness for product planning. Analytics can be motivators for product managers to achieve goals for market positioning, meeting quality-in-use (i.e. customer and user satisfaction) and improving product quality (usability, functional suitability, maintainability, reliability and performance efficiency). Therefore, even limited list of analytics will be helpful to gain good support for taking planning decisions aligned with the product goals. In the case that analytics shows any deviation from the product goal, the product manager takes a constructive decision to prevent its occurrence or, at least, decrease negative effects. The analytics-based model can be used in various application domains rather than SaaS, when collecting the customized analytics for a particular domain is applicable.

Acknowledgments. Parts of this work have been done with the support of the SUPERSEDE project funded by the European Union's ICT 2014 under grant agreement no 644018.

Appendix: Tables of Qualitative Analysis

Table 3. Constraining analytics[a]

Product characteristics	Constraints
Product maturity	*"When you are creating an immature product, it is hard to base your decision based on these kinds of statistics. Instead of analytics for creating decision for an immature product, we create a prototype and test the prototype. But for tuning functionality and enhancing, these statistics can have benefits."* *"From a second release to third release, definitely analytics can be helpful. Product-use [measurement] affects their allocation of feature in third release. But not from first release to second, because first release is mainly about how to build a product."*
Product users	*"Referral source attribute is not important because our users are from all over the world as they use their mobile phone."* *"End users are within some specific organizations so statistics about referral sources are not important."* *"Statistics about new user are not important because we are dealing with available users, not new users."*
Being Web based	*"Technology and channel [measurement] is very important because the product is a web-based tool."* *"Technology and channel data is less important. We need to support all browsers and cover related technology as it is a web based product."*
Network type	*"For our specific product, error and response time could be used, and others [other healthiness measurements] did not have a role in the intranet-based product."*
Product context	*"Dos and worm attacks are not important in an IPhone application."*

(*Continued*)

Table 3. (*Continued*)

Product characteristics	Constraints
Product technology	*"Technology and channel data are less important. We have to support all browsers and cover related technology as it is a web based product."* *"Inside our organization it is clear which OS or browsers the product has to work with, so we did not have too many challenges about it [Technology and channels measurement attributes]"*
Product features	*"Language attribute is not important. Our product only supports English language, and there is no different to know what languages have the users."*

[a]Words given in the brackets (i.e. []) have not been directly mentioned in the quotes, and were added to make the interviewees quotes more clear.

Table 4. Examples of Analytics Interpretation for product goals and the constraints that a product goal provides for analytics

Product goal characteristics	Interpretation	Constraint
Market positioning	*"Statistics about campaign are important because they show how efficient various marketing campaigns are in bringing visitors to be customers."* *"Referral source measurements can be interesting as we can learn about the structure of the market and then they can map it to the feature use, by that make it an input for prioritizing features for further development. So in combination with other studies of a market, it is important but alone and in isolated manner."* *"Our goal is to increase web users, if product use is not too many then action should be taken to find the reason.."*	*"For referral source measures, if I can find out in what segment the user belongs to then it is very important. If from the measure I find out from which country they use it, it is mostly less important."* *"Referral source is not importance since we sell product to an organization not end users. So they do not care where the customers are coming from."*
Customer Satisfaction	*"Our main role is to create customer benefit to the product and give them functionality that is useful. For example by analytics, finding errors can be seen very quickly and repaired in each month release."*	*"In our product, it is good to create more customer benefit which are got from an interview with customers and customer feedback from their service organizations. If we agree on prioritizing feature, the statistics are not useful for them."*

(*Continued*)

Table 4. (*Continued*)

Product goal characteristics	Interpretation	Constraint
Functional Suitability	*"Referral source measure attributes are important because you can help to adapt User Interfaces."* *"Statistics in Technology and channels are important because we do not want to support all versions and will support technologies that are used more."* *"Technology and channels statistics are very important- Depending on which mobile they have accessed from they have to provide a service according to that."*	*"Technology is a tricky category, what do you mean by technology? Technology that used for development, or technology that is related to users. They are different with each other. For development part the analytics is not important, although for user side that plays important role."*
Reliability	*"Product healthiness [analytics] is very important. If we cannot achieve desire reliability and performance we can go home."*	*"All healthiness measures are important, especially error, people do not accept faulty product and error."*

Table 5. Examples of shifting from constraining analytics use to interpretation of analytics for product planning

Product characteristics	Constrain (by product characteristics)	Interpretation	Product goal	Constraint (by product goal)
Social ERP (Business oriented product)	*"Exit and entrance feature is mostly good to know when you have a product like a website. For other product it might be different entrances and exits, and might not so differ to each other."* *"Referral source measurements are not so interesting. I think they are mostly useful for websites, like online shopping to know the source of customers. For us, the current users location is clear."*	*"Quality adds value to the product. If not, you [i.e. your products] are definitely dead. Faulty product ends in no user satisfaction. So It's good to know before lose all users."* *"Feature measurements Provide a good picture of interesting features"*	*"Planning a high quality product is that makes users satisfied is important."*	*"Product user is very important to monitor the popularity level of product during time period."*

(*Continued*)

Table 5. (*Continued*)

Product characteristics	Constrain (by product characteristics)	Interpretation	Product goal	Constraint (by product goal)
SaaS-based Knowledge Management (Information display and transaction entry product type)	*"End users are inside some specific organizations, so referral source measurements are not important for us. Also inside each organization it is clear which OS or browser are available so we do not have too much challenges about it."*	*"Lead users have special roles in patterns related to gathering tacit knowledge in the organizations. So it is important to understand who are the lead users to target specific users. So user classification based on their activities on the product is useful."* *"Depth of use analytic helps us to understand that users are involved with the product and do not have random visiting."*	*"The product suppose to grab tacit knowledge in the organization so it was important that adequate number of users would engaged in different parts of the system."*	*"Feature use is very important because it shows which parts of the system the users are engaged."*

References

1. Rajlich, V.C.T., Bennett, K.H.: A staged model for the software life cycle. Computer **33**, 66–71 (2000)
2. Lehman, M.M.: Programs, life cycles, and laws of software evolution. Proc. IEEE **68**, 1060–1076 (1980)
3. Gold, N., Mohan, A., Knight, C., Munro, M.: Understanding service-oriented software. IEEE Softw. **21**, 71–77 (2004)
4. Choudhary, V.C.: Software as a service: implications for investment in software development. In: 40th Annual Hawaii International Conference on System Sciences, HICSS 2007, Waikoloa, Big Island, Hawaii (2007)
5. Denne, M., Cleland-Huang, J.: The incremental funding method: Data-driven software development. IEEE Softw. **21**, 39–47 (2004)
6. Ottum, B.D., Moore, W.L.: The role of market information in new product success/failure. J. Prod. Innov. Manag. **14**, 258–273 (1997)
7. Fricker, S.A.: Software Product Management. In: Maedche, A., Botzenhardt, A., Neer, L. (eds.) Software for People, pp. 53–81. Springer, Heidelberg (2012)
8. Kittlaus, H.-B., Clough, P.N.: Software Product Management and Pricing: Key Success Factors for Software Organizations. Springer-Verlag New York Inc., New York (2009)

9. Bekkers, W., van de Weerd, I., Spruit, M., Brinkkemper, S.: A framework for process improvement in software product management. In: Riel, A., O'Connor, R., Tichkiewitch, S., Messnarz, R. (eds.) EuroSPI 2010. CCIS, vol. 99, pp. 1–12. Springer, Heidelberg (2010)
10. Cooper, R.G., Edgett, S.J., Kleinschmidt, E.J.: New product portfolio management: practices and performance. J. Prod. Innov. Manag. **16**, 333–351 (1999)
11. Phaal, R., Farrukh, C.J., Probert, D.R.: Technology roadmapping—a planning framework for evolution and revolution. Technol. Forecast. Soc. Change **71**, 5–26 (2004)
12. Svahnberg, M., Gorschek, T., Feldt, R., Torkar, R., Saleem, S.B., Shafique, M.U.: A systematic review on strategic release planning models. Inf. Softw. Technol. **52**, 237–248 (2010)
13. Ebert, C.: The impacts of software product management. J. Syst. Softw. **80**, 850–861 (2007)
14. Phaal, R., Farrukh, C.J., Probert, D.R.: Strategic roadmapping: a workshop-based approach for identifying and exploring innovation issues and opportunities. Eng. Manag. J. **19**, 3–12 (2007)
15. Krueger, R.A.: Focus Groups: A Practical Guide for Applied Research. Sage, Los Angeles (2009)
16. Fowler, F.J.: Survey Research Methods. Sage, Los Angeles (2009)
17. Lynna, G.S., Akgünb, A.E.: Project visioning: Its components and impact on new product success. J. Prod. Innov. Manag. **18**, 374–387 (2001)
18. Robson, C.: Real World Research: A Resource for Social Scientists and Practitioner-Researchers. Blackwell, Oxford (2002)
19. Howard, J.A., Sheth, J.N.: The Theory of Buyer Behavior. Wiley, New York (1969)
20. Milne, A., Maiden, N.: Power and politics in requirements engineering: embracing the dark side? Requir. Eng. **17**, 83–98 (2012)
21. Zhang, D., Dang, Y., Lou, J.-G., Han, S., Zhang, H., Xie, T.: Software analytics as a learning case in practice: Approaches and experiences. In: International Workshop on Machine Learning Technologies in Software Engineering, pp. 55–58. Lawrence, Kansas (2011)
22. Davenport, T.H., Harris, J.G.: Competing on Analytics: The New Science of Winning. Harvard Business Press, Boston (2007)
23. Buse, R., Zimmermann, T.: Analytics for software development. In: Foundations of Software Engineering (FSE)/SDP Workshop on Future of Software Engineering Research. ACM, Santa Fe (2010)
24. Buse, R., Zimmermann, T.: Information needs for software development analytics. In: International Conference on Software Engineering, ICSE 2012, pp. 987–996. IEEE Press, Zurich (2012)
25. Elo, S., Kyngäs, H.: The qualitative content analysis process. J. Adv. Nurs. **62**, 107–115 (2008)
26. Brinkkemper, S.: Method engineering: engineering of information systems development methods and tools. Inf. Softw. Technol. **38**, 275–280 (1996)
27. Fotrousi, F., Izadyan, K., Fricker, S.A.: Analytics for product planning: in-depth interview study with SaaS product managers. In: IEEE 6th International Conference on Cloud Computing, Santa Clara Marriott, CA, USA (2013)
28. Cooper, A.: What is analytics? Definition and essential characteristics. CETIS Anal. Ser. **1**, 1–10 (2012)
29. Gorchels, L.: The Product Manager's Handbook: The Complete Product Management Resource. NTC Business Books, Illinois (2000)
30. Fricker, S., Schumacher, S.: Release planning with feature trees: industrial case. In: Regnell, B., Damian, D. (eds.) REFSQ 2011. LNCS, vol. 7195, pp. 288–305. Springer, Heidelberg (2012)

31. Cusumano, M.A.: The changing software business: Moving from products to services. Computer **41**, 20–27 (2008)
32. Menasce, D.A.: QoS issues in web services. IEEE Internet Comput. **6**, 72–75 (2002)
33. Srivastava, J., Cooley, R., Deshpande, M., Tan, P.-N.: Web usage mining: Discovery and applications of usage patterns from web data. ACM SIGKDD Explor. Newslett. **1**, 12–23 (2000)
34. Clifton, B.: Advanced Web Metrics with Google Analytics. Wiley. com, New York (2012)
35. Kohavi, R., Rothleder, N.J., Simoudis, E.: Emerging trends in business analytics. Commun. ACM **45**, 45–48 (2002)
36. Holsapple, C., Lee-Post, A., Pakath, R.: A unified foundation for business analytics. Decis. Support Syst. **64**, 130–141 (2014)
37. Shung, K.P., Junyu, M.C.: Application of analytics in business strategy. Bus. Intell. J. **5**, 190–193 (2012)
38. Guest, G., Bunce, A., Johnson, L.: How many interviews are enough? An experiment with data saturation and variability. Field Methods **18**, 59–82 (2006)
39. Clements, P., Bass, L.: Using business goals to inform a software architecture. In: 18th IEEE International on Requirements Engineering Conference (RE 2010), Sydney, NSW, Australia (2010)
40. Ebert, C., Brinkkemper, S.: Software product management–An industry evaluation. J. Syst. Softw. **95**, 10–18 (2014)
41. Herrera, M., Moraga, M.Á., Caballero, I., Calero, C.: Quality in use model for web portals (QiUWeP). In: Facca, F.M., Daniel, F. (eds.) ICWE 2010. LNCS, vol. 6385, pp. 91–101. Springer, Heidelberg (2010)
42. Olsson, H.H., Bosch, J.: Climbing the "Stairway to Heaven": evolving from agile development to continuous deployment of software. In: Bosch, J. (ed.) Continuous Software Engineering, pp. 15–27. Springer, New York (2014)

Ecosystems Here, There, and Everywhere

A Barometrical Analysis of the Roots of 'Software Ecosystem'

Arho Suominen[1(✉)], Sami Hyrynsalmi[2], and Marko Seppänen[3]

[1] VTT Technical Research Centre of Finland, Innovations, Economy, and Policy, Espoo, Finland
arho.suominen@vtt.fi

[2] Department of Information Technology, University of Turku, Turku, Finland
sthyry@utu.fi

[3] Department of Pori, Tampere University of Technology, Tampere, Finland
marko.seppanen@tut.fi

Abstract. This study structures the ecosystem literature by using a bibliometrical approach in analysing theoretical roots of ecosystem studies. Several disciplines, such as innovation, management and software studies have established own streams in the ecosystem research. This paper reports the results of analysing 601 articles from the Thomson Reuters Web of Science database, and identifies ten separate research communities which have established their own thematic ecosystem disciplines. We show that five sub-communities have emerged inside the field of software ecosystems. The software ecosystem literature draws its theoretical background from (1) technical, (2) research methodology, (3) business, (4) management, and (5) strategy oriented disciplines. The results pave the way for future research by illustrating the existing and missing links and directions in the field of the software ecosystem.

Keywords: Business ecosystem · Software ecosystem · Bibliometric

1 Introduction

Managerial fads and fashions come and go (see [1,2]). The recent, even hyped buzzword "ecosystem" has its conceptual roots in 1930s in the context of biological ecosystems [3], and re-established and reinforced by Moore as business ecosystems in 1990s [4]. A vast amount of scholarly and other literature have been published around the topic and scholars are still arguing on the conceptual definitions and even foundations. However, this conceptual underdevelopment has not restrained any consultant or manager using the concept for their own purposes; one of the key characteristics of handy management concept is its intellectual and content-wise flexibility.

There are several sub-types of ecosystems, coined and defined for different purposes; business ecosystem (e.g. [5]), industrial ecosystem (e.g. [6]), innovation ecosystem (e.g. [7]), knowledge ecosystem [8], mobile ecosystem (e.g. [9]),

A. Maglyas and A.-L. Lamprecht (Eds.): ICSOB 2016, LNBIP 240, pp. 32–46, 2016.
DOI: 10.1007/978-3-319-40515-5_3

and software ecosystem (e.g. [10]). These sub-types usually have some common roots, and their definitional overlapping is remarkable. In this paper, we focus on exploring and making sense on the recent trends and trajectories of software ecosystem by using bibliographical methods to analyze and demonstrate the development and show possible future research avenues.

We use bibliometric approach integrated with a qualitative analysis on the selected core documents. The data was gathered from Thomson Reuters Web of Science database in January 2016. The internal structures the sample publications was examined using two bibliometric approaches: bibliographic coupling and co-citation analysis. Bibliographic coupling reveals to what extent the publication use shared intellectual background whereas the co-citation analysis was used to explore what is the shared background for the publications.

It seems that the concepts of ecosystems do have some theoretical and practical value, especially since the economy is transforming into a full-pull economy. In other words, the traditional economy has been dominated by a mass market, economies of scale and 'pushing' goods and services to customers. The Internet has enabled firms to target customers at the individual level. Thus, "now every company is a software company"[1] and analyzing the software ecosystem will provide us a better understanding how and where the scholarly attention has been developing, and more importantly, where the current research gaps are that academia should be targeting to fulfill.

2 Background

The complex relationships in business have, for a long time, been explained and studied with metaphors derived from the nature. Whereas the metaphors such as 'jungle' and 'rainforest' [11] have not been widely adapted, the 'business ecosystem' metaphor by Moore [4] in 1993 is nowadays widely used both in academia as well as in industry. A business ecosystem, according to Moore [12, p. 26], is *"an economic community supported by a foundation of interacting organizations and individuals-the organisms of the business world."* According to his view, ecosystems are born from companies working around an innovation [4]. The business ecosystem research field was later remarkably advanced by Iansiti and Levien [13,14] with their definition of healthiness of a business ecosystem.

Since the introduction of the concept, a series of different artificial ecosystems has been presented; e.g. 'software ecosystems' [10,15,16], 'mobile ecosystems' [9,17,18], 'innovation ecosystems' [19–21], 'digital ecosystems' [22–24] in addition to those mentioned in earlier. However, the relationship between different types of ecosystems are not clear [25], nor it has been defined what are the boundaries between different ecosystems [26]. As an example, under the umbrella term 'software ecosystem', there have been research on ecosystems

[1] Kirkpatrick, D. Now Every Company Is A Software Company. http://www.forbes.com/sites/techonomy/2011/11/30/now-every-company-is-a-software-company/#1505e9a21100.

formed around a geographical location [27–29] as well as on closed marketplaces [25,30]. These two types represent almost the different ends of the spectrum where software ecosystem conceptualization has been applied.

Previously there have been attempts to organize the emerged ecosystem literature by literature reviews [10,31,32] as well as identify the theoretical backgrounds of the studies [33]. However, recently there have been discussions what is the relationship between, e.g., the concept of software and business ecosystems [25,32]. We contribute this ongoing discussion by analyzing the different ideological backgrounds of the published studies with a bibliometrical approach.

3 Data and Research Method

The study follows bibliometric approach integrated with a qualitative analysis of selected core documents. The data was downloaded from Thomson Reuters Web of Science (WoS) database in January 2016. WoS database was selected as a source as, with Scopus, it is one of the largest science publication database both by volume and coverage. The selection between Scopus and WoS is in many cases irrelevant as the results derived from either correlate highly [34]. A more important aspect in the selection is the access to data, which is proprietary, and the authors had broadest access to WoS supporting its selection as datasource. The dataset was compiled by searching with one of the terms "innovation ecosystem(s)", "business ecosystem(s)", "software ecosystem(s)" being used in the title, abstract, author keywords or the WoS enhanced metadata Keywords Plus® field. These are the among largest artificial ecosystem fields. The search resulted in 601 articles. This includes all type of articles indexed in WoS e.g. journal publications, conference proceedings, reviews, and letters.

Since 2005 there has been a rapid increase in publication volume relating to the search terms (Fig. 1). The first publications in the dataset was published in 1991 is by Zeleny et al. [35] titled *"Applying a new set of lenses – implications for managers of managing in the business ecosystem"*. The most highly cited article in the set is by Teece [36] on dynamic capabilities. Roughly 1/6 of the articles were published in 2014, as seen in Fig. 1. The downturn in publishing in 2015 may be explained by the fact that conference proceedings for 2015 will be added to the WoS during 2016, thus increasing the 2015 publications count.

The 11 most active publication outlets have published roughly 1/4 of the publications in the dataset. Most active has been the *Proceedings of the International Conference on Digital Ecosystems and Technologies* (DEST) followed by two Springer lecture notes series, which also originate from a number of conferences. Major journal outlets are *Journal of Systems and Software* and *Technology and Innovation Management* among other mentioned in Table 1.

The knowledge structure of the before mentioned 601 publications was studied using two established bibliometric approaches. First, Bibliographic coupling [37] was used to study the shared intellectual background of publications. BC measures the shared intellectual background among documents, where a strength value is calculated between each document in the dataset based on the

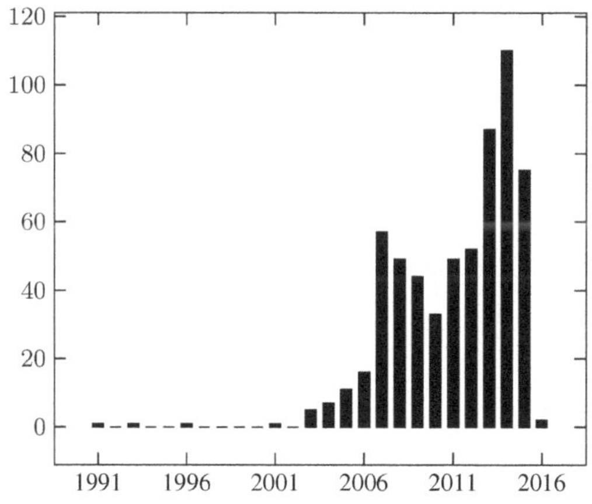

Fig. 1. Histogram of article publication by years

Table 1. The largest, by volume, research outlets for the sample publications. The list is limited the outlets having more than 10 publications. Full table available at http://goo.gl/qJ03tB

Publication forums	Publications
International Conference on Digital Ecosystems and Technologies	45
Lecture Notes in Business Information Processing	27
Lecture Notes in Computer Science	14
The Technology Innovation Management Review	10

number of shared references. [37] states that "...a single item of reference shared by two documents is defined as a unit of coupling between them". Based on these definition of a unit we can create a network of documents mentioned in the references of the dataset, where a vertices is formed between two documents if there is one or more times the documents co-occur in a reference list. Edges are also weighted by the count of occurrences of the two documents in the dataset, where weight is [1,601]. The BC approach works on the assumption that the more shared references, the stronger theoretical foundation the two documents share. By this process, BC method has been shown to be able identify documents with a shared research focus [38]. Calculating the BC weight to all documents in the dataset, we can cluster and visualize a network of shared knowledge.

After identifying the cluster relevant to software ecosystem, we use a co-citation (CoC) analysis [39] to show what is the shared background that the publications use. In CoC two documents are co-cited if there is one or more documents that cite both articles. The weight of co-citation is based on the count of articles that co-cite the two documents. CoC creates a network of cited documents rather than linking the documents in the dataset. [40] When identifying the software ecosystem community, similar clustering and visualization where done to cited publications than BC analysis. We used the VOSviewer software [41] to pre-process the WoS data and calculate the bibliographic coupling and co-citation weights. VOSviewer also transformed the original data to a network based on the bibliographical links between documents. The parameters for the analysis are given in Table 2.

Table 2. Parameters used in the bibliometric analysis.

Analysis	Unit of analysis	Counting methods
Bibliographic coupling	Documents	Full Counting
Co-citation analysis	Cited references	Full Counting

Additional network metrics were calculated using Gephi network visualization software. Latent patterns in the network were uncovered using a Modularity algorithm developed by Blonder et al. [42]. The Modularity algorithm was run using randomized, edge weighted and a resolution of 1.0 as parameters. Searching for central nodes in the network was done by two approaches. First we calculated the Eigenvector Centrality for each node. In graph theory and network analysis, centralilty is used as a measure to identify the most important vertices within a graph. The Eigenvector Centrality measure assigns a score for each node based on its connections with the concept that connections to high-scoring nodes contribute more to the Eigenvector Centrality score of a node than connections to low-scoring nodes. To create a more comprehensive picture of important nodes, we also used an algorithm developed by Kleinberg [43] to find authoritative nodes in a network. The algorithm, originally developed for hyperlink analysis, searches for hub and authorities in a network. A hub is a node that points to many other nodes, an authority is a page that is by many hubs. In this we look for authoritative nodes, publications, in the network and compare the results to Eigenvector Centrality results.

The graph is visualized using the Force Layout algorithm using Gephi. The visualization was used to qualitative evaluate the structure of different research communities identified and to communicate the results. For each main stream, or community produced by the Modularity algorithm, of the literature the most central publications were selected for qualitative evaluation. Documents were selected by ranking documents based on community it belongs, Eigenvector Centrality and Authority value. The documents selected from each community were used to create a qualitative narrative to each of the main research streams.

4 Results

Analyzing the 601 publications by the means of BC revealed a portion of articles not linked to the majority of the sample. The largest set of connected articles has 470 articles, leaving 131 articles that are not connected to the core sample.

These 131 articles were excluded for any further analysis. For the 470 articles remaining publications, VOSViewer was used to calculate BC weight values for each node and the coupling strength between documents. The highest BC weight in the set is by Weber and Hine [5] titled *"Who inhabits a business ecosystem? The technospecies as a unifying concept"* (weight = 601). The average BC weight is 103,29 (N=470, s.d. 119,26).

Employing the Modularity algorithm we identify 10 communities in the BC network seen in Fig. 2 and described in Table 3. We focus on the four largest communities: Community 1 in blue (N=133), Community 2 in orange (N=111), Community 5 in lilac (N=109), and Community 9 in green (N=91) seen in Fig. 2. From the communities, Community 9 is most connected with approximately 30 edges per node and Community 9 has the highest number of edges to nodes.

Literature in Community 1 focuses on industry platforms, ecosystem dynamics and value creation in ecosystem. This community is not specific to the software ecosystem concept, but analyses the ecosystem concept at a more general

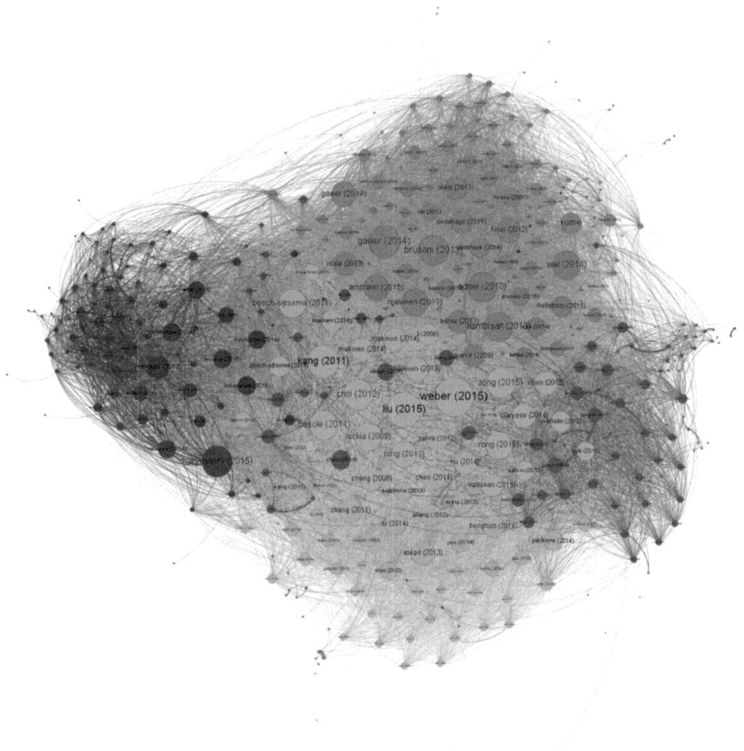

Fig. 2. Bibliographic coupling network of 470 publications relating to software and innovation ecosystems. Data: WoS. Graph is available online for a more in-depth analysis of labels at http://goo.gl/NytKiG (Color figure online)

Table 3. Largest communities in the sample data. Top publications by bibliographic coupling weight are given for each community. Data: WoS. Full table available at http://goo.gl/xTa8EN

Community	Nodes	Edges	Top publications by BC weight
1	133	2321	Gawer 2014 [44], Brusoni 2013 [45], Adner 2010 [46]
2	111	987	Nikayin 2013 [47], Shang 2013 [48], Gueguen 2009 [49]
5	109	1518	Hyrynsalmi 2015 [32], Manikas 2013 [10], Crooymans 2015 [50]
9	91	2728	Weber 2015 [5], Liu 2015 [51], Kang 2011 [52]

level. Community 2 focuses on service innovation and digital ecosystem. Topics range from service quality management to mobile handset ecosystems. Community 5 focuses specifically on software ecosystem and the majority of publications in the community clearly highlight the software ecosystem concept. The most interconnected sub-network in the dataset is Community 9 that focuses on business ecosystems broadly. The publications highlight the dynamics and evolutionary processes in business ecosystems.

Table 4 shows central and authoritative publications for each of the core clusters. These clusters are not central in the sense that they would be highly cited as the calculations are based on the BC analysis. The central publications describe more, what are publications that are central in that they reference key literature to the specific community. For example for Community 1, [46,53,54] references key literature for the community and by analyzing these we are able to further understand the content of the cluster.

The central publications support our analysis of the content of communities. In Community 1 [46,53] focus on value creation and competitive dynamics of ecosystem at an general level. [54] looks at open source innovation practises in non–software domains and is more loosely connected to [46,53]. Central publications for Community 2 focuses on business models and ecosystems [55,56] and the digital and mobile domain [49]. For Community 5, the central documents focus specifically on software ecosystem [57,58] and on service innovation

Table 4. The most central publications for each of the four core communities. Centrality is evaluated by both HITS algorithm and Eigenvector centrality.

Com.	Authoritative Publication	Authority	Central publications	Centrality
1	Adner 2010 [46], Pierce 2009 [53]	0.009 & 0.008	Taney 2007 [54], Pierce 2009 [53]	0.75 & 0.72
2	Fragidis 2007 [55], Gueguen 2009 [49]	0.007 & 0.007	Fragidis 2007 [55], Fan 2004 [56]	0.79 & 0.7
5	Popp 2010 [57], Kabbedijk 2011 [58]	0.007 & 0.007	Arndt 2006 [59], Popp 2010 [57]	0.43 & 0.37
9	Kang 2011 [52], Zhang 2008 [60]	0.011 & 0.010	Scarlat 2007 [61], Zhang 2008 [60]	1 & 0.99

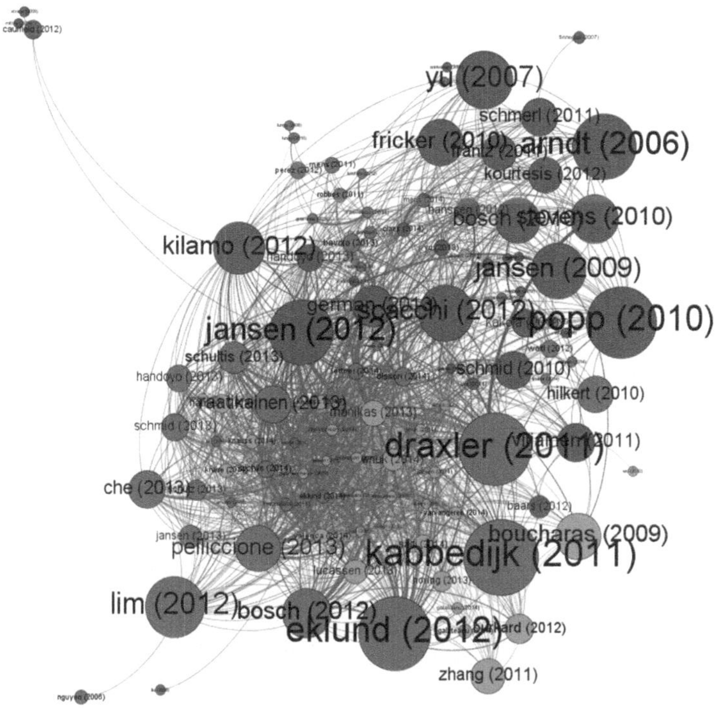

Fig. 3. Bibliographic coupling subnetwork for Community 5. Data: WoS

specifically in information system [59]. For the final core community, Community 9, our evaluation of the BC weight suggested that the community focuses on business ecosystems broadly. Looking at the central publications [52] does just this, but [60,61] clearly focus on the digital and mobile domains. This suggest that in parts the content of the community is more focused.

Focusing on the software context our focus turns towards Community 5, seen in Fig. 3. In the figure, the nodes are sized based on the Eigenvector Centrality. This reduces the size of the review article by [32] and highlights articles that are at by definition most important vertices within a graph. The subnetwork seen in Fig. 3 has been clustered using the Modularity algorithm highlighting four subcommunities.

Finally we reflect on the BC analysis by looking at the CoC results. Understanding the shared knowledge bases of the sample publications, we highlight the citations, not the publications. This shows what is the underlying shared background of the software ecosystem literature. This background is seen in Fig. 4.

The total amount of cited references for the 109 publications is 2357. Due to the unpracticality of visualizing a network so large, we set the minimum number of citations a cited reference has to have to 2. This excludes a significant amount of references that occur in the network only once, leaving the final analysis data with 273 cited publications. For these, we created a network based on

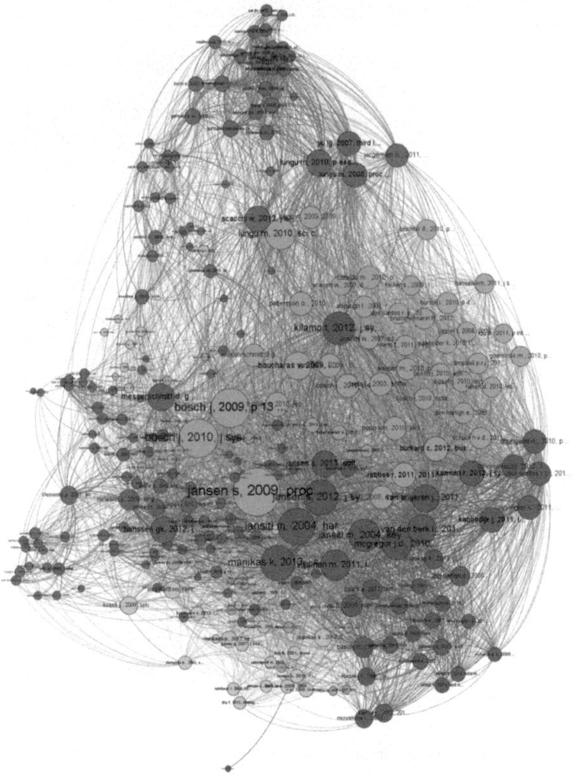

Fig. 4. Co-citation network of 273 publications core to software ecosystem literature (defined as Community 5). Data: WoS. The graph is available online at http://goo.gl/SMCHus (Color figure online)

co-citations. Using VOSviewer we identified that 2 documents from the 273 were not connected to the rest of the network and the largest set of connected nodes is 271. We excluded the two singular nodes, keeping the rest for the analysis.

The modularity algorithm highlighted five communities, seen in Fig. 4, of background literature in software ecosystems; Community 1 in red (N=55), Community 2 in blue (N=74), Community 3 in green (N=31), Community 4 in light green (N=60) and Community 5 in lilac (N=51). The size of the nodes reflects the number of connections to each node (Degree).

Analyzing the content of the communities further we identify thematic differences between the clusters. Community 1 (red,top) is the most technically oriented. In this the term software ecosystem refers to technical ecosystems exemplified by for example [62] focusing on open source ecosystems. Community 2 (blue, left) is based on case study research work. Central articles to the community focus on reporting case study research in software engineering [63] and the handbook to software ecosystems [64]. Community 3 (green, right) highlights background articles such as [65], which are at the core of strategic management literature. This stream of background literature ties the software ecosystem literature to the business ecosystem literature where publications, such as the before mentioned article by Gawer and Henderson, has received a significant interest. The central article to the community is Zhu's [66] strategic management article on entering platform markets. Community 4 (light green, bottom middle) focuses on modeling the ecosystem structures. This is exemplified by background on ecosystem modelling [67] and architecture [68]. Community 5 (lilac, bottom right) draws heavily from the management literature. Background highlights Moore's seminal article of Predator Pray competition as well as other management publications (e.g. [13,69]).

5 Discussion and Conclusions

Managerial and business strategy is riddled with fashionable terms – currently the ecosystem analogy by Moore [4] is very much in fashion. With the plethora of literature on the topic, we assume that the concept creates theoretical and practical value. There is, however, a clear need to identify what that value is and which communities are taking this analogy to use.

We used well-established bibliometric methods to uncover thematic differences in innovation, business and software ecosystem literature. These difference highlighted four larger thematic areas, one of which is software related. Looking at Table 4, we notice that the most central articles in Community 5 have a low Eigenvector centrality in the overall network. This suggest that when analyzing software ecosystem literature in its broader context it remains as more isolated than other communities. Using weather terminology, we may see how and where these low-pressure areas have emerged, and what is the current reading at the barometer, equaling the speed of development in that particular area.

Looking deeper to the sub–network of software ecosystem we uncovered five bibliographically coupled sub–communities seen in Fig. 3. We remain skeptical whether the figure is able to elaborate on the underlying structure of scientific research in software ecosystems. This suggests that we should look at the documents cited by the sub–community to create further insight.

The co-citation analysis highlighted the theoretical origins of software ecosystem research papers. It is apparent that the literature has a more technically oriented stream, but this is smaller in size comparison to the managerial and business oriented areas. The technically oriented research stream can also explain the isolation of the community seen in Table 4 as literature in this stream does not draw from the innovation and business ecosystem literature.

We also identifies a stream of literature focusing on research methods, specifically case study research in software engineering. This highlights the need for structured case studies, but also the large quantity of case study work published in recent years. Finally, we see three larger sub–communities focusing on managerial, strategy and business aspect of software ecosystems. This broad community need further analysis to understand the thematic differences between the communities. This is left for future work.

The study is limited by the selection of key search terms for the bibliometric analysis – as this also impacts the later qualitative analysis. Adding term, such as "mobile ecosystem" or "digital ecosystem" would have produced an different type of thematic clustering. A test of adding terms suggest that by adding more focused terms, such as the before mentioned, we would increase the document volume by approximately 25 %. We argue that our approach covers the largest artificial ecosystem fields, but further work should consider the possibility that a broader scope could create more insight to the structure or the field.

As a summary, our results highlighted that the "innovation ecosystem(s)", "business ecosystem(s)", "software ecosystem(s)" literature draws from four major thematical areas based on their background. One distinct area is the software ecosystem literature. The software ecosystem literature draws its theoretical background from five communities, one more technically oriented, one research methodology oriented and three business, management and strategy oriented themes. The barometer shows that there are several developing areas, and likely new ones are to be formed from the current ones.

References

1. Abrahamson, E.: Managerial fads and fashions: the diffusion and rejection of innovations. Acad. Manage. Rev. **16**(3), 586–612 (1991)
2. Furnham, A.: Fads and fashions in management (2015)
3. Tansley, A.G.: The use and abuse of vegetational concepts and terms. Ecology **16**(3), 284–307 (1935)
4. Moore, J.F.: Predators and prey: a new ecology of competition. Harvard Bus. Rev. **71**(3), 75–86 (1993)
5. Weber, M.L., Hine, M.J.: Who inhabits a business ecosystem? the technospecies as a unifying concept. Technol. Innov. Manage. Rev. **5**(5), 31–44 (2015)
6. Frosch, R.A., Gallopoulos, N.E.: Strategies for manufacturing. Sci. Am. **261**(3), 144–152 (1989)
7. Dedehayir, O., Ortt, J.R., Seppänen, M.: Reconfiguring the innovation ecosystem: an explorative study of disruptive change. In: International ICE Conference on Engineering, Technology and Innovation (ICE), pp. 1–9. IEEE (2014)
8. Clarysse, B., Wright, M., Bruneel, J., Mahajan, A.: Creating value in ecosystems: crossing the chasm between knowledge and business ecosystems. Res. Policy **43**(7), 1164–1176 (2014)
9. Basole, R.C.: Visualization of interfirm relations in a converging mobile ecosystem. J. Inf. Technol. **24**(2), 144–159 (2009)
10. Manikas, K., Hansen, K.M.: Software ecosystems – a systematic literature review. J. Syst. Softw. **86**(5), 1294–1306 (2013)
11. Håkansson, H., Ford, D., Gadde, L.E., Snehota, I., Waluszewski, A.: Business in Networks. Wiley, Chichester (2009)
12. Moore, J.F.: The Death of Competition: Leadership and Strategy in the Age of Business Ecosystems. Harper Business, New York (1996)
13. Iansiti, M., Levien, R.: Strategy as ecology. Harvard Bus. Rev. **82**(3), 68–78 (2004)
14. Iansiti, M., Levien, R.: The Keystone Advantage: What the New Dynamics of Business Ecosystems Mean for Strategy, Innovation, and Sustainability. Harvard Business School Press, Boston (2004)

15. Bosch, J.: From software product lines to software ecosystems. In: Proceedings of the 13th International Software Product Line Conference, SPLC 2009, pp. 111–119. Carnegie Mellon University, Pittsburgh (2009)
16. Jansen, S., Finkelstein, A., Brinkkemper, S.: A sense of community: A research agenda for software ecosystems. In: 31st International Conference on Software Engineering – Companion Volume, ICSE-Companion 2009, pp. 187–190. IEEE, May 2009
17. Basole, R.C., Karla, J.: On the evolution of mobile platform ecosystem structure and strategy. Bus. Inf. Syst. Eng. **3**, 313–322 (2011)
18. Hyrynsalmi, S., Suominen, A., Mäkilä, T., Knuutila, T.: The emerging mobile ecosystems: an introductory analysis of Android Market. In: Proceedings of the 21st International Conference on Management of Technology, IAMOT 2012, pp. 1–16. International Association for Management of Technology, Hsinchu, March 2012
19. Adner, R.: Match your innovation strategy to your innovation ecosystem. Harvard Bus. Rev. **84**(4), 98–107 (2006)
20. Rohrbeck, R., Hözle, K., Gemünden, H.G.: Opening up for competitive advantage – how Deutsche Telekom creates an open innovation ecosystem. R&D Manage. **39**(4), 420–430 (2009)
21. Adner, R., Kapoor, R.: Innovation ecosystems and the pace of substitution: re-examining technology s-curves. Forthcoming, December 2011
22. Briscoe, G., De Wilde, P.: Digital ecosystems: evolving service-orientated architectures. In: Proceedings of the 1st International Conference on Bio Inspired Models of Network, Information and Computing Systems, BIONETICS 2006, pp. 1–6. ACM, New York (2006)
23. Dini, P., Lombardo, G., Mansell, R., Razavi, A.R., Moschoyiannis, S., Krause, P., Nicolai, A., León, L.R.: Beyond interoperability to digital ecosystems: regional innovation and socio-economic development led by SMEs. Int. J. Technol. Learn. Innov. Dev. **1**(3), 410–426 (2008)
24. Stanley, J., Briscoe, G.: The ABC of digital business ecosystems. Commun. Law – J. Comput. Media Telecommun. Law **15**(1), 12–25 (2010)
25. Hyrynsalmi, S.:Letters from the war of ecosystems — an analysis of independentsoftware vendors in mobile application marketplaces. Doctoral dissertation, University of Turku, Turku, Finland, TUCS Dissertations No 188, December 2014
26. Gueguen, G., Isckia, T.: The borders of mobile handset ecosystems: is coopetition inevitable? Telematics Inform. **28**(1), 5–11 (2011)
27. Larrucea, X., Nanclares, F., Santamaria, I.: A method for defining a regional software ecosystem strategy: colombia as a case study. Technol. Forecast. Soc. Change **104**, 247–258 (2016)
28. Ben Hadj Salem Mhamdia, A.: Performance measurement practices in software ecosystem. Int. J. Prod. Perform. Manage. **62**(5), 514–533 (2013)
29. den Hartigh, E., Visscher, W., Tol, M., Salas, A.J.: Measuring the health of a business ecosystem. In: Jansen, S., Brinkkemper, S., Cusumano, M.A. (eds.) Software Ecosystems: Analyzing and Managing Business Networks in the Software Industry, pp. 221–246. Edward Elgar Publisher Inc., Northampton (2013)
30. Hyrynsalmi, S., Suominen, A., Mäntymäki, M.: The influence of developer multi-homing on competition between software ecosystems. J. Syst. Softw. **111**, 119–127 (2016)

31. Barbosa, O., dos Santos, R.P., Alves, C., Werner, C., Jansen, S.: A systematic mapping study on software ecosystems from a three-dimensional perspective. In: Jansen, S., Brinkkemper, S., Cusumano, M.A. (eds.) Software Ecosystems: Analyzing and Managing Business Networks in the Software Industry, pp. 59–81. Edward Elgar Publisher Inc., Northampton (2013)
32. Hyrynsalmi, S., Seppänen, M., Nokkala, T., Suominen, A., Järvi, A.: Wealthy, healthy and/or happy — what does 'ecosystem health' stand for? In: Fernandes, J.M., Machado, R.J., Wnuk, K. (eds.) Software Business. LNBIP, vol. 210, pp. 272–287. Springer, Heidelberg (2015)
33. Hanssen, G.K., Dybå, T.: Theoretical foundations of software ecosystems. In: Jansen, S., Bosch, J., Alves, C.F. (eds.) Proceedings of the International Workshop on Software Ecosystems, CEUR Workshop Proceedings, vol. 879, pp. 2–13. MIT Sloan School of Management, Cambridge, June 2012. CEUR-WS
34. Archambault, É., Campbell, D., Gingras, Y., Larivière, V.: Comparing bibliometric statistics obtained from the web of science and scopus. J. Am. Soc. Inf. Sci. Technol. **60**(7), 1320–1326 (2009)
35. Zeleny, M., Cornet, R., Stoner, J.: Applying the new set of lenses - implications for managers of managing in the business ecosystem. In: Hennessy, J.E., Robins, S. (eds.) Managing toward the millennium. Fordham Univ Press (1991)
36. Teece, D.J.: Explicating dynamic capabilities: the nature and microfoundations of (sustainable) enterprise performance. Strateg. Manage. J. **28**(13), 1319–1350 (2007)
37. Kessler, M.: An experimental study of bibliographic coupling between technical papers (corresp.). IEEE Trans. Inf. Theory **9**(1), 49–51 (1963)
38. Peters, H.P., Braam, R.R., van Raan, A.F.: Cognitive resemblance and citation relations in chemical engineering publications. J. Am. Soc. Inf. Sci. **46**(1), 9 (1995)
39. Small, H.: Co-citation in the scientific literature: a new measure of the relationship between two documents. J. Am. Soc. Inf. Sci. **24**(4), 265–269 (1973)
40. Garfield, E.: From bibliographic coupling to co-citationanalysis via algorithmic historio-bibliography: a citationist's tribute to belverc. griffith. Drexel University, Philadelphia, PA (2001)
41. van Eck, N., Waltman, L.: Software survey: vosviewer, a computer program for bibliometric mapping. Scientometrics **84**(2), 523–538 (2009)
42. Blondel, V.D., Guillaume, J.L., Lambiotte, R., Lefebvre, E.: Fast unfolding of communities in large networks. J. Stat. Mech. Theory Exp. **2008**(10), P10008 (2008)
43. Kleinberg, J.M.: Authoritative sources in a hyperlinked environment. J. ACM (JACM) **46**(5), 604–632 (1999)
44. Gawer, A., Cusumano, M.A.: Industry platforms and ecosystem innovation. J. Prod. Innov. Manage. **31**(3), 417–433 (2014)
45. Brusoni, S., Prencipe, A.: The organization of innovation in ecosystems: problem framing, problem solving, and patterns of coupling. Adv. Strat. Manage. **30**(2013), 167–194 (2013)
46. Adner, R., Kapoor, R.: Value creation in innovation ecosystems: How the structure of technological interdependence affects firm performance in new technology generations. Strat. Manage. J. **31**(3), 306–333 (2010)
47. Nikayin, F., De Reuver, M., Itälä, T.: Collective action for a common service platform for independent living services. Int. J. Med. Inform. **82**(10), 922–939 (2013)
48. Shang, T., Shi, Y.: The dynamics of business ecosystems in the context of industrial emergence. In: GMC 2013: Proceedings of the Ninth International Symposium on Global Manufacturing and China, pp. 168–172 (2013)

49. Gueguen, G., Isckia, T.: The borders of mobile handset ecosystems: is coopetition inevitable? In: Hesselman, C., Giannelli, C. (eds.) Mobile Wireless Middleware, Operating Systems, and Applications-Workshops, vol. 12, pp. 45–54. Springer, Heidelberg (2009)
50. Crooymans, W., Pradhan, P., Jansen, S.: Exploring network modelling and strategy in the dutch software business ecosystem. In: Fernandes, J.M., Machado, R.J., Wnuk, K. (eds.) Software Business. LNBIP, vol. 210, pp. 45–59. Springer, Heidelberg (2015)
51. Liu, G., Rong, K.: The nature of the co-evolutionary process complex product development in the mobile computing industrys business ecosystem. Group Organ. Manage. **40**(6), 809–842 (2015)
52. Kang, C., Hong, Y.S., Kim, K.J., Park, K.T., et al.: Representation and analysis of business ecosystems co-specializing products and services. In: DS 68–4: Proceedings of the 18th International Conference on Engineering Design (ICED 2011), Impacting Society through Engineering Design, vol. 4. Product and Systems Design, Lyngby/Copenhagen, 15–19 August 2011
53. Pierce, L.: Big losses in ecosystem niches: How core firm decisions drive complementary product shakeouts. Strat. Manage. J. **30**(3), 323–347 (2009)
54. Tanev, S.: Toward a methodology for studying the application of open source innovation practices in non-software domains. In: Saratov Fall Meeting 2006: Optical Technologies in Biophysics and Medicine VIII, p. 65350T. International Society for Optics and Photonics (2007)
55. Fragidis, G., Tarabanis, K., Koumpis, A.: Conceptual and business models for customer-centric business ecosystems. In: Digital EcoSystems and Technologies Conference, DEST 2007. Inaugural IEEE-IES, pp. 94–99. IEEE (2007)
56. Fan, B.: Competitive strategy: a business eco-system perspective. In: ISMOT 2004: Proceedings of the Fourth International Conference on Management of Innovation and Technology: Managing Total Innovation in the 21st Century, pp. 281–284 (2004)
57. Popp, K.M., Meyer, R.: Profit from Software Ecosystems: Business Models, Ecosystems and Partnerships in the Software Industry. Books on Demand GmbH, Norderstedt (2010)
58. Kabbedijk, J., Jansen, S.: Steering insight: an exploration of the ruby software ecosystem. In: Regnell, B., van de Weerd, I., De Troyer, O. (eds.) ICSOB 2011. LNBIP, vol. 80, pp. 44–55. Springer, Heidelberg (2011)
59. Arndt, J.M., Dibbern, J.: Co-innovation in a service oriented strategic network. In: IEEE International Conference on Services Computing, SCC2006, pp. 285–288. IEEE (2006)
60. Zhang, J., Huo, Y., Liang, X.J.: Business ecosystem strategies of mobile network operators in the 3G era: the case of china mobile. China Commun. **5**(3), 114–118 (2008)
61. Scarlat, E.: From virtual enterprises to digital business ecosystems: a survey on the modeling and simulation methods. Econ. Comput. Econ. Cybern. Stud. Res. **41**(1–2), 17–29 (2007)
62. Scacchi, W., Alspaugh, T.A.: Understanding the role of licenses and evolution in open architecture software ecosystems. J. Syst. Softw. **85**(7), 1479–1494 (2012). Software Ecosystems special issue
63. Runeson, P., Host, M., Rainer, A., Regnell, B.: Case Study Research in Software Engineering: Guidelines and Examples. Wiley, Hoboken (2012)
64. Messerschmitt, D.G., Szyperski, C.: Software Ecosystem: Understanding an Indispensable Technology and Industry. The MIT Press, Cambridge (2003)

65. Gawer, A., Henderson, R.: Platform owner entry and innovation in complementary markets: evidence from intel. J. Econ. Manage. Strat. **16**(1), 1–34 (2007)
66. Zhu, F., Iansiti, M.: Entry into platform-based markets. Strat. Manage. J. **33**(1), 88–106 (2012)
67. Boucharas, V., Jansen, S., Brinkkemper, S.: Formalizing software ecosystem modeling. In: Proceedings of the 1st International Workshop on Open Component-Ecosystems, IWOCE 2009, pp. 41–50. ACM, New York (2009)
68. Anvaari, M., Jansen, S.: Evaluating architectural openness in mobile software platforms. In: Proceedings of the Fourth European Conference on Software Architecture: Companion Volume, ECSA 2010, pp. 85–92. ACM, New York (2010)
69. Viljainen, M., Kauppinen, M.: Software ecosystems: a set of management practices for platform integrators in the telecom industry. In: Regnell, B., van de Weerd, I., De Troyer, O. (eds.) ICSOB 2011. LNBIP, vol. 80, pp. 32–43. Springer, Heidelberg (2011)

PDISC – Towards a Method for Software Product DISCovery

Type: Exploratory Paper

Karl Werder[1(✉)], Benedikt Zobel[2], and Alexander Maedche[3]

[1] University of Mannheim, Mannheim, Germany
werder@es.uni-mannheim.de
[2] Osnabrueck University, Osnabrueck, Germany
benedikt.zobel@uni-osnabrueck.de
[3] Karlsruhe Institute of Technology, Karlsruhe, Germany
alexander.maedche@kit.edu

Abstract. For the creation of software products, the idea of iterative and incremental development and design is widely accepted and embedded in various methodologies. However, earlier activities within software projects are often the cause for the projects termination. Such activities are often described as the product discovery phase. Therefore, this study develops PDISC, a method for software product discovery. Following a design science research approach, a systematic literature review extracts design requirements and method fragments from literature. The method fragments describe early activities and are documented using process deliverable diagrams. Collectively, such method fragments form a method database that is used to develop PDISC. PDISC helps practitioners to conduct early activities in a systematic way in order to create a product vision.

Keywords: Software product · Discovery · Method engineering · Product vision

1 Introduction

Product discovery phase is the term used to describe early activities collectively in order to create a viable, desirable and feasible product vision. These early activities provide a different set of challenges and our understanding of their precise influence on a product remains unclear [1, 2]. Hence, practitioners require actionable guidance in the form of a method for the discovery of software products [1, 2]. Such method can help practitioners to structure their early activities. Moreover, it assures the correct shaping and documentation of the product idea in the form of a product vision.

More recently, scholars explore the combination of different methodologies. For example, the combination of agile software development (ASD) and user-centered design (UCD), i.e. blending practices and techniques for development with those established in the design discipline (e.g. [1, 3, 4]). Fox et al. [3] for example, suggest a method combining ASD and UCD through a cycle zero and parallel yet interwoven tracks. Focusing on the individual, da Silva [5] worked extensively to identify the role of

A. Maglyas and A.-L. Lamprecht (Eds.): ICSOB 2016, LNBIP 240, pp. 47–62, 2016.
DOI: 10.1007/978-3-319-40515-5_4

UX designers within agile teams and the integration of interaction design into ASD [6]. In a similar vein, Ferreira, Noble, and Biddle [7] suggest steps towards the cooperation of user experience designers and agile developers. Brhel et al. [1] identified five principles along the processes and practices of UCD and ASD domains, establishing a user-centered agile software development approach. However, we lack systematic knowledge on how to conduct early activities and deliverables during the product discovery phase [1, 2]. The objective of such phase is the creation of a product vision that improves the software's success. To the author's knowledge, there is no discovery method for software products suggested in the literature.

Therefore, we follow calls for more research on product discovery [1, 2, 8] and seek to develop a method for software product discovery. Our research objectives are to: (a) review existing literature on methods regarding the discovery of software products, (b) extract and formalize existing methods from such literature to establish clear design requirements and design principles, and (c) translate those design requirements into a formalized method for software product discovery. We formulate the following research question: *How to design a method for a software product discovery phase?*

The paper contributes to practice and theory. The practical contribution is PDISC, a method for software product discovery. Such method helps practitioners to articulate needed activities and deliverables when discovering software products. In addition, it provides a checklist in the form of a comprehensive list of activities and deliverables during such process. While processes within firms may vary depending on situational factors, such list creates awareness of fundamental activities and deliverables of product discovery. The theoretical contribution of the paper is the systematic extraction of design requirements and subsequent formulation of clear design principles. These principles categorize the requirements along product-, user- and team-related aspects and therefore, address concerns of viability, desirability and feasibility of the envisioned product. We establish clear phases within product discovery that form a framework for future research.

2 Foundations and Related Work

The term product discovery has been heavily used in the pharmaceutical domain and the area of drug discovery (e.g. [9]). However, in recent years the term is used to describe a phase of upfront activities preceding the product development and product design phases [1]. In the field of new product development, it describes the ideation generation stage [10]. Others highlight the importance of this phase to determine the actual need for such a product and the existence of a user base on the one hand, and the actual feasibility of such a solution on the other hand [11].

As shown in Fig. 1, ASD is one possible representation of product development phase, while UCD serves as representation of product design. Product design is a key element in various software development methodologies. Some authors describe it as conceptualization of a solution prior to programming activities [12]. Product development, in turn, describes the creation or implementation of software artifacts, e.g. by programming [13]. In iterative or agile frameworks these two phases are executed multiple times, and are thus depicted as parallel to one another (e.g. [1, 3]).

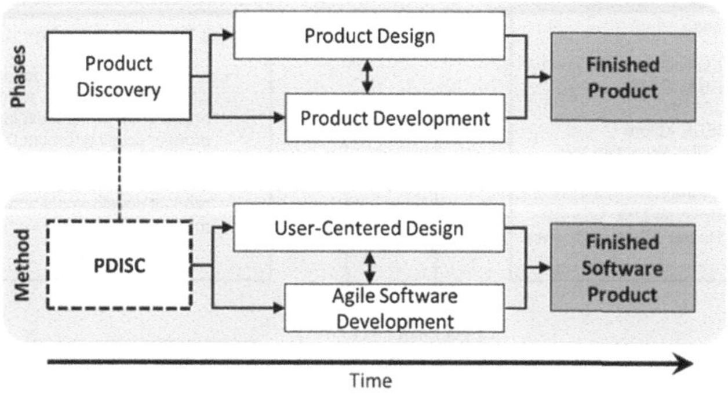

Fig. 1. Placement of a method for product discovery in existing methods and phases

The combination of ASD and UCD becomes more and more a research stream by itself. In ASD and UCD, the strict separation of upfront and development and design phase (as it is done e.g. in waterfall-models) was changed to an iterative process, leaving early activities mostly out of scope [1, 3, 12, 14]. Scrum as methodology proposing concrete guidelines for agile development in formulating teams and roles also does not focus on activities prior to building software artifacts [15, 16]. More insights could stem from the not software-related areas of New Product Development and Innovation Management. In these, Product Discovery was introduced as so called front-end phases, with buzzwords such as "fuzzy front-end" and "front-end innovation" [17–19]. The key goal of these phases is to reduce uncertainty and equivocality that is largely present at the early stages of product development [17–21]. Therefore, a method summarizing and structuring early activities related to software development and design is entitled PDISC.

3 Research Method

For the development of the software product discovery method, we opt for a design science research (DSR) approach [22, 23] in combination with the discipline of method engineering [24–26]. The study investigates the method for product discovery as its central artifact. Moreover, the study aims at solving a practical problem by designing an appropriate artifact [27]. First, the problem is identified (cf. Sect. 1). In order to define the solutions objective, the study reviews the literature, defines the term software product discovery and extracts design requirements. Next, the study develops design principles that guide the design and development of PDISC. For the design and development, the study relies on a method database.

In order to extract design requirements and method fragments, the study starts with a systematic literature review (SLR) [28, 29]. A systematic process and transparent documentation of the literature allows the reader to assess the completeness of the review [29]. Hence, the first step in conducting a SLR is the development of a study protocol. The protocol documents the main research questions, key decisions along the scope (e.g. search strategy; databases; inclusion, exclusion, and quality criteria), and a concept-matrix. Figure 2 presents the search strategy. Hereafter, the studies inclusion

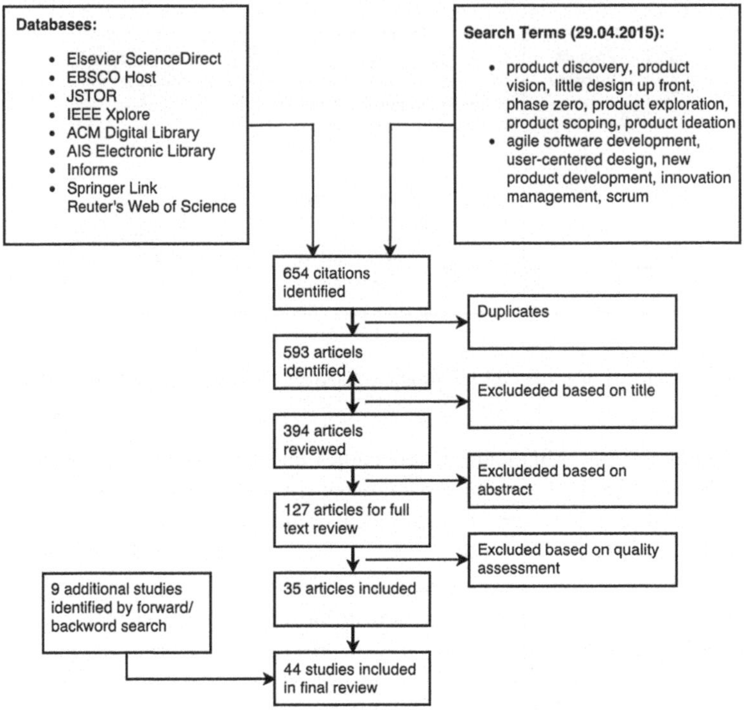

Fig. 2. Search strategy diagram

and exclusion criteria, the data sources and search strategy, and the data extraction and analysis process are described in more details.

3.1 Inclusion and Exclusion Criteria

The study includes articles that provide insights on potential shortcomings w.r.t. the product discovery phase of software products. In addition, articles that describe possible solutions and/or recommendations of a product discovery phase are included. The investigated timeframe is from 1997 until mid-2015, given the origins of agile as an established reference methodology. After the initial query of the databases, the exclusion of duplicates reduces the initial set of 654 articles to 593 articles. Thereafter, the exclusion based on the title, e.g. with an irrelevant industrial focus such as biology and pharmacy or industrial engineering, leads to a selection of 394 articles. Following, reading the abstracts excludes those articles that do not focus or contribute to product discovery. Consequently, 127 articles remain for further assessment. Based on this assessment, every paper receives a score on a 5-point Likert scale assessing their applicability to four questions. The questions assess whether a goal is mentioned by the authors, whether there is an empirical part of this paper, whether shortcomings or challenges related to product discovery are mentioned and whether recommendation to product discovery are documented. The study excludes articles that receive a score of less than three. As a result, 35 articles are relevant for this study. Conducting a forward and backward search leads to the inclusion of another nine articles, resulting in 44 articles.

3.2 Data Sources and Search Strategy

The sources focus on databases that include publications from the field of information systems discipline, computer science and general management. Hence, following a rather inclusive approach in response to some critics and therefore, also identifying less impactful yet still relevant publications in the search results [30]. We include the following nine databases: Elsevier ScienceDirect, EBSCO Host, JSTOR, IEEE Xplore, ACM Digital Library, AIS Electronic Library, Informs, Springer Link and Reuter's Web of Science. Given that different synonyms exist for the term product discovery, a preceding exploratory literature search identifies the keyword-matrix. In order to assure that the correct keywords are in the search string and the study identifies relevant articles, we conduct a pilot test using IEEE as the sample database. We analyze the resulting 134 articles for plausibility and soundness. Thereafter, the keyword-matrix builds the basis for the search string in order to identify and evaluate prevalent matches in research literature. Consequently, we formulated the following search string:

```
("product discovery" OR "product vision" OR "little design up
front" OR "phase zero" OR "product exploration" OR "product
scoping" OR "product ideation")
AND
("agile software development" OR "user-centered design" OR "new
product development" OR "innovation management" OR "scrum")
```

3.3 Data Extraction and Data Analysis

In order to extract information, the study analyzes 44 articles for their shortcomings and proposed actions related to product discovery. Clusters start to form and the articles build groups along identified commonalities (see Table 1). During the full text review, the authors highlight critical sections and aggregate them in order to transfer them into the research database. The database documents key information, such as the dimension, the corresponding activity, phase and methodology, and their use in design requirements and design principles. While 28 articles suggest shortcomings of current practices in a discovery phase, 30 articles provide suggestions on the implementation of early activities. Articles proposing activities are potential contributions towards the method database. Thereafter, nine articles with concrete and multiple activities form the method database. A Process-Deliverable-Diagram (PDD) models and documents the activities of each article. Documenting the activities using a PDD enriches the methods' understanding and structures the method fragments.

4 Results

From the final list of articles, we identify eight common challenges (see Table 1). Overall, we see three related groups of challenges, i.e. product-related, user-related and team-related. First, challenges related to the product, i.e. the need to define the product

Table 1. Challenges related to the discovery of products mentioned in primary articles.

Challenges	References
Product vision needs to be defined earlier and clearer that it is current practice	Ferreira, Noble, & Biddle, 2007 [7]; Heikkilä et al., 2015 [15]; Hildenbrand & Meyer, 2012 [30]; Hollis & Maiden, 2013 [31]; Kajko-Mattsson & Nyfjord, 2009 [32]; Kakar & Carver, 2012 [20]; Nyfjord & Kajko-Mattsson, 2008 [33]; Qumer & Henderson-Sellers, 2007 [34]; Sarpong & Maclean, 2012 [35]; Sibghatullah & Hussain, 2006 [36]; Stevens, 2014 [17]; Tessarolo, 2007 [37]; Vanhanen, Itkonen, & Sulonen, 2003 [38]
User involvement as early as possible	Brhel, Meth, Maedche, & Werder, 2015 [3]; Cloyd, 2001 [39]; T. S. Da Silva, Martin, Maurer, & Silveira, 2011 [8]; Ferreira et al., 2007 [7]; Fox, Sillito, & Maurer, 2008 [1]; Hildenbrand & Meyer, 2012 [30]; Kuusinen, 2014 [16]; Patton, 2002 [40]; Rejeb, Boly, & Morel-Guimaraes, 2008 [41]; Salah, Paige, & Cairns, 2014 [42]; Sibghatullah & Hussain, 2006 [36]; Sohaib & Khan, 2010 [14]
Conduct little design upfront	Adikari, McDonald, & Campbell, 2009 [43]; Brhel et al., 2015 [3]; T. S. Da Silva et al., 2011 [8]; Ferreira et al., 2007 [7]; Kuusinen, 2014 [16]; Miller, 2005 [44]; Salah et al., 2014 [45]; Salah, Paige, & Cairns, 2014 [42]
Utilize fuzzy front end and front end innovation	Frishammar, Florén, & Wincent, 2011 [18]; Kakar & Carver, 2012 [20]; Khurana & Rosenthal, 1998 [21]; Knoll & Horton, 2011 [46]; Oliveira & Rozenfeld, 2010 [47]; Rejeb et al., 2008 [41]; Sperry & Jetter, 2009 [19]; Stevens, 2014 [17]
Establish a sprint zero	Adikari et al., 2009 [43]; Heikkilä et al., 2015 [15]; Inayat, Salim, Marczak, Daneva, & Shamshirband, 2015 [48]; Kajko-Mattsson & Nyfjord, 2009 [32]; Loniewski, Armesto, & Insfran, 2011 [49]; Sibghatullah & Hussain, 2006 [36]
Developing a low-fidelity prototype	Cloyd, 2001 [39]; T. S. da Silva et al., 2011 [6]; Fox et al., 2008 [1]; Salvador, Nakasone, & Pow-Sang, 2014 [50]
Moving items from product vision to product backlog	Cloyd, 2001 [39]; Hildenbrand & Meyer, 2012 [30]; Qumer & Henderson-Sellers, 2007 [34]; Vanhanen et al., 2003 [38]
Using the concept of design thinking	Hildenbrand & Meyer, 2012 [30]

vision early and communicate its practice clearly. Second, when working with users, developers and designer face a common challenge, i.e. early user involvement. Organizations often delay such involvement, resulting in negative consequences. Third, teams need to adopt the correct practices, such as little design upfront and the development of low-fidelity prototypes.

5 Designing a Method for Software Product Discovery

Product Related Requirements. While ASD is an established method with a focus on the software's functionality, it is vague about the starting conditions. Examples are the desirable upfront-activities that are not planned in development projects [43]. As a result, these steps often lack time and budget during their execution [43, 46, 48]. Other appeals include calls for a clearer position of exploratory activities in software development projects, insufficiently addressed by current agile methods [52], as well as calls for less uncertainty and ignorance within pre-implementation phases of agile projects [34]. Furthermore, reflecting mentions criticize the implementation of operational planning activities only in later development phases, and a lack of describing activities required for the creation of product visions or product backlogs, even in cases the notion of these documents is used by scholars [15, 31]. Hence, we formulate the first Design Requirement (**DR1**): *A method for Software Product Discovery should articulate early activities that improve the software product development environment.*

Idea generation is a key activity in a proposed pre-phase 0 [21], executed prior to the development of a new product, and prior to the identification of detailed customer needs, technological capabilities, or core product requirements [17]. Menor, Tatikonda, and Sampson [53] describe a similar idea generating activity in the area of new service development. An initial ideation step as well as idea generation technique is also used in new product development [19, 47]. Therefore, we formulate (**DR2**): *A method for Software Product Discovery should collect initial product ideas.*

Some sources mention that agile practices only start after a vision or more concrete artifacts are established [31]. According to Sarpong and Maclean [36], a product vision can be defined as the "mental image of a yet to be realized product". Others try to conceptualize ways to reach a useful vision. An extended envisioning process is suggested as a way to identify high-level requirements [32]. More explicitly, the product vision serves as a key input element for all further activities [39]. Kajko-Mattsson and Nyfjord [33] even describe a product vision planning phase in detail, aiming at identifying a so-called product vision plan. Sibghatullah and Hussain [37] introduce the so-called product vision statement as a result of visioning activities, and state that the product vision becomes more important, the higher the uncertainty or complexity of the product goal is. Using the term "High-Level Product Scope", others propose the up-front activity of building a visionary scope initially, and revising it through all iterations to come [49]. In design thinking, the vision is frequently enriched in the ideate-phase [31]. Furthermore, counting towards a vision is the "holistic design vision" as a result of an iteration 0 [43]. As a result of a pre-phase 0 different kinds of a version can be possible, for example for the business, a project, and a product simultaneously [21]. Kakar and Carver [20] state that the creation of a clearly defined product concept is important in order to effectively manage the software development process. Tessarolo [38] states that a product vision can further be important for on-time performance. The process of product vision planning is described by Nyfjord and Kajko-Mattsson [34]. A developed vision can be used for sharing a unified picture, for example, with the developers [54]. This in turn constitutes towards a unified understanding of the product in the project team [55]. Ferreira et al. [7] recommend that usability concerns should be a part of the vision, while Ebert [56] sees translated market needs as input for the vision. In order to include this upfront visioning work in the product discovery phase, we derive (**DR3**): *A method for Software Product Discovery should form a product vision.*

When taking a closer look at the results of the process, scholars mention that agile development practices should pay more attention to usability concerns. Literature often states that either pragmatic and hedonic qualities do not play a role at all [1, 3, 14, 41, 44], or only at a time much too late to have a major impact on the resulting product [40, 51]. One goal should thus be to include a user-focus during the process. This is supported by the statement that User-Centered Design would be "a perfect fit for an agile environment" [57], and that "requirements should be based on what users would be doing with the product". Hence, we derive (**DR4**): *A method for Software Product Discovery should extract users' needs for pragmatic and hedonic qualities.*

To improve software product development process and environment early activities have to be embedded and clearly articulated (DR1). A focus on the software product is broken down into elements, stating that a first instance collects initial product ideas (DR2). Such ideas will be developed into and form a concrete product vision (DR3). Furthermore, the two basic requirements of a software product, i.e. the software needs to be usable and useful are to be considered. As these four Design Requirements all share the focus of the software product itself, the first Design Principle (**DP1**) summarizes them: *Product context, goals, purposes and key requirements require clarification in order to improve product success.*

User Related Requirements. In ASD as well as UCD, users and customers play a larger role through a principle called "frequent stakeholder involvement" in comparison to traditional development or design techniques. Stakeholders are important in every development project. While there are many stakeholders available, the user is one of the most important ones. However, the creation process of a software product often neglects the user. For example, ASD does not provide concrete guidance on how to develop software that is user-friendly [43]. However, this poses difficulties during the development, especially in terms of software's usability. Often, a reason for the lack of usability is the low prioritization of usability during the development. In addition, there is often no guidance on user experience activities [16]. Some point out that the lack of user-focus in agile practices is a key reason for a lack in innovation management [42]. In order to cope with this issue, the literature presents different suggestions. One example is a condensed up-front user analysis [40, 45]. Therefore, we derive (**DR5**): *A method for Software Product Discovery should improve the adoption of practices for researching users' needs.*

Eventually, user requirements have to be collected and evaluated [58]. Hildenbrand and Meyer [31] mention that even mature processes, such as lean thinking do not provide descriptions on how to gain knowledge of user requirements. Sohaib and Khan [14] ask how user requirements could be gained from the stakeholders usually involved in agile feedback rounds. In most cases, this is the customer rather than the end-user. Sy [54] propose their version of a cycle zero, also incorporating user research. In order to process such requirements effectively, they need to a proper documentation. We identify (**DR6**): *A method for Software Product Discovery should properly document and record user requirements as a basis for further design and development activities.*

Building on the two prior design requirements, both, practices and documentation need to be integrated into the ongoing developments [50]. Even without starting actual programming activities, it is still necessary to prepare for a later phase. It ensures the ability to integrate collected requirements. For cycle zero, Sy [54] proposes the detailed inquiry of collecting data in order to support later phases. For example, the provision of exact target user descriptions. The process following the design thinking principles can also help to include the users' wishes into the finished product [31]. Other agile techniques, such as user-goal-analysis followed by prototyping activities, also try to improve this process [35, 40]. Following, we identify (**DR7**): *A method for Software Product Discovery should enable the integration of user requirements and user-centered practices into further design and development activities.*

The need to improve the adoption of user research practices (DR5) and the proper documentations of their results (DR6) provides a sound basis. However, these also need a successful integration into further design and development activities (DR7). As these requirements are user related and aim to include the user into the design and development activities, they are summarized into **DP2**: *A method of Software Product Discovery should provide methods to research and integrate specific users' needs and demands into the software product design and development process in order to the product's usability and user experience.*

Team Related Requirements. Furthermore, we find shortcomings of the overall understanding or "picture" by the design and development team. For example, da Silva et al. [8] points out that the "big picture" of what is expected is gone missing at some point in time throughout the project. This issue can be attributed to the fact that either there is not enough detail of the concepts to begin with, or the formulated product vision poses inconsistencies [33, 38, 39]. Countermeasures propose the constitution of a shared vision amongst all project members [18, 43, 46, 54, 59]. Hence, we suggest (**DR8**): *A method for Software Product Discovery should enable the product team to develop a unified understanding of the product.*

Hollis & Maiden [32] and Adikari et al. [44] further focus on requirements and requirements engineering, and how these processes lack creative thinking and a dedicated focus when implemented today. In current development projects, a lack of guidance can be observed that leads to either bad quality or longer development times [37]. The challenging combination of creative thinking and structured stepwise progress comes from fundamental difference between design and development. While the design emphasizes the creative part that can be hard to articulate and document, development stemming from the engineering disciplines builds on stepwise and sequential process improvements. A design and development team needs to master both. Hence, we derive (**DR9**): *A method for Software Product Discovery should enable the product team to master both, development maturity and creative thinking.*

The lack of up-front activities as mentioned in the literature (e.g. [43, 46]) can be rooted back to a lack of management support and appreciation [52]. Consequently, a lack of other elements, such as maintenance, is found in the literature [33]. In describing general problems in ASD, Hollis & Maiden [32] state that the principle of simplicity found throughout agile processes has been taken too far to still provide any contribution towards innovation, while Ebert [56] finds fault with agile cycle times being too long to still be productive. In addition, the coordination in agile teams between the different functions leads to project delays [56]. Both, cycle time and project coordination are common management decisions. From a different perspective, Gamble & Hale [60] describe that scalability is difficult or problematic to achieve in ASD projects. Also, UCD is prone to management challenges. For example, Salah et al. [43] often find a lack of support by management roles towards user-centered activities, making it difficult for the team to execute them. Summarizing, we formulate (**DR10**): *A method for Software Product Discovery should assure management support for the product team.*

Furthermore, the need to clearly separate product discovery from product creation has been stressed in literature [1]. Such separation helps to clearly separate roles and responsibilities. For example, within UCD it is important to distinguish between the researcher and a prototyper [57]. Within ASD, the importance of clearly upfront specified roles and responsibilities have been suggested [55]. Given its importance, we also find it rooted in SCRUM, one example method of ASD. Therefore, we suggest (**DR12**): *A method for Software Product Discovery should clearly distinguish different roles and their responsibilities for the product team.*

Gaining a unified understanding of the product in planning (DR9), providing thorough guidance for designers and developers (DR10), ensuring management support (DR11) as well was specifying and separating team roles and responsibilities (DR12) are design requirements focusing on the team, i.e. all human resources involved. The last design principle **DP3** summarizes these team requirements: *A method of Software Product Discovery should guide a diverse team of specialists to develop a unified understanding of the product and its importance.*

6 The PDISC Method

Following the extraction of the methods and method fragments from prior literature, PDISC - a method for product discovery – is built. Starting with an initial idea generation (cf. [21, 39, 53]), each stakeholder can make suggestions in order to develop an idea pool. Interviews or focus groups help to gather ideas early on. Thereafter, an iterative process allows the execution of activities multiple times. Three main activities follow and can be executed in parallel. First, users are engaged and integrated into the discovery process [21, 31, 37, 40, 43, 54]. Marketers or developers use general or contextual interviews, task analysis or other practices to engage the user and collect requirement. Second, a central product vision document is created, so that a common

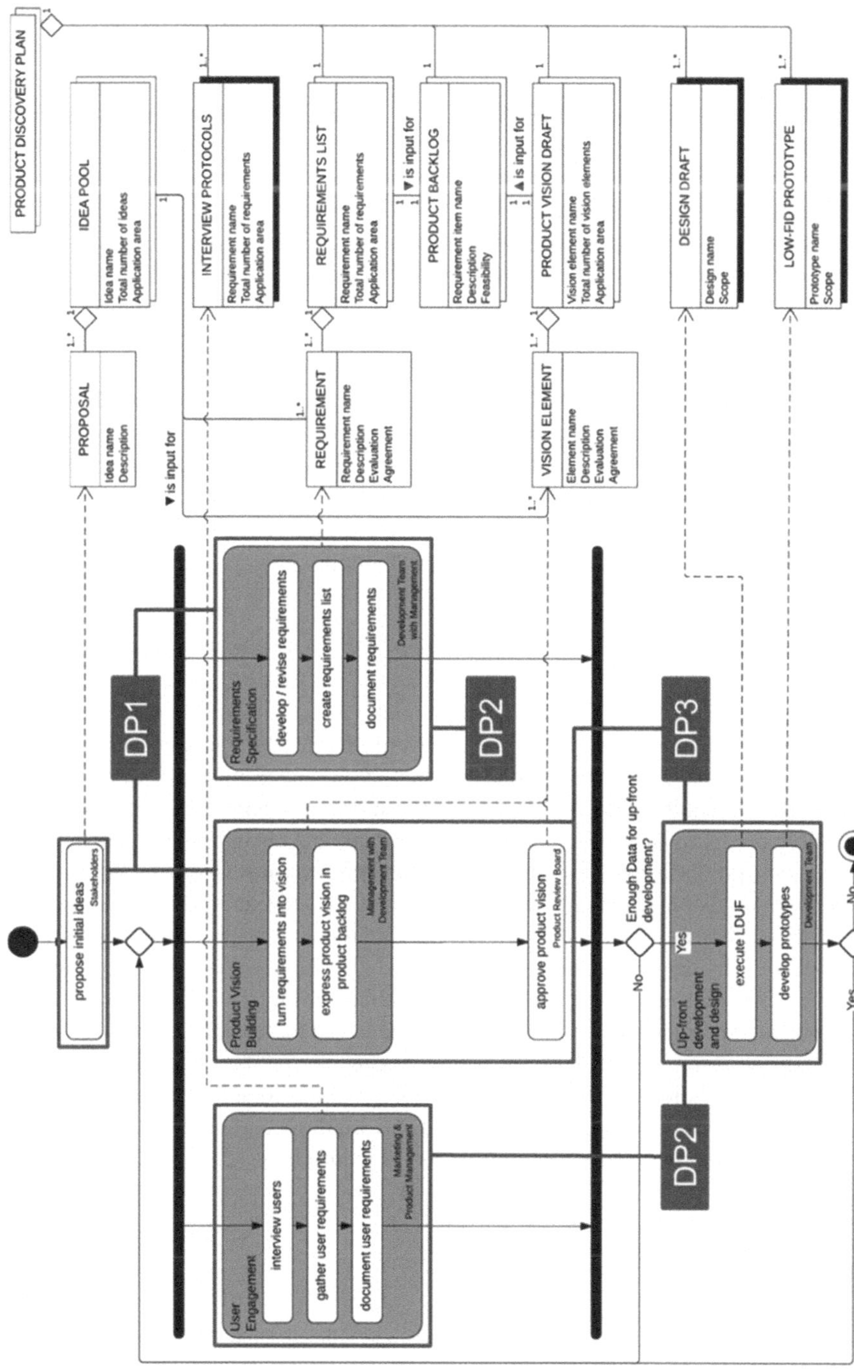

Fig. 3. PDISC, method for software product discovery. Described as a PDD with an overlay of the associated design principles related to the activities.

understanding is developed and documented for management approval [33, 37, 39, 54]. Management and the development team use prioritization techniques to select requirements and convert them into the product backlog. Third, requirements are generated, initially based on the idea pool [21, 31, 33, 37, 43]. In later iterations, such requirements are refined using the results from the user engagement. The documentation of user stories or scenarios can help the development team to communicate such requirements to management (Fig. 3).

The product vision draft and the requirements list form the product backlog [33, 39]. Until this point, the product backlog is the central element combining different activities and serving as input for any later phases. While this rather technical pool of functionality provides a valuable source for developers, different roles might need other types of documentation. The iterative cycle of the main activities ends when sufficient information for an initial design draft or low-fidelity prototype are available [31, 37, 43]. Design drafts are generated using sketching or mock-up applications. Early prototypes are created using paper. Later, tools help to create digital and interactive prototypes. However, the up-front development and design activities can only start after there are user inputs or requirements. However, once a design suggestion is available, feedback and a jump to the beginning of the iterative cycle are possible.

7 Conclusion

The study successfully derives design principles for a software product discovery method. Their implementation leads to the design of PDISC. Our theoretical contribution is the design principles, which categorizes product-, user- and team-related requirements. PDISC balances requirements for all three areas in order to deliver a viable, desirable, and feasible product vision. The product-related requirements help the organization to design a viable product. Implementing user-related requirements into the method assures that the product vision proposes a desirable product. In addition, team-related requirements of the method suggest the design of a feasible product. The design principles allow practitioners to challenge their own processes for comprehensiveness and completeness. While they may not implement all steps, depending on the size of the organization, PDISC helps practitioners to design a product that is viable, feasible and desirable. If a product falls short on any of these three dimensions, the product's success is at risk. Furthermore, the implementation and individual activities provide stepwise tutorial for creating a product vision. This is especially valuable for those organizations that yet have to define a software product discovery process for themselves.

References

1. Fox, D., Sillito, J., Maurer, F.: Agile methods and user-centered design: how these two methodologies are being successfully integrated in industry. In: Agile 2008 Conference, pp. 63–72. IEEE Computer Society, Toronto (2008)
2. The Standish Group: Chaos Report, Las Vegas, NV, US (2014)

3. Brhel, M., Meth, H., Maedche, A., Werder, K.: Exploring principles of user-centered agile software development: a literature review. Inf. Softw. Technol. **61**, 163–181 (2015)
4. Barksdale, J.T., McCrickard, D.S.: Software product innovation in agile usability teams: an analytical framework of social capital, network governance, and usability knowledge management. Int. J. Agile Extreme Softw. Dev. **1**, 52 (2012)
5. da Silva, T.S., Silveira, M.S., de O. Melo, C., Parzianello, L.C.: Understanding the UX designer's role within agile teams. In: Marcus, A. (ed.) DUXU 2013, Part I. LNCS, vol. 8012, pp. 599–609. Springer, Heidelberg (2013)
6. da Silva, T.S., Silveira, M., Maurer, F.: Best practices for integrating user-centered design and agile software development. In: 10th Brazilian Symposium on Human Factors in Computing Systems and the 5th Latin American Conference on Human-Computer Interaction, pp. 43–45. Brazilian Computer Society, Porto Alegre, Brazil (2011)
7. Ferreira, J., Boyland, J., Biddle, R.: Up-Front Interaction Design in Agile Development. In: Concas, G., Damiani, E., Scotto, M., Succi, G. (eds.) XP 2007. LNCS, vol. 4536, pp. 9–16. Springer, Heidelberg (2007)
8. da Silva, T.S., Martin, A., Maurer, F., Silveira, M.S.: User-centered design and agile methods: a systematic review. In: 2011 AGILE Conference, pp. 77–86. IEEE, Salt Lake City (2011)
9. Nwaka, S., Hudson, A.: Innovative lead discovery strategies for tropical diseases. Nat. Rev. Drug Discov. **5**, 941–955 (2006)
10. Cooper, R.G.: Winning at New Products: Creating Value Through Innovation. Basic Books, New York (2011)
11. Cagan, M.: Product Discovery. http://www.svpg.com/product-discovery
12. Freeman, P., Hart, D.: A science of design for software-intensive systems. Commun. ACM **47**, 19 (2004)
13. Boehm, B.W.: A spiral model of software development and enhancement. Computer (Long. Beach. Calif.) **21**, 61–72 (1988)
14. Sohaib, O., Khan, K.: Integrating usability engineering and agile software development: a literature review. In: 2010 International Conference on Computer Design and Applications, pp. V2-32–V2-38. IEEE, Qinhuangdao (2010)
15. Heikkilä, V.T., Paasivaara, M., Rautiainen, K., Lassenius, C., Toivola, T., Järvinen, J.: Operational release planning in large-scale Scrum with multiple stakeholders–A longitudinal case study at F-Secure Corporation. Inf. Softw. Technol. **57**, 116–140 (2015)
16. Kuusinen, K.: Improving UX work in scrum development: a three-year follow-up study in a company. In: Sauer, S., Bogdan, C., Forbrig, P., Bernhaupt, R., Winckler, M. (eds.) HCSE 2014. LNCS, vol. 8742, pp. 259–266. Springer, Heidelberg (2014)
17. Stevens, E.: Fuzzy front-end learning strategies: exploration of a high-tech company. Technovation **34**, 431–440 (2014)
18. Frishammar, J., Florén, H., Wincent, J.: Beyond managing uncertainty: insights from studying equivocality in the fuzzy front end of product and process innovation projects. IEEE Trans. Eng. Manag. **58**, 551–563 (2011)
19. Sperry, R., Jetter, A.: Theoretical framework for managing the front end of innovation under uncertainty. In: Portland International Conference on Management of Engineering & Technology, pp. 2021–2028. IEEE, Portland (2009)
20. Kakar, A., Carver, J.: Best practices for managing the fuzzy front-end of software development (SD): insights from a systematic review of new product development (NPD) literature. In: Proceedings of International Research Workshop on IT Project Management, p. 14., AISeL, Orlando, FL, US (2012)
21. Khurana, A., Rosenthal, S.R.: Towards holistic front ends in new product development. J. Prod. Innov. Manag. **15**, 57–74 (1998)

22. Kuechler, B., Vaishnavi, V.: On theory development in design science research: anatomy of a research project. Eur. J. Inf. Syst. **17**, 489–504 (2008)
23. Peffers, K., Tuunanen, T., Rothenberger, M.A., Chatterjee, S.: A design science research methodology for information systems research. J. Manag. Inf. Syst. **24**, 45–77 (2007)
24. Brinkkemper, S., Saeki, M., Harmsen, F.: Meta-modelling based assembly techniques for situational method engineering. Inf. Syst. **24**, 209–228 (1999)
25. Brinkkemper, S.: Method engineering: engineering of information systems development methods and tools. Inf. Softw. Technol. **38**, 275–280 (1996)
26. Hevner, A.R., March, S.T., Park, J., Ram, S.: Design science in information systems research. Manag. Inf. Syst. Q. **28**, 75–105 (2004)
27. Kitchenham, B., Charters, S.: Guidelines for performing systematic literature reviews in software engineering (2007)
28. Brocke, J. vom, Simons, A., Niehaves, B., Reimer, K., Plattfaut, R., Cleven, A.: Reconstructing the giant: on the importance of rigour in documenting the literature search process. In: European Conference on Information Systems, p. 161. AISeL, Verona, IT (2009)
29. Boell, S.K., Cecez-Kecmanovic, D.: On being systematic in literature reviews in IS. J. Inf. Technol. **30**, 161–173 (2015)
30. Hildenbrand, T., Meyer, J.: Intertwining lean and design thinking: software product development from empathy to shipment. In: Maedche, A., Botzenhardt, A., Neer, L. (eds.) Software for People, pp. 217–237. Springer, Heidelberg (2012)
31. Hollis, B., Maiden, N.: Extending agile processes with creativity techniques. IEEE Softw. **30**, 78–84 (2013)
32. Kajko-Mattsson, M., Nyfjord, J.: A model of agile evolution and maintenance process. In: 42nd Hawaii International Conference on System Sciences, pp. 1–10. IEEE, Big Island (2009)
33. Nyfjord, J., Kajko-Mattsson, M.: Degree of agility in pre-implementation process phases. In: Wang, Q., Pfahl, D., Raffo, D.M. (eds.) ICSP 2008. LNCS, vol. 5007, pp. 234–245. Springer, Heidelberg (2008)
34. Qumer, A., Henderson-Sellers, B.: Construction of an agile software product-enhancement process by using an agile software solution framework (ASSF) and situational method engineering. In: 31st Annual International Computer Software and Applications Conference, vol. 1, pp. 539–542. IEEE, Beijing (2007)
35. Sarpong, D., Maclean, M.: Mobilising differential visions for new product innovation. Technovation **32**, 694–702 (2012)
36. Sibghatullah, M., Hussain, S., Hussain, S.: An approach to effective product development life cycle. In: International Conference on Emerging Technologies, pp. 719–726. IEEE, Peshawar (2006)
37. Tessarolo, P.: Is integration enough for fast product development? An empirical investigation of the contextual effects of product vision. J. Prod. Innov. Manag. **24**, 69–82 (2007)
38. Vanhanen, J., Itkonen, J., Sulonen, P.: Improving the interface between business and product development using agile practices and the cycles of control framework. In: Proceedings of the Agile Development Conference, pp. 71–80. IEEE, Salt Lake City (2003)
39. Cloyd, M.H.: Designing user-centered web applications in web time. IEEE Softw. **18**, 62–69 (2001)
40. Patton, J.: Hitting the target: adding interaction design to agile software development. In: OOPSLA 2002 Practitioners Reports, Salt Lake City, p. 7 (2002)

41. Ben Rejeb, H., Boly, V., Morel-Guimaraes, L.: A new methodology based on Kano model for the evaluation of a new product acceptability during the front-end phases. In: 32nd Annual IEEE International Computer Software and Applications Conference, pp. 619–624. IEEE, Turku (2008)
42. Salah, D., Paige, R., Cairns, P.: A practitioner perspective on integrating agile and user centred design. In: 28th International BCS Human Computer Interaction Conference, Southport, UK, pp. 100–109 (2014)
43. Adikari, S., McDonald, C., Campbell, J.: Little design up-front: a design science approach to integrating usability into Agile requirements engineering. In: Jacko, J.A. (ed.) HCI International 2009, Part I. LNCS, vol. 5610, pp. 549–558. Springer, Heidelberg (2009)
44. Miller, L.: Case study of customer input for a successful product. In: Agile Conference, pp. 225–234. IEEE, Denver (2005)
45. Salah, D., Paige, R.F., Cairns, P.: A systematic literature review for agile development processes and user centred design integration. In: 18th International Conference on Evaluation and Assessment in Software Engineering, pp. 1–10. ACM Press, New York (2014)
46. Knoll, S.W., Horton, G.: The impact of stimuli characteristics on the ideation process: an evaluation of the change of perspective "Analogy." In: 44th Hawaii International Conference on System Sciences, pp. 1–10. IEEE, Kauai (2011)
47. Oliveira, M.G., Rozenfeld, H.: Integrating technology roadmapping and portfolio management at the front-end of new product development. Technol. Forecast. Soc. Change **77**, 1339–1354 (2010)
48. Inayat, I., Salim, S.S., Marczak, S., Daneva, M., Shamshirband, S.: A systematic literature review on agile requirements engineering practices and challenges. Comput. Hum. Behav. **51**, 915–929 (2015)
49. Loniewski, G., Armesto, A., Insfran, E.: An architecture-oriented model-driven requirements engineering approach. In: Model-Driven Requirements Engineering Workshop, pp. 31–38. IEEE, Trento (2011)
50. Salvador, C., Nakasone, A., Pow-Sang, J.A.: A systematic review of usability techniques in agile methodologies. In: 7th Euro American Conference on Telematics and Information Systems, pp. 1–6. ACM Press, New York (2014)
51. Ferre, X., Medinilla, N.: How a human-centered approach impacts software development. In: Jacko, J.A. (ed.) HCI 2007. LNCS, vol. 4550, pp. 68–77. Springer, Heidelberg (2007)
52. Menor, L.J., Tatikonda, M.V., Sampson, S.E.: New service development: areas for exploitation and exploration. J. Oper. Manag. **20**, 135–157 (2002)
53. Sy, D.: Adapting usability investigations for agile user-centered design. J. Usability Stud. **2**, 112–132 (2007)
54. Jain, R., Suman, U.: A systematic literature review on global software development life cycle. ACM SIGSOFT Softw. Eng. Notes **40**, 1–14 (2015)
55. Ebert, C.: Understanding the product life cycle: four key requirements engineering techniques. IEEE Softw. **23**, 19–25 (2006)
56. Williams, H., Ferguson, A.: The UCD perspective: before and after agile. In: Agile Conference, pp. 285–290. IEEE, Washington, D.C. (2007)
57. Liskin, O.: How artifacts support and impede requirements communication. In: Fricker, S. A., Schneider, K. (eds.) REFSQ 2015. LNCS, vol. 9013, pp. 132–147. Springer, Heidelberg (2015)

58. Gaubinger, K., Rabl, M.: Structuring the front end of innovation. In: Gassmann, O., Schweitzer, F. (eds.) Management of the Fuzzy Front End of Innovation, pp. 15–30. Springer International Publishing, Cham (2014)
59. Gamble, R.F., Hale, M.L.: Assessing individual performance in Agile undergraduate software engineering teams. In: IEEE Frontiers in Education Conference, pp. 1678–1684. IEEE, Oklahoma City (2013)

Supporting the Evolution of Research in Software Ecosystems: Reviewing the Empirical Literature

Konstantinos Manikas(✉)

Department of Computer Science, University of Copenhagen,
Copenhagen, Denmark
kmanikas@di.ku.dk

Abstract. The field of software ecosystems is gradually transiting towards an established means of software development and distribution, counting numerous areas of applicability. However, research in software ecosystems, although the activity of over 10 years, is still characterized as premature with significant lack of software ecosystem specific theories that are solid, mature, generic, and detailed enough to be measurable and transferable. In this study, we intent to come closer to an evolution of the field by supporting the "localization" of research, i.e. the focus on specific types of software ecosystems. To do so, we investigate the literature of empirical, non open source ecosystem studies and intent to identify the various aspects and perspectives studied.

In total, we review 56 empirical studies that investigate 55 software ecosystems. Our analysis confirms the assumption that proprietary software ecosystem studies lack deeper investigation of technical and collaborative aspects. Moreover, we identify an increased focus on organizational aspects and a rather limited focus on business. Furthermore, we identify common technology as the component investigated most in the ecosystems, both from the technical aspects, but also as means of applying orchestration. Finally, comparing the main areas with the overall ecosystem literature, we identify that empirical studies lack representation of health, motivation, actor activity, reusability, integration, and quality of ecosystems.

Keywords: Software ecosystems · Literature review · Empirical study review · Proprietary software ecosystems

1 Introduction

The field of software ecosystems has arguably moved from a new and upcoming field to an established means of developing and distributing software products, functions, or services. Currently, it is the most viable option of software product development in several domains and is counting examples in numerous other. Although the field has been active in research in the course of more than ten years, it can be argued that research is still scratching the surface of the field. The field can be characterized as one that is counting numerous and constantly

A. Maglyas and A.-L. Lamprecht (Eds.): ICSOB 2016, LNBIP 240, pp. 63–78, 2016.
DOI: 10.1007/978-3-319-40515-5_5

increasing studies that might go into depth in a specific aspect and/or type of software ecosystems, but find it challenging to make contributions that robust, while abstract enough to be applied to different types of ecosystems.

The case of software ecosystem *health* is a representative example of the evolution that theories in the field have been following. Software ecosystem health can be described as "the ability of the ecosystem to endure and remain variable and productive over time" [1]. It has been defined in the context of natural (biological) ecosystems and has appeared in software ecosystems mainly inspired by business ecosystems health[1]. Health, has been of focus and an important aspect from the early times of software ecosystem research [7], however the work on this aspect can be mainly characterized as either (a) too abstract, and thus not directly applicable (e.g. [1,8,9]), or (b) too specific, and thus challenging to be transfered to other (types of) ecosystems (e.g. [10–12]). Similar challenges can be noted in the *governance*[2] of software ecosystems [15–18].

This has as a result that, although theories and concepts evolve in the field, software ecosystems are still lacking a basic level of knowledge that is tailored to the specific needs of problems in the field. These theories are not solid and specific enough to allow for measurable results, while being abstract enough to allow for transferability (i.e. applied on ecosystems of different characteristics). This becomes magnified when taking into consideration the big variability in and differentiation of types of ecosystems existing.

This lack of specific theories is something that is also noted in the most recent and extensive systematic literature study of software ecosystems. [19] studies the literature of the field consisting of a total of 231 papers, spanning form 2007 to 2014. While examining the evolution of the field to characterize, among other, the field maturity, it is identified that the existing literature can be categorized as: **empirical but specific**, where one or more ecosystems are studied as means of addressing a problem, while the problem or the solution being highly coupled to these ecosystems; **temperature measuring**, where different theories, tools, or methods, usually imported from another field, investigate a problem that results in interpreting results based on assumptions. Furthermore, two steps for the evolution of research in the field towards its better maturity are proposed: (i) **research scoping**, where research should set more focus on defining the specific ecosystem parameters that study results are applicable, and (ii) **theory building**, where research should focus on defining theories that are designed for the specific characteristics and problems of software ecosystems. In order for (i) to be accelerated and have better results, some "ground-work" should be done on identifying and defining sets of parameters that separate the different types of ecosystems and their variability.

In this study, we intent to contribute towards an arguably higher level of maturity in the field by supporting work towards a better scoping of future research, as mentioned in (i). Our aim is to investigate the work studying

[1] E.g. [2–6].

[2] An arguably more accurate term is *orchestration* [13,14] that better describes more "loose" organizational structures or ecosystems with voluntary contributions.

existing ecosystems and identify what aspects of (existing) software ecosystems are (empirically) studied. One of the most common differentiation of ecosystem types is the separation between ecosystems that are driven or supported by free and open source software (FOSS) and ecosystems that are driven or supported by proprietary software. Literature studying FOSS ecosystems, as identified by [7], tends to have deeper study of technical and collaborative aspects but might lack organizational and business perspectives. On the other hand, proprietary ecosystem studies tend to have do the opposite. In reality, the boarders of this polarization tend to be more obscure, as there are several ecosystems that support both FOSS and proprietary contributions or are based on both FOSS or proprietary common technologies.

In this study, we focus on proprietary ecosystems and intent to identify the various aspects and perspectives studied. More specifically, we review the empirical literature of proprietary software ecosystems, i.e. the literature of that studies some aspect(s) of an existing non-FOSS software ecosystem, to identify what ecosystem characteristics are defined. We do so, by reviewing 56 papers that study a total of 55 existing and non-FOSS software ecosystems. Our results reveal an increased focus in organizational aspects of software ecosystems, a restricted focus on business, with rather limited aspects of revenues and monetization. Moreover, our analysis confirms the view of proprietary ecosystem studies having limited access to proprietary information, such as source code, with a distinct lack of studies of the software perspectives of ecosystem contributions. The literature puts the most focus on the common technology both from the technical perspective but also as a means to apply orchestration to the ecosystem. Another main focus of the studies is the actors of the ecosystem and the relations among them. Finally, we compare the main areas of the empirical studies with the overall ecosystem literature and identify that ecosystem aspects such as health, motivation, actor activity, reusability, integration, and quality are not represented.

2 Related Work

The field of software ecosystems counts a number of secondary studies, but to our knowledge, none with primary focus on investigating the implications of empirical studies of existing software ecosystems. The systematic literature review of [7] identifies, among other, 42 software ecosystems in a literature body of 90 papers from 2007 to 2012. Manikas [19] expands this list to 108 for a literature body of 231 papers from 2007 to 2014.

In the context of secondary studies, Barbosa and Alves [20] conduct a mapping study of the literature of software ecosystems up to 2010 identifying 44 papers. Among their findings, they note that 10 studies were based on case studies. Santos et al. [21] combining the literature from that study and their previous study [22], identify four dimensions of software ecosystems: technical, business, social, and management - engineering. Hansen and Dybå [23] intent to build an overview of theories used in the literature. By reviewing a literature body of 40 papers, they identify a set of theoretical areas while using the concept of "organizational ecology". Handoyo et al. [24] use the roles identified [7] and [20] to create a classification of ecosystem roles. Manikas and Hansen [1] focus on the context of health and review the literature of software ecosystem health and related areas. They find that software ecosystem health is heavily inspired from business ecosystems and propose a framework for the measurable definition of software ecosystem health. Fotrousi et al. [25] map the literature of software ecosystems to identify key performance indicators used in software ecosystems. They map 34 papers from software and digital ecosystems and identify right measurement attributes spread across seven entities. Franco-Bedoya et al [26] review part of the literature of open source software ecosystems (a total of 17 papers) to identify quality measures and provide input to their proposed quality model.

3 Method

In this study, we review the empirical literature of software ecosystems that is not build on a FOSS ecosystem, i.e. the academic literature that includes the study or investigation of an existing proprietary software ecosystem. This literature was identified as part of the analysis of the software ecosystem literature in the systematic literature study of [19]. This literature study was designed according to the guidelines of Kitchenham and Charters [27], using a similar protocol with the second most recent and extensive systematic literature study of software ecosystems [7]. This protocol includes the literature search in a list of academic libraries[3]. Moreover, the literature body was expanded with the papers from the International Workshop of Software Ecosystem (IWSECO) for years 2007-2004, the Workshop on Ecosystem Architectures (WEA) for years 2013-2014, the special issue on software ecosystems of the Journal of Systems and Software, and the special issue on software ecosystems of the Journal of Information Technology. All the identified literature contains the words "software ecosystem(s)" in either of the fields title, abstract, or keywords.

After we define the collected literature, we analyze it using the three structures of *"software ecosystem architecture"*, proposed by [28], and the ecosystem components, proposed by [29].

Christensen et al. in [28] investigate means of modeling software ecosystems where, based on the design of a software ecosystem, they propose the ecosystem analysis and modeling using the concept of software ecosystem architecture. This concept consists of three main structures that are necessary for the design and well-functioning of a software ecosystem:

Organizational structure. That covers aspects of the ecosystem related to the orchestration of the ecosystem elements, such as actor and software elements, as much as possible connections and interactions among these elements.

[3] The digital libraries are: IEEE Explore, SpringerLink, ACM Digital Library, ScienceDirect, and Web of Science.

Business structure. That covers aspects of the ecosystem related to the creation of value. This is examined both from the perspective of the ecosystem, i.e. how is value added to the ecosystem, and the perspective of the ecosystem element, e.g. how is an actor gaining value from the contribution to the ecosystem.

Software structure. Covers aspects that relate to the software elements of the ecosystem, such as the structure of the common technology or the contributions to the ecosystem.

Moreover, in order to be specific and identify what elements of the ecosystems are studied, we use the approach of the ecosystem components. Knodel and Manikas in [29] propose a typification of software ecosystems challenging the existing ecosystems definitions. In this work they identify a number of components that ecosystems are consisted of[4]. They describe that an ecosystem is build on top of a **common technology**, that supports the interaction of a set of **actors**. The actors are part of the ecosystem by having an activity that results in one or several **contributions** to the ecosystem. The contributions can be of variable nature such as a (software) product or component, a service, or data (information). Each actor's activity in the ecosystem is motivated by one or several **incentives**. Moreover, the ecosystem exists and operates on a specific **environment**. The environment might include the domain of the ecosystem and the physical or digital aspects surrounding the ecosystem, while it can pose different requirements, or constraints to the ecosystem.

We use the three ecosystem structures and the five ecosystem components to analyze the ecosystem studies. Each study was analyzed and categorized according to what structure(s) it addresses and what are the main components investigated. One study can be categorized in more than one structure (e.g. both organizational and business) and have up to three components. The components classification was prioritized, e.g. a study can primarily focus on the common technology of an ecosystem with (secondary) focus on contributions.

4 Analysis

Our literature body includes 56 studies spanning from 2008 to 2014[5]. In total the literature studies 37 different, existing, named, software ecosystems and 18 anonymized.

Figure 1, shows how the papers are distributed in the three structures and what ecosystem components are the main focus for each structure. As it can be seen, the organizational structure has the largest focus with roughly 61 % of the total literature, while business has 37 %, and software 39 %[6].

---

[4] In their work, they are mentioned as "ecosystem building blocks".

[5] The count of papers per year is 2008:2, 2009:2, 2010:6, 2011:7, 2012:6, 2013:11, 2014:22.

[6] One paper can be categorized in more than one structure.

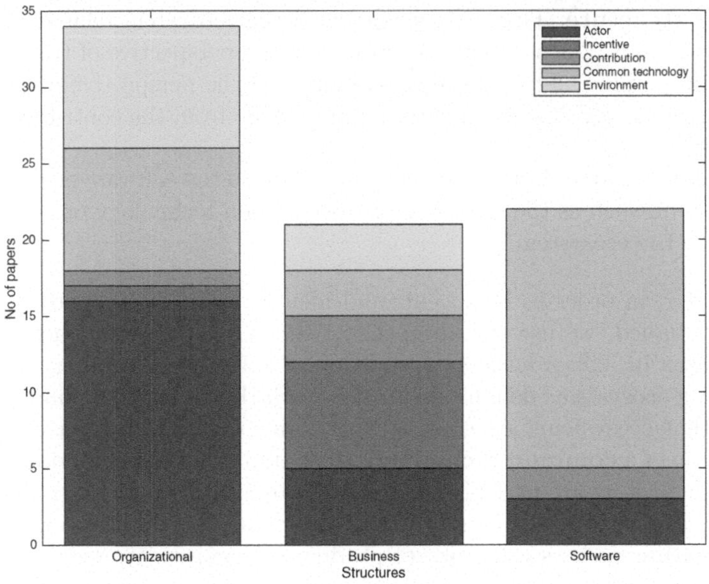

Fig. 1. Number of papers and ecosystem components according to ecosystem structures (Color figure online).

The most common component analyzed in the studies focusing on organizational structures is the 'actor', being the main focus of approximately 47 % of the studies within this structure. The most common second component appearing after actor in the organizational structure is 'incentive' and the third 'common technology'. This gives a good indication that many of the studies have been focusing on the network and relationships of actors and examining those from two main perspectives: the actor incentives and the common platform as means of facilitating actor relationship. In the business structure, it is not a surprise that the most common component is 'incentive' (33 % of the studies in the structure). As expected, the most common component that comes with 'incentive' is 'actor'. In the software structure, the most common component is 'common technology' (77 %) with most of those studies having 'contribution' as the second component.

If we examine the components independently from the architecture structures, we note that 'common technology' is the most common component[7]. Common technology usually has as a second component 'contribution' and that is mainly in the studies belonging to the software structure. These studies typically investigate the influence of software engineering aspects, such as software architecture, to the ecosystem. Another component that comes (to a less extent than the contribution) is 'environment'. These studies typically investigate the technical aspects of the common technology and how it poses additional restrictions,

[7] The percentage distribution of components is common technology: 34 %, actor: 30 %, environment: 14 %, incentive: 13 %, and contribution: 9 %.

limitations, or specific rules to the ecosystem. The second most common component studied is 'actor'. Actor usually has a second component 'incentive' and, to a less extent, 'common technology'. What might come as a surprise in this context is the fact that contribution is not one of the most common components coming after actor. So there is not many studies[8] that investigate the actors and their contributions in this data set. This can be explained by two reasons: (i) the nature of the empirical sets, i.e. non-FOSS ecosystems, make it hard to study specific contributions in detail and (ii) the contribution component is in general not very studied (possibly also due to (i)).

Table 1 contains the identified main foci of the studies according to the ecosystem structures and components. Looking at the table, our first remark is that incentive and environment do not appear in the software structure. Moreover, the contribution component is not very studied in this structure. That, in combination with what is actually studied in the software structure, makes the statement of the nature of the ecosystems not allowing for deep analysis into contributions even stronger.

Examining the organizational structure, we note that actor, environment, and common technology are of focus. The representation of the common technology here provides the view of a common technology used as a means of imposing orchestration rules and strategies.

Looking at the business structure, we note a more spread distribution in the foci of components with the other two structures. This implies that different aspects of the business and value creation on software ecosystem are investigated. From the other side, it is notable that the central aspects of business, i.e. monetization and revenues, are arguably under-represented. While, intersection of business structures and organizational structure is more emphasized in the studies. This is also explained by the fact that many (52 %) of the business structure studies are also categorized as organizational structure.

Finally, when examining the focus areas of all the studies, we notice that there are several perspectives[9] that appear across components and structures. Furthermore, we notice that some of the ecosystem aspects that the literature has been focusing, including non-empirical literature, are not represented here. Comparing with the analysis of [19], that analyzes the literature and identifies trends, we note the following:

Organizational structure is lacking or is under-represented in studies of the aspects of *health*, and *actor activity*.

Business structure lacks focus on *motivation*, *process*, and *innovation*.

Software structure is focusing on the software architecture only in the level of the common technology (not contribution). Moreover, aspects like *reusability*, *evolution*, *integration*, and *quality* are not adequately represented.

[8] Less than 4 % of the total.

[9] An example of this is the partnerships modeling/management/networks.

Table 1. Analysis of software ecosystem structures and components.

Category	Organizational	Business	Software
Actor	- Partnership model - Vendor modeling - Software supply network - Actor relationships - involvement - participation - Modeling co-innovation service systems - Concept building - Ecosystem characteristics - Inner source - Actor and software networks - Health - Actor (vendor - reseller) relationships - Network analysis - Collaboration models - Partner management [30–45]	- Vendor modeling - Software supply network - Actor (vendor - reseller) relationships - Partner management - Actor participation [31, 32, 40, 43, 45]	- Developer information needs - Inner source in small team organizations - Actor and software networks [37, 38, 46]
Incentive	- Partnership models [47]	- Partnership models - Business model analysis for new SECOs - Value chain models - Actor motivation - Business and value chain challenges - Revenue models - Actor incentive influence [47–53]	NA
Contribution	- Product requirement information flow [54]	- Multi-homing - User feedback [54–56]	- Variability modeling - Software implementation [57, 58]
Common technology	- Software service supply chain model and architecture - Creating SECO for embedded software	- Architectural decisions - App Stores	- Architectural decisions - Software service supply chains

Table 1. *(Continued)*

Category	Organizational	Business	Software
	- Ecosystem establishment - App Stores - Cloud-based platform description - Ecosystem modeling - Multiple software product lines - Partnership impact in requirements engineering [59–66]	- SECO process [62,67,68]	- Software portability - Platform boundary resources - Infrastructure architecture - Variability issues - Ecosystem establishment - SECO process - Co-development in the cloud - Cloud-based platform description - Development and variability management - Evolution in industrial automation - Reverse engineering - Ecosystem modeling - Platform architecture - Multiple software product lines - Partnership impact in requirements [59,61,63–77]
Environment	- Ecosystem description - Ecosystem modeling - Strategic network (planning) - Collaboration and value creation challenges - Modeling ecosystems - Knowledge propagation - Ecosystem management - Governance framework [9,17,78–83]	- Strategic network (planning) - Collaboration and value creation challenges - Governance framework [17,80,81]	NA

5 Summary

In this study we review the empirical literature of existing proprietary (non-FOSS) software ecosystems to identify studied ecosystem aspects and perspectives. We identify a literature body of 56 empirical studies, studying a total of 55 software ecosystems. Our analysis includes the use of the concept of software ecosystem architecture and the three structures of software ecosystem modeling: organizational, business, and software structures. Moreover, we identify the main components studied in software ecosystem using the five ecosystem components: actor, incentive, common technology, contribution, and environment.

Our study confirms the assumption that proprietary software ecosystem studies lack deeper investigation of technical and collaborative aspects. Moreover, it reveals an increased focus on organizational structures and a rather limited focus on business with lack of revenue and monetization aspects. The most investigated ecosystem component is common technology, that is studied both as a technical but also as an orchestration element. Furthermore, actors, their incentives, and their influence to and from the common technology is also of focus in the studies. Finally, we compare the main areas of the empirical studies with the overall ecosystem literature and identify that ecosystem aspects such as health, motivation, actor activity, reusability, integration, and quality are not represented.

Acknowledgments. This work has been supported by the SCAUT (http://www.scaut.dk/) project, partially funded by Innovation Fund Denmark, grant #72-2014-1.

Appendix: Literature body

[9,17,30–83]

References

1. Manikas, K., Hansen, K.M.: Reviewing the health of software ecosystems-a conceptual framework proposal. In: Alves, C.F., Hanssen, G.K., Bosch, J., Jansen, S. (eds.) Proceedings of the 5th International Workshop on Software Ecosystems, Potsdam, Germany, June 11, 2013, vol. 987, pp. 33–44 (2013)
2. Iansiti, M., Levien, R.: Keystones and Dominators: Framing Operating and Technology Strategy in a Business Ecosystem. Harvard Business School, Boston (2004)
3. Iansiti, M., Richards, G.L.: The information technology ecosystem: structure, health, and performance. Antitrust Bull. **51**, 77 (2006)
4. Iansiti, M., Levien, R.: Strategy as ecology. Harvard Bus. Rev. **82**(3), 68–81 (2004)
5. Iansiti, M., Levien, R.: The Keystone Advantage: What the New Dynamics of Business Ecosystems Mean for Strategy, Innovation, and Sustainability. Harvard Business Press, Boston (2004)
6. den Hartigh, E., Tol, M., Visscher, W.: The health measurement of a business ecosystem. In: Proceedings of the European Network on Chaos and Complexity Research and Management Practice Meeting (2006)

7. Manikas, K., Hansen, K.M.: Software ecosystems-a systematic literature review. J. Syst. Softw. **86**(5), 1294–1306 (2013)
8. Hyrynsalmi, S., Seppänen, M., Nokkala, T., Suominen, A., Järvi, A.: Wealthy, healthy and/or happy—what does 'Ecosystem Health' stand for? In: Fernandes, J.M., Machado, R.J., Wnuk, K. (eds.) Software Business. LNBIP, vol. 210, pp. 272–287. Springer, Heidelberg (2015)
9. Berk, I.v.d., Jansen, S., Luinenburg, L.: Software ecosystems: a software ecosystem strategy assessment model. In: Proceedings of the Fourth European Conference on Software Architecture: Companion Volume, ECSA 2010, pp. 127–134. ACM, New York (2010)
10. Eckhardt, E., Kaats, E., Jansen, S., Alves, C.: The merits of a meritocracy in open source software ecosystems. In: Proceedings of the 2014 European Conference on Software Architecture Workshops, ECSAW 2014, pp. 7:1–7:6. ACM, New York (2014)
11. Jansen, S.: Measuring the health of open source software ecosystems: beyond the scope of project health. Inf. Softw. Technol. **56**(11), 1508–1519 (2014)
12. Lingen, S.V., Palomba, A., Lucassen, G.: On the software ecosystem health of open source content management systems. In: Alves, C.F., Hanssen, G.K., Bosch, J., Jansen, S. (eds.) Proceedings of the 5th International Workshop on Software Ecosystems, Potsdam, Germany, June 11, 2013, vol. 987, pp. 45–56. CEUR-WS.org (2013)
13. Jansen, S., Finkelstein, A., Brinkkemper, S.: A sense of community: a research agenda for software ecosystems. In: 31st International Conference on Software Engineering-Companion, ICSE-Companion 2009, vol. 2009, pp. 187–190, May 2009
14. Manikas, K.: Analyzing, Modelling, and Designing Software Ecosystems - Towards the Danish Telemedicine Software Ecosystem. Ph.D. thesis, University of Copenhagen (2015)
15. Albert, B., Santos, R., Werner, C.: Software ecosystems governance to enable it architecture based on software asset management. In: 2013 7th IEEE International Conference on Digital Ecosystems and Technologies (DEST), pp. 55–60, July 2013
16. Jansen, S., Cusumano, M.: Defining software ecosystems: a survey of software platforms and business network governance. In: Jansen, S., Bosch, J., Alves, C. (eds.) Proceedings of the Forth International Workshop on Software Ecosystems, Cambridge, MA, USA, June 18th, 2012, vol. 879, pp. 40–58. CEUR-WS.org (2012)
17. Wnuk, K., Manikas, K., Runeson, P., Lantz, M., Weijden, O., Munir, H.: Evaluating the governance model of hardware-dependent software ecosystems – a case study of the axis ecosystem. In: Lassenius, C., Smolander, K. (eds.) ICSOB 2014. LNBIP, vol. 182, pp. 212–226. Springer, Heidelberg (2014)
18. Manikas, K., Wnuk, K., Shollo, A.: Defining decision making strategies in software ecosystem governance. Technical report, Department of Computer Science, University of Copenhagen (2015)
19. Manikas, K.: Revisiting software ecosystems research: a longitudinal literature study. J. Syst. Softw. **117**, 84 (2016)
20. Barbosa, O., Alves, C.: A systematic mapping study on software ecosystems. In: Third International Workshop on Software Ecosystems (IWSECO-2011), pp. 15–26. CEUR-WS (2011)
21. Santos, R., Werner, C., Barbosa, O., Alves, C.: Software ecosystems: trends and impacts on software engineering. In: 2012 26th Brazilian Symposium on Software Engineering (SBES), pp. 206–210, Sept 2012

22. Santos, R.P., Werner, C.M.L.: A proposal for software ecosystem engineering. In: Third International Workshop on Software Ecosystems (IWSECO-2011), pp. 40–51. CEUR-WS (2011)
23. Hanssen, G.K., Dybå, T.: Theoretical foundations of software ecosystems. In: Jansen, S., Bosch, J., Alves, C. (eds.) Proceedings of the Forth International Workshop on Software Ecosystems, Cambridge, MA, USA, June 18th, 2012, vol. 879, pp. 6–17. CEUR-WS.org (2012)
24. Handoyo, E., Jansen, S., Brinkkemper, S.: Software ecosystem roles classification. In: Herzwurm, G., Margaria, T. (eds.) ICSOB 2013. LNBIP, vol. 150, pp. 212–216. Springer, Heidelberg (2013)
25. Fotrousi, F., Fricker, S.A., Fiedler, M., Le-Gall, F.: KPIs for software ecosystems: a systematic mapping study. In: Lassenius, C., Smolander, K. (eds.) ICSOB 2014. LNBIP, vol. 182, pp. 194–211. Springer, Heidelberg (2014)
26. Franco-Bedoya, O., Ameller, D., Costal, D., Franch, X.: Queso a quality model for open source software ecosystems. In: 2014 9th International Conference on Software Engineering and Applications (ICSOFT-EA), pp. 209–221, Aug 2014
27. Kitchenham, B., Charters, S.: Guidelines for performing systematic literature reviews in software engineering. Engineering 2(EBSE 2007–001) (2007)
28. Christensen, H.B., Hansen, K.M., Kyng, M., Manikas, K.: Analysis and design of software ecosystem architectures - towards the 4s telemedicine ecosystem. Inf. Softw. Technol. **56**(11), 1476–1492 (2014)
29. Knodel, J., Manikas, K.: Towards a typification of software ecosystems. In: Fernandes, J.M., Machado, R.J., Wnuk, K. (eds.) Software Business. LNBIP, vol. 210, pp. 60–65. Springer, Heidelberg (2015)
30. van Angeren, J., Jansen, S., Brinkkemper, S.: Exploring the relationship between partnership model participation and interfirm network structure: an analysis of the office365 ecosystem. In: Lassenius, C., Smolander, K. (eds.) ICSOB 2014. LNBIP, vol. 182, pp. 1–15. Springer, Heidelberg (2014)
31. Boucharas, V., Jansen, S., Brinkkemper, S.: Formalizing software ecosystem modeling. In: Proceedings of the 1st International Workshop on Open Component Ecosystems, IWOCE 2009, pp. 41–50. ACM, New York (2009)
32. Costa, G., Silva, F., Santos, R., Werner, C., Oliveira, T.: From applications to a software ecosystem platform: an exploratory study. In: Proceedings of the Fifth International Conference on Management of Emergent Digital EcoSystems, MEDES 2013, pp. 9–16. ACM, New York (2013)
33. Hilkert, D., Wolf, C.M., Benlian, A., Hess, T.: The "as-a-service"-paradigm and its implications for the software industry–insights from a comparative case study in CRM software ecosystems. In: Tyrväinen, P., Jansen, S., Cusumano, M.A. (eds.) ICSOB 2010. LNBIP, vol. 51, pp. 125–137. Springer, Heidelberg (2010). doi:10.1007/978-3-642-13633-7_11
34. Janner, T., Schroth, C., Schmid, B.: Modelling service systems for collaborative innovation in the enterprise software industry-the st. gallen media reference model applied. In: IEEE International Conference on Services Computing, SCC 2008, vol. 2, pp. 145–152, July 2008
35. Jansen, S., Brinkkemper, S., Finkelstein, A.: Business network management as a survival strategy: a tale of two software ecosystems. In: First International Workshop on Software Ecosystems (IWSECO-2009), pp. 34–48. Citeseer (2009)
36. Lettner, D., Angerer, F., Prähofer, H., Grünbacher, P.: A case study on software ecosystem characteristics in industrial automation software. In: Proceedings of the 2014 International Conference on Software and System Process, ICSSP 2014, pp. 40–49. ACM, New York (2014)

37. Linåker, J., Krantz, M., Höst, M.: On infrastructure for facilitation of inner source in small development teams. In: Jedlitschka, A., Kuvaja, P., Kuhrmann, M., Männistö, T., Münch, J., Raatikainen, M. (eds.) PROFES 2014. LNCS, vol. 8892, pp. 149–163. Springer, Heidelberg (2014)
38. Manikas, K., Hansen, K.M.: Characterizing the danish telemedicine ecosystem: making sense of actor relationships. In: Proceedings of the Fifth International Conference on Management of Emergent Digital EcoSystems, MEDES 2013, pp. 211–218 (2013)
39. Monteith, J.Y., McGregor, J.D., Ingram, J.E.: Proposed metrics on ecosystem health. In: Proceedings of the 2014 ACM International Workshop on Software-defined Ecosystems. BigSystem 2014, pp. 33–36. ACM, New York (2014)
40. Riis, P., Schubert, P.: Upgrading to a new version of an erp system: a multilevel analysis of influencing factors in a software ecosystem. In: 2012 45th Hawaii International Conference on System Science (HICSS), pp. 4709–4718, Jan 2012
41. Scholten, U., Fischer, R., Zirpins, C.: The dynamic network notation: harnessing network effects in paas-ecosystems. In: Proceedings of the Fourth Annual Workshop on Simplifying Complex Networks for Practitioners, SIMPLEX 2012, pp. 25–30. ACM, New York (2012)
42. Schultis, K.B., Elsner, C., Lohmann, D.: Architecture challenges for internal software ecosystems: a large-scale industry case study. In: Proceedings of the 22nd ACM SIGSOFT International Symposium on Foundations of Software Engineering, FSE 2014, pp. 542–552. ACM, New York (2014)
43. Schütz, S.W., Kude, T., Popp, K.M.: The impact of software-as-a-service on software ecosystems. In: Herzwurm, G., Margaria, T. (eds.) ICSOB 2013. LNBIP, vol. 150, pp. 130–140. Springer, Heidelberg (2013)
44. Molder, J., van Lier, B., Jansen, S.: Clopenness of systems: the interwoven nature of ecosystems. In: Third International Workshop on Software Ecosystems (IWSECO-2011), pp. 52–64. CEUR-WS (2011)
45. Wnuk, K., Runeson, P., Lantz, M., Weijden, O.: Bridges and barriers to hardware-dependent software ecosystem participation-a case study. Inf. Softw. Technol. **56**(11), 1493–1507 (2014)
46. Haenni, N., Lungu, M., Schwarz, N., Nierstrasz, O.: A quantitative analysis of developer information needs in software ecosystems. In: Proceedings of the 2014 European Conference on Software Architecture Workshops, ECSAW 2014, pp. 12:1–12:6. ACM, New York (2014)
47. Andresen, K., Brockmann, C., Drager, C.: A classification of ecosystems of enterprise system providers - an empirical analysis. In: 2013 46th Hawaii International Conference on System Sciences (HICSS), pp. 4034–4044, Jan 2013
48. Axelsson, J., Papatheocharous, E., Andersson, J.: Characteristics of software ecosystems for federated embedded systems: a case study. Inf. Softw. Technol. **56**(11), 1457–1475 (2014)
49. Handoyo, E., Jansen, S., Brinkkemper, S.: Software ecosystem modeling: the value chains. In: Proceedings of the Fifth International Conference on Management of Emergent Digital EcoSystems, MEDES 2013, pp. 17–24. ACM, New York (2013)
50. Howison, J., Herbsleb, J.D.: Incentives and integration in scientific software production. In: Proceedings of the 2013 Conference on Computer Supported Cooperative Work, CSCW 2013, pp. 459–470. ACM, New York (2013)
51. Olsson, H.H., Bosch, J.: Ecosystem-driven software development: a case study on the emergingchallenges in inter-organizational R&D. In: Lassenius, C., Smolander, K. (eds.) Software Business. Towards Continuous Value Delivery. LNBIP, vol. 182, pp. 16–26. Springer, Switzerland (2014)

52. Popp, K.M.: Hybrid revenue models of software companies and their relationship to hybrid business models. In: Third International Workshop on Software Ecosystems (IWSECO-2011), pp. 77–88. CEUR-WS (2011)
53. Ververs, E., van Bommel, R., Jansen, S.: Influences on developer participation in the debian software ecosystem. In: Proceedings of the International Conference on Management of Emergent Digital EcoSystems, MEDES 2011, pp. 89–93. ACM, New York (2011)
54. Knauss, E., Damian, D., Knauss, A., Borici, A.: Openness and requirements: opportunities and tradeoffs in software ecosystems. In: 2014 IEEE 22nd International Requirements Engineering Conference (RE), pp. 213–222, Aug 2014
55. Idu, A., van de Zande, T., Jansen, S.: Multi-homing in the apple ecosystem: why and how developers target multiple apple app. stores. In: Proceedings of the International Conference on Management of Emergent Digital EcoSystems, MEDES 2011, pp. 122–128. ACM, New York (2011)
56. Schneider, K., Meyer, S., Peters, M., Schliephacke, F., Mörschbach, J., Aguirre, L.: Feedback in context: supporting the evolution of IT-ecosystems. In: Ali Babar, M., Vierimaa, M., Oivo, M. (eds.) PROFES 2010. LNCS, vol. 6156, pp. 191–205. Springer, Heidelberg (2010). doi:10.1007/978-3-642-13792-1_16
57. Brummermann, H., Keunecke, M., Schmid, K.: Formalizing distributed evolution of variability in information system ecosystems. In: Proceedings of the Sixth International Workshop on Variability Modeling of Software-Intensive Systems, VaMoS 2012, pp. 11–19. ACM, New York (2012)
58. Keunecke, M., Brummermann, H., Schmid, K.: The feature pack approach: systematically managing implementations in software ecosystems. In: Proceedings of the Eighth International Workshop on Variability Modelling of Software-Intensive Systems, VaMoS 2014, pp. 20:1–20:7. ACM, New York (2013)
59. Aoyama, M.: Model and its management architecture of software service supply chains. In: Mochimaru, M., Ueda, K., Takenaka, T. (eds.) Serviceology for Services, pp. 181–189. Springer, Japan (2014)
60. Eklund, U., Bosch, J.: Introducing software ecosystems for mass-produced embedded systems. In: Cusumano, M.A., Iyer, B., Venkatraman, N. (eds.) ICSOB 2012. LNBIP, vol. 114, pp. 248–254. Springer, Heidelberg (2012)
61. Hanssen, G.K.: A longitudinal case study of an emerging software ecosystem: implications for practice and theory. J. Syst. Softw. **85**(7), 1455–1466 (2011)
62. Jansen, S., Bloemendal, E.: Defining app stores: the role of curated marketplaces in software ecosystems. In: Herzwurm, G., Margaria, T. (eds.) ICSOB 2013. LNBIP, vol. 150, pp. 195–206. Springer, Heidelberg (2013)
63. Kruize, J., Wolfert, S., Goense, D., Veenstra, T., Scholten, H., Beulens, A.: Integrating ICT applications for farm business collaboration processes using fi space. In: 2014 Annual SRII Global Conference (SRII), pp. 232–240, April 2014
64. McGregor, J.D.: A method for analyzing software product line ecosystems. In: Proceedings of the Fourth European Conference on Software Architecture: Companion Volume, ECSA 2010, pp. 73–80. ACM, New York (2010)
65. Urli, S., Blay-Fornarino, M., Collet, P., Mosser, S., Riveill, M.: Managing a software ecosystem using a multiple software product line: a case study on digital signage systems. In: 2014 40th EUROMICRO Conference on Software Engineering and Advanced Applications (SEAA), pp. 344–351, Aug 2014
66. Valenca, G., Alves, C., Heimann, V., Jansen, S., Brinkkemper, S.: Competition and collaboration in requirements engineering: a case study of an emerging software ecosystem. In: 2014 IEEE 22nd International Requirements Engineering Conference (RE), pp. 384–393, Aug 2014

67. Anvaari, M., Conradi, R., Jaccheri, L.: Architectural decision-making in enterprises: preliminary findings from an exploratory study in norwegian electricity industry. In: Drira, K. (ed.) ECSA 2013. LNCS, vol. 7957, pp. 162–175. Springer, Heidelberg (2013)
68. Järvinen, J., Huomo, T., Mikkonen, T., Tyrväinen, P.: From agile software development to mercury business. In: Lassenius, C., Smolander, K. (eds.) ICSOB 2014. LNBIP, vol. 182, pp. 58–71. Springer, Heidelberg (2014)
69. Bhowmik, T., Alves, V., Niu, N.: An exploratory case study on exploiting aspect orientation in mobile game porting. In: Bouabana-Tebibel, T., Rubin, S.H. (eds.) Integration of Reusable Systems. Advances in Intelligent Systems and Computing, vol. 263, pp. 241–261. Springer, Switzerland (2014)
70. Dal Bianco, V., Myllarniemi, V., Komssi, M., Raatikainen, M.: The role of platform boundary resources in software ecosystems: a case study. In: 2014 IEEE/IFIP Conference on Software Architecture (WICSA), pp. 11–20, April 2014
71. Bosch, J., Bosch-Sijtsema, P.: From integration to composition: on the impact of software product lines, global development and ecosystems. J. Syst. Softw. **83**(1), 67–76 (2010)
72. Brummermann, H., Keunecke, M., Schmid, K.: Variability issues in the evolution of information system ecosystems. In: Proceedings of the 5th Workshop on Variability Modeling of Software-Intensive Systems, VaMoS 2011, pp. 159–164. ACM, New York (2011)
73. Kourtesis, D., Bratanis, K., Bibikas, D., Paraskakis, I.: Software co-development in the era of cloud application platforms and ecosystems: the case of CAST. In: Camarinha-Matos, L.M., Xu, L., Afsarmanesh, H. (eds.) Collaborative Networks in the Internet of Services. IFIP AICT, vol. 380, pp. 196–204. Springer, Heidelberg (2012)
74. Lettner, D., Petruzelka, M., Rabiser, R., Angerer, F., Prähofer, H., Grünbacher, P.: Custom-developed vs. model-based configuration tools: experiences from an industrial automation ecosystem. In: Proceedings of the 17th International Software Product Line Conference Co-located Workshops, SPLC 2013 Workshops, pp. 52–58. ACM, New York (2013)
75. Lettner, D., Angerer, F., Grunbacher, P., Prahofer, H.: Software evolution in an industrial automation ecosystem: an exploratory study. In: 2014 40th EUROMICRO Conference on Software Engineering and Advanced Applications (SEAA), pp. 336–343, Aug 2014
76. Lungu, M.: Towards reverse engineering software ecosystems. In: IEEE International Conference on Software Maintenance, ICSM 2008, pp. 428–431 (2008)
77. Schultis, K.B., Elsner, C., Lohmann, D.: Moving towards industrial software ecosystems: are our software architectures fit for the future? In: 2013 4th International Workshop on Product Line Approaches in Software Engineering (PLEASE), pp. 9–12, May 2013
78. Alves, A.M., Pessôa, M.: Brazilian public software: beyond sharing. In: Proceedings of the International Conference on Management of Emergent Digital EcoSystems, MEDES 2010, pp. 73–80. ACM, New York (2010)
79. Bosch, J., Bosch-Sijtsema, P.: ESAO: a holistic ecosystem-driven analysis model. In: Lassenius, C., Smolander, K. (eds.) ICSOB 2014. LNBIP, vol. 182, pp. 179–193. Springer, Heidelberg (2014)
80. Nordström, H., Sääksjärvi, M.: Application service provisioning as a strategic network. In: Lamersdorf, W., Tschammer, V., Amarger, S. (eds.) Building the E-Service Society. IFIP, vol. 146, pp. 171–186. Springer, US (2004)

81. Pichlis, D., Raatikainen, M., Sevón, P., Hofemann, S., Myllärniemi, V., Komssi, M.: The challenges of joint solution planning: three software ecosystem cases. In: Jedlitschka, A., Kuvaja, P., Kuhrmann, M., Männistö, T., Münch, J., Raatikainen, M. (eds.) PROFES 2014. LNCS, vol. 8892, pp. 310–313. Springer, Heidelberg (2014)
82. van der Schuur, H., Jansen, S., Brinkkemper, S.: The power of propagation: on the role of software operation knowledge within software ecosystems. In: Proceedings of the International Conference on Management of Emergent Digital EcoSystems, MEDES 2011, pp. 76–84. ACM, New York (2011)
83. Viljainen, M., Kauppinen, M.: Software ecosystems: a set of management practices for platform integrators in the telecom industry. In: Regnell, B., van de Weerd, I., De Troyer, O. (eds.) ICSOB 2011. LNBIP, vol. 80, pp. 32–43. Springer, Heidelberg (2011)

A Survey of Modeling Approaches for Software Ecosystems

Oskar Pettersson(✉) and Jesper Andersson

Linnaeus University, Växjö, Sweden
oskar.pettersson@lnu.se, jesper.andersson@lnu.se

Abstract. Software ecosystems is one promising strategy for organizations to find new market segments, new innovative value propositions creating new value streams. However, understanding internal and external actors, resources and relationships that could be leveraged in a SECO is critical for their strategic decisions. The consequence of mistakes may be costly failures that can force an organization to move out of a market. This paper describes a systematic mapping study that targets description of software ecosystems. Our conjecture is that adequate description support leads to modeling, which will improve information and in turn strategic decisions. The survey searches existing literature for description techniques and their application for comprehensive description.

The study identifies and maps 63 primary studies out of 937 candidates according to their degree of modeling support and several other important aspects for SECO description. The analysis indicates that no approach fully supports comprehensive SECO descriptions, supporting domain specific and view specific modeling of ecosystem concerns. The analysis is used to highlight areas for a future research agenda.

Keywords: Software ecosystems · Mapping study · Domain specific · View

1 Introduction

Recent technology development has triggered strategy development for how companies collaborate with end users, partners, and other stakeholders on their markets. For software intensive systems, organizations apply strategies that define Software Ecosystems (SECO). As a consequence SECOs have become a part of companies daily operations, peoples daily life, and thus it has attracted the interest of researchers [1]. SECOs have contributed to new and innovative value propositions for new and old customer segments creating new revenue streams for players active in a SECO. The importance of understanding the business landscape your organization is active in is emphasized in the business literature. Johnson et al. [2] describe business model comprehension as a critical success criterion for any business model innovation activities.

Failures where organisations overshoot their targeted platform, partially or completely, could mean the demise of a product [3]. SECOs are encompassing far

A. Maglyas and A.-L. Lamprecht (Eds.): ICSOB 2016, LNBIP 240, pp. 79–93, 2016.
DOI: 10.1007/978-3-319-40515-5_6

more than a business model and a software platform with its APIs. Full comprehension of a SECO requires understanding of many more dimensions [4]. These dimensions are arguably well understood when they are contained within one organisation [5], but when they are cross-cutting multiple organizations, comprehension is a much more complex endeavor. Risk management is critical from a business perspective, that is first identifying risks and then understand the consequences. For example, before deciding to open up a platform and set up a SECO that involves external parties, all consequences should be known. Adequate modeling support is critical for such activities, supporting both business and technical decisions concerning a SECOs and its core assets.

Several literature surveys have investigated the definition of SECOs [6,7]. Jansen et al. [8], presents findings regarding modeling approaches based on Manikas et al. [6] data. It is however unclear from existing research how SECOs are modeled, what is included in a SECO model and which notations practitioners and researchers have used. It is however clear that no consensus or standard exist. To that end we performed a systematic mapping of existing literature where we attempt to pin-point how SECOs are currently modeled. Adequate modeling support assist SECO stakeholder communication and as a consequence augments decision-making.

The survey shows that mainly three entities are modeled for SECOs; actors, static relationships, and dynamic flows. It also identifies three focal points for modeling; social networking models, goal oriented models, and software supply networks. The study indicates that current modeling approaches not fully capture all aspects of SECO architectures [9]. The root cause is that models adopted from other areas are not designed to account for the interconnected and inter-organizational aspects of SECOs [10].

The remainder of the paper is organized as follows. Section 2 describes the study's setup, including research questions and research methodology. In Sect. 3, we describe the data we extracted, the maps created, and map the studies accordingly. Section 4 answers the research questions. In Sect. 5 we conclude and discuss future research.

2 Systematic Mapping Study

In this section we describe the research context, research goals, and questions. We also describe the planning for the mapping study, including the selection process and how the data extraction performed.

2.1 Research Context

We have adopted Perry and Wolf's model of architecture [11] as a theoretical description framework for our research. Perry and Wolf defines architecture as a model consisting of elements, form, and rationale. Our conjecture is that this model can act as a basis for ecosystem description.

The model defines three elements; data, processing, and connecting elements. Data elements define and hold data, processing elements transform data elements, while connecting elements connects them. The architecture's form capture how elements are structured, while the rationale include information concerned with architecture decisions.

Our research goal is to provide a framework for SECO modeling and description. Complete modeling support for software ecosystem is required for maximum benefit. Completeness implies support more modeling all concerns relevant for different stakeholders. Completeness also implies modeling support for different context and different domains. A framework must ensure consistent usage of terminology, models, and hierarchies in this multi faceted modeling landscape. As a first step in the research project we set the goal to survey the state-of-research and state-of-practice.

2.2 Research Questions

We reformulated our research goal into three research questions.

RQ1. *What constitutes a Software Ecosystem and how may it be documented?* Documentation or description is broad and include both models and techniques for populating the models. It could also be part of a methodology or based on meta-models that frames a problem or domain.

RQ2. *What domains are primarily described in a SECO?* We would like to understand if domain specific variations exists and characterize them

RQ3. *To what degree are established standards used in these descriptions?* Standards play an increasingly important role in software and system documentation. We would like to incorporate standard notations and techniques in a description framework.

2.3 Systematic Mapping

We decided to conduct a systematic mapping [12] to better understand the field. A systematic mapping is a research method which is suitable for charting an area where an overview is lacking, providing structure to existing research and results. The systematic mapping analyzes a set of primary studies, which are retrieved from databases using a search-string. The set retrieved from the databases is pruned in multiple steps based on inclusion criteria. The selection results in the set of primary studies, which are studied and analyzed more in-depth. We deviate from the rules of a systematic mapping slightly and created a mapping scheme based on our research questions in advance. The intention was to guide both our primary and in-depth analysis. We depict the mapping scheme in Fig. 1.

2.4 Search String

A systematic mapping starts with a broad search in multiple databases to populate the set of candidate studies. We use our research goal and research questions to formulate a search string. `(''software ecosystem'' OR ''software`

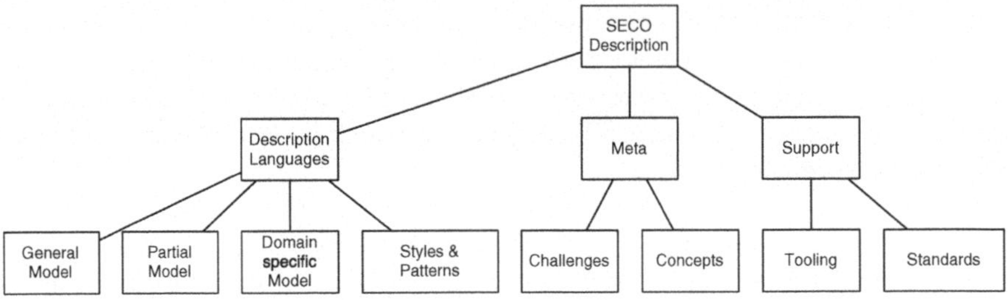

Fig. 1. The hierarchical mapping scheme

`ecosystems'') AND (Documentation OR Model OR Modeling OR Documenting OR View OR Viewpoint OR ''ISO42010'')`. We apply the search string on three digital databases; ACM, IEEE, and Science Direct. We also include all IWSECO proceedings not indexed by these three databases. These are the 2009 and 2011 to 2013 editions.

2.5 Inclusion Criteria

We apply four criteria to decide whether a candidate study should be included in the analysis or not. These criteria focus the selection further and remove studies that can not contribute to the result.

1. Does the study describe a Software Ecosystem?
2. Does the study explicitly describe a description approach for SECOs in one or more domains?
3. Is the study already included in the set of primary studies?
4. Is the study written in English?

In addition we applied a publication type filter that excluded book chapters, introductions or summaries of conferences, proposals, technical reports.

2.6 Selection Process

The selection process contains four steps. The first step retrieves the documents that satisfy the search string from three digital databases. The title, abstract, and keywords are extracted from matching studies. The second step applies the inclusion criteria based on reading of the abstract and keywords. Step three is similar to step number two, however in step three the full paper is read before the criteria is applied. The final stage looks for duplicates such as papers from the same authors with a similar content and papers published as conference papers first and then as journal papers. In that case, journal papers were prioritized.

2.7 Data Extraction

The next step in a mapping study is data extraction from the publications in the set of primary studies. The mapping structure in Fig. 1 was derived based on our understanding of general modeling. Based on this model we defined four data extraction criteria that maps research questions to the mapping structure. The first data extraction criterion (DE1) to find out how SECOs are described in the primary studies, which is important for RQ1. The second goal was to understand SECO description constituents and how these are combined in comprehensive documentation. DE2 focuses on what domain the information relevant for answering RQ2. DE3 and DE4 targets aspects of documentation, such as standards and how domains, which will be used to answer RQ3.

DE1. Strategies for describing a SECO
Description strategies could include models, frameworks, tools, views or elements.
DE2. Domains the work is conducted in.
That is, if the authors explicitly place the work in a domain.
DE3. Established standards used or proposed
Standards here refers to common standards and concepts in architecture description. The terms specifically searched for here are SysML, Enterprise Architecture, TOGAF, Zachman framework, ISO 19439, ISO 42010, UML, and SPEM.
DE4. Systematic approaches to accounting for domains
In short, how does the description strategy account for what domains it describes.

3 Data Collection and Mapping

In this section we describe the data collection and mapping of primary studies. The map consists of three main categories and eight subcategories. A complete index for the mapping is available online[1].

The collection and selection process is depicted in Table 1. Applying the inclusion criteria to the candidates sets reduced the numbers from the initial 937 publications to 63. The study identified publications from 2007 and onwards, 55 of the 63 studies were conference, symposium or workshop papers. We found in total studies from thirty-two venues.

3.1 Map Description

We conducted an initial analysis of the primary studies, applying the pre-defined map. The map defines three categories for an initial classification;meta, descriptions, and support. We provide a high-level description of the categories below and continue with a more detailed description of subcategories for a more precise characterization (Table 2).

The meta category is focused on things that define descriptions, but does not describe how to describe or document an ecosystem. Studies in this category can be further categorized into concepts or challenges. Concept publications

[1] https://github.com/oskarp/icsob2016/blob/master/index.pdf.

Table 1. Number of studies per database and inclusion criteria.

Database	Publications	Filter 1	Filter 2	Filter 3
ACM	352	42	28	25
Science Direct	126	12	7	7
IEEE Explore	434	42	21	18
IWSECO-09&11-13	25	12	12	12
Total	*937*	*109*	*69*	***63***

describe SECOs using high-level concepts and can be used to guide descriptions. Examples include general views on SECOs and ecosystem life-cycles. Challenges describe limitations or impediments for SECO description. These are described as areas where a best-practice is not known or areas where no feasible practices exist.

Descriptions contains studies that include a description or application of at least one of element, form, and rationale in a SECO description. This category can be further decomposed into four subcategories; general, partial, domain specific, and styles & patterns. General refers to studies that claim support for describing complete SECOs, while partial refers to studies with specialized descriptions for an aspect or part of a SECO. For example, ecosystem roles or requirements. The 'domain specific' subcategory includes studies that target descriptions for a particular domain, for example, embedded systems. This does however not imply that the description is domain specific per se, it merely under-lines that the description approach has been applied to a single domain. Patterns & Styles include publications that utilize or derive patterns or styles for SECO descriptions.

The third category is support, which has two subcategories; tooling and standards. Tooling refers to tools available for describing SECOs. These tools come in many forms, however the criterion is that it can be used to at least partially describe a SECO. The standards subcategory include studies that describe or discuss standards in connection to SECOs.

3.2 Meta Categories

Concepts. The study identified seven publications that are concerned with description concepts. These can be characterized as addressing views, life-cycles or elements. Campbell [4] identifies three views, business, social, and architecture for SECOs. The discussion on the social view is extended by dos Santos [13]. Yakakami [14] proposes a view set containing consortium, code management, and open source. A life-cycle for SECOs is described by Hartmann [15]. It focuses on the openness in consumer electronics software and how openness impacts the software architecture. Kazman [16] introduces the metropolis model for commons-based peer production. Both life-cycle models highlights challenges related to managing external contributions in open organisations. In the elements

Table 2. Primary studies — Complete map.

Category	Characteristic	Papers
Meta	Concepts	S37, S38, S39, S40, S41, S42, S53, S54, S56, S60, S61
	Challenges	S43, S44, S45 , S46 , S47 , S48 , S49, S50 , S51
Descriptions	General	S3, S4, S5, S6, S57, S63
	Partial	S8, S9, S10, S11, S12, S13, S14, S15, S16, S17, S18, S19, S20, S21, S22, S7, S52, S55, S58, S59, S62
	Domain specific	S23, S24 , S25 , S26, S27, S28, S29 , S30 , S31
	Styles	S2
	Patterns	S1
Support	Tooling	S32, S33 , S34, S35, S36
	Standards	

Table 3. Primary studies — Concepts map

Characteristic	Area	Publication
Elements	User generated content	S38
	Activity Theory	S42
Life-cycle	Openness	S40
	Metropolis life-cycle	S39
Views	Business, Social, Architecture	S37, S54, S56, S60
	Social	S17
	Business	S53, S61
	Consortium, Management, Open source	S41

category, Musil [17] discusses user generated content and elements in a stigmergic information system, while Uden [18] attempts to map SECOs onto activity theory elements (Table 3).

Challenges. The studies that primarily focus on challenges are mapped in Table 4. The challenges found can be related to the software and social views specifically, or challenges spanning multiple views. Challenges related to general architecture are common in the primary studies, one example is patterns and anti-patterns for SECO architecture, which is discussed by two of primary studies. For the social view, Schultis et al. [19] identify the need for collaboration models in order to augment SECO platforms. Serebrenik and Mens [20] point at the need to investigate domain specific aspects of SECOs. Furthermore, both Jansen [21], and Serebrenik and Mens [20] request more understanding and further investigation of quality attributes in SECOs.

Table 4. Primary studies — Challenges map

View	Challenge	Publication
Software	General Architecture	S43, S44, S50, S48, S45
	Patterns	S49, S47
Social	Collaboration models	S45
Multiple	Domain Specific Ecosystems	S46
	Quality attributes	S47, S46
	Topics	S51

Table 5. Primary studies — General approaches map.

Ref	Element	Connectors	Form	Rationale
S4	Agent, Medium, Object	Communication	Logical, channel and organization	-
S5, S57	Soft & Hard goals, Resource, Task	Means-ends, Decomposition, Dependency	Role, Stage	-
S6	Agents, Features	-	Context	-
S3	Product, Product of Interest, Platform product, Hardware Product	Medium	SEM	-
S3	Company of Interest, Supplier, Customer, Intermediary, Customer's Customer	Flow, OR, XOR	SEM	-
S63	Project, Organization	Dependency, Contribution	Business, Software, Innovation	-

3.3 Description Categories

In this section we describe the mapping of primary studies to the description subcategories; general, partial, domain-specific, and patterns & styles.

General. The study found six publications describing general description approaches. Janner et al. [22] present a methodology where they adapt the St. Gallen Media Reference for SECO modeling. Boucharas et al. [23] propose that software supply networks and product deployment contexts can be used to model SECOs. The I* modeling framework is used by Sadi and Yu [24]. Fontana et al. suggests an agent based approach where a set of tasks, agents and their context aware activation describe a SECO [25]. The final study from Monteith et al. [26] adapts the STREAM framework to a SECO context. We map the studies in this category onto the elements suggested by Perry and Wolf [11]. Table 5 maps the studies onto elements, form, and rationale [11].

Janner et al. [22] describe communities of co-creation through elements of agents and objects that are connected trough a communication medium. Such communication media is constrained by three different components, logical space,

Table 6. Primary studies —"Partial" descriptions map

View	Publication
Social	S17, S7
Software	S20, S21, S19, S13, S11, S9, S8, S52, S62
Business	S10, S14, S15, S16, S18, S58, S58
Roles	S22, S12, S55

Table 7. Primary studies — "Domain specific" descriptions map.

Domain	Publication
Enterprise resource planning	S23
Embedded systems	S24, S26, S27
Technology-enhanced Learning	S25
Mobile Learning	S28
Mashups	S29
Collective intelligence	S30
Service ecosystem	S31

channel system, and organization. The I* extensions by Sadi and Yu [24] set up soft goals, hard goals, resources, and tasks as elements to describe a SECO, connected trough either means-ends, decomposition or dependencies and put into configurations for each stage of the SECO. Fontana et al. [25] present an approach that decouples the computation from coordination. This approach is not at the same level of abstraction as the others found by the survey, its more software than ecosystem. It utilizes agents with features that can be instantiated in different contexts. Monteith et al. [26] gives a high level overview of projects, organizations and their interactions over three different views. They argue for an iterative and view based method of modeling SECOs. Boucharas et al. [23] propose two approaches combined describe SECOs: SSN (Software Supply Networks) and PDC (Product Deployment Contexts). SSNs specifies the product, product of interest, platform product, and hardware product elements, which use a medium as a connector. A medium specify a stack for each connection. The PDC specifies elements such as company of interest, supplier, customer, intermediary, and customer's customer. It connects these trough flows that can have either OR or XOR gates.

Partial. We categorized sixteen of the primary studies as partial descriptions. Table 6 maps them onto the principal view they are describing. In the map we have seven studies in the software system category, six studies with a business model focus, two with a focus on social ecosystems and two focusing entirely on roles. A majority of the studies focus on software and business. Roles are in most of the other studies included in one of the other principal dimensions, that is as an aspect of software, business, or social views. However, two studies explicitly address the roles as a separate view.

Domain Specific. The sub category 'domain' specific includes studies concerned with ecosystems for a specific application domain. We identified nine publications included in the set of primary studies, which primarily described SECOs in relation to a specific domain. These are mapped onto the domains in Table 7. The domains are covering a wide spectra. One possible interpretation is that SECOs are investigated in many different areas of research. Embedded systems appear as the most popular domain with about one-third of the primary studies.

Table 8. Primary studies — Tools map

Domain	Publication
Product line / Variability	S34, S35, S33
Visualization	S36
Architecture spec. support	S32

Styles & Patterns. We included the 'styles & patterns category to specifically identify studies with that focus. The study identified one primary study that was categorized as architectural styles and one classified as architectural patterns. Styles are proposed by Taylor [27], as a foundation for multiple stakeholders that independently would like to extend an ecosystems platform. More specifically the COAST architectural style might be that foundation. The single publication that addresses patterns is a literature study from Syeed et al. [28], which investigates the benefits of the plug-in pattern in a SECO environments.

3.4 Support Categories

In this section we describe the mapping of publications for the support categories tools and standards.

Tools. Five publications describing documentation tools for SECOs were identified among the primary studies. Three however describe faucets of the same tool, the EASY-producer [29]. This tool is an Eclipse plug-in that aids the design of variability-rich product line SECOs. Lungu et al. [30] present an approach for visualizing SECOs using a tool called the small project observatory. The fifth and final publication in this category mentions a collection of tools to support architectural design decisions and merely touches ecosystem concerns (Table 8).

Standards. Another area of interest in our map are studies that address standards. The map use 'standard', characteristic, and usage for a more fine-grained categorization. Standard refers to which standard a study is concerned with. Characteristic maps the primary study to the meta and description categories. Usage can be either implementation, proposal, challenge or related research. Implementation include studies that illustrate that applies (parts of) a standard. Proposal means that the study proposes an implementation of the standard, while related research means that the study compares some aspect of standard to position itself.

We found a discussion on standards in seven of the primary studies. UML appeared in three studies covering implementation, proposal and related research. A further analysis revealed that the studies explicitly referred to UML for their models. The ISO 42010 Standard for architecture documentation was identified in three publications. Both Musil et al. [31], and Ruokolainen and Kutvonen [32] show implementations of the standards, while Pelliccione [9]

Table 9. Primary studies — Standards map

Standard	Characteristic	Usage	Publication
UML	Domain Specific	Implementation	S30, S31, S25
	General	Related research	S3
	Challenges	Proposal	S50
ISO42010	Domain Specific	Implementation	S30, S31
	Challenges	Proposal	S50
SPEM	General	Related research	S5
	Domain Specific	Implementation	S25
Enterprise architecture	Domain Specific	Challenge	S27

proposes it as a part of solution. The two implementations are both explicitly demonstratinghow the standard can be implemented for their respective domains. One of the studies proposes both ISO42010 and UML as part of a solution. The Software & Systems Process Engineering Meta-model (SPEM) was discussed in two studies. Pettersson et al. [33] provide an actual implementation, where SPEM is used to describe SECO views. Sadi and Yu [24] position their work to SPEM discussing it as related research. None of the established enterprise architecture standards was found in the study. However enterprise architecture was identified as a challenge by Axelsson et al. [34] (Table 9).

4 Analysis

The data we extracted and mapped in the previous section, is further analyzed in this section to answer our research questions.

4.1 RQ1: Software Ecosystem Architecture Documentation

The study has found a large number of primary studies concerned with SECO description. It is difficult to identify recurring patterns, directions or trends for how to best describe SECOs in the primary studies after an initial review. However, a more in-depth analysis of the five general approaches we identified, more specifically investigating elements, connectors, form, and rationale, reveals several similarities at more abstract levels. All approaches in these studies provide mechanisms for describing functionality and making connections. Further, all approaches, except SSN/PDC, utilize form to provide different spaces, contexts or stages to their models. None of the general approaches however addressed rationale explicitly.

The partial descriptions focus primarily on software and business views. Social views and pure role views have also been identified in the map. These views are all discussed in the studies that proposed either I*, SSN/PDC or the St. Gallen Media Reference Model, however without any demonstration. The I* and St Gallen approaches also attempt to model user generated content, which mapped in concept category. Life cycles in general and support for a diverse set of views are not discussed by any study. The studies point at patterns and quality attributes as principal, SECO documentation challenges.

The analysis paints a diverse landscape where the general approaches apparently does not provide comprehensive support for modeling all specific domains or facets of ecosystems. Our analysis shows that it is impossible to claim generality without supporting openness and flexibility to support concern specific ecosystem views.

4.2 RQ2: SECO Domains

The study identifies seven domains in the domain-specific studies. If we consider mobile learning as a sub-field of TEL we see that all domain specific implementations can be found in studies that implement SECOs to a principal domain.

What is notable is that four out of seven [31–33,35] of the proposed description approaches include explicit meta-models of the domain they describe. In addition they are adopting the common views, such as business, software, and social. This is an indication that support for domain specific descriptions that can be tailored, expanded, compared and transferred between domains is highly desirable. In order to be able to achieve that openness, flexibility, and some standardization of these descriptions are required. Openness and flexibility appear as key properties to support domain specific ecosystem modeling.

4.3 RQ3: Standardization

The study indicates that the domain specific approaches are more open to adopt established standards. We include I* and the St Gallen Media Reference Model among the standards, although each is found in one study.

The study indicates that UML is the most widely used notation standard. In addition, ISO42010 is applied in all studies that implements UML. The open definition of viewpoints and views in ISO42010 lead to several viewpoints using UML notations. SPEM on the other hand is mentioned once as related research and implemented in one approach. Enterprise architecture is mentioned once as a challenge, its complete absence from SECO descriptions is somewhat surprising. The ISO42010 appears to be a good starting point for standardization as would allow for the inclusion of any other standard notation for models in the viewpoints. It supports definition of viewpoints and configuration of description frameworks by including or excluding viewpoints in the description frameworks. This would provide for concern and stakeholder specific configuration, supporting different domains and their specific requirements.

5 Conclusions

This study describes a systematic mapping of software ecosystem description and documentation. The goal is to gain a deeper understanding of the area and guide future research on SECO modeling and documentation. The primary studies are mapped onto three principal categories covering description, concepts and challenges, and support categories. The study covers one decade and while we can see that the community has converged towards a consensus in recent years, no widely adopted approach for SECO description and documentation has been found. The map points at important aspects of SECO description and documentation, which combines into requirements on a SECO documentation framework. These make up a roadmap for future research and contributions. The framework must support modeling of complete ecosystems, support different views and SECO domains. The key requirements for this are openness and flexibility. The framework should be configurable for domains and specific modeling concerns. The use of standards is an example of important knowledge for continued activities. Standards frame the documentation with strict guidelines for what is included and not, and how models are specified. Future research and development activities in this field must take this into account to be relevant for practitioners.

Some of the domain specific approaches have adopted the ISO42010 for system and software architecture. Our analysis indicates that this standard is a good starting point, being open providing support for flexible viewpoint inclusion and exclusion. Specific viewpoints for SECOs may be added to a viewpoint library. In our ongoing and future research we now use the ISO42010 as a foundation, developing a methodology for creating domain specific SECO documentation frameworks. The approach defines processes and activities that define the domain specific framework and later populate the views for a specific SECO in that domain. We believe that an open and configurable framework approach based on standards best support precise modeling, which is a prerequisite for correct and informed strategic business decisions in the software intensive industries.

References

1. Messerschmitt, D.G., Szyperski, C.: Software Ecosystem: Understanding an Indispensable Technology and Industry. The MIT Press, Cambridge (2005). Number 0262633310 in MIT Press Books
2. Johnson, M.W., Christensen, C.M., Kagermann, H.: Reinventing your business model. Harvard Bus. Rev. **86**(12), 50–59 (2008)
3. Anvaari, M., Jansen, S.: Evaluating architectural openness in mobile software platforms. In: Proceedings of the Fourth European Conference on Software Architecture: Companion Volume. ECSA 2010, pp. 85–92. ACM, New York (2010)
4. Campbell, P.R.J., Ahmed, F.: A three-dimensional view of software ecosystems. In: Proceedings of the Fourth European Conference on Software Architecture: Companion Volume, ECSA 2010, pp. 81–84. ACM, New York (2010)
5. Fowler, M.: Patterns of Enterprise Application Architecture. Addison-Wesley Longman Publishing Co. Inc, Boston (2002)
6. Manikas, K., Hansen, K.M.: Software ecosystems a systematic literature review. J. Syst. Softw. **86**(5), 1294–1306 (2013)
7. Dc Lima Fontao, A., Pereira Dos Santos, R., Dias-Neto, A.: Mobile software ecosystem (mseco): a systematic mapping study. In: 2015 IEEE 39th Annual Computer Software and Applications Conference (COMPSAC), vol. 2, pp. 653–658 (2015)

8. Jansen, S., Handoyo, E., Alves, C.: Scientists' needs in modelling software ecosystems. In: Proceedings of the 2015 European Conference on Software Architecture Workshops, ECSAW 2015, pp. 44:1–44:6. ACM, New York (2015)
9. Pelliccione, P.: Open architectures and software evolution: the case of software ecosystems. In: 2014 23rd Australian Software Engineering Conference (ASWEC), pp. 66–69, April 2014
10. Schultis, K.B., Elsner, C., Lohmann, D.: Moving towards industrial software ecosystems: are our software architectures fit for the future?. In: 2013 4th International Workshop on Product Line Approaches in Software Engineering (PLEASE), pp. 9–12, May 2013
11. Perry, D.E., Wolf, A.L.: Foundations for the study of software architecture. ACM SIGSOFT Softw. Eng. Notes **17**(4), 40–52 (1992)
12. Kitchenham, B., Charters, S.: Guidelines for performing systematic literature reviews in software engineering. Technical report, Technical report, Ver. 2.3 EBSE Technical Report. EBSE (2007)
13. dos Santos, R., Werner, C.: Treating social dimension in software ecosystems through reuseecos approach. In: 2012 6th IEEE International Conference on Digital Ecosystems Technologies (DEST), pp. 1–6, June 2012
14. Yamakami, T.: A three-dimensional view model of open source-aware software development for large-scale mobile software platforms. In: 2010 4th IEEE International Conference on Digital Ecosystems and Technologies (DEST), pp. 130–135, April 2010
15. Hartmann, H., Trew, T., Bosch, J.: The changing industry structure of software development for consumer electronics and its consequences for software architectures. J. Syst. Softw. **85**(1), 178–192 (2012). Dynamic Analysis and Testing of Embedded Software
16. Kazman, R., Chen, H.M.: The metropolis model and its implications for the engineering of software ecosystems. In: Proceedings of the FSE/SDP Workshop on Future of Software Engineering Research, FoSER 2010, pp. 187–190. ACM, New York (2010)
17. Musil, J., Musil, A., Winkler, D., Biffl, S.: A first account on stigmergic information systems and their impact on platform development. In: Proceedings of the WICSA/ECSA 2012 Companion Volume, WICSA/ECSA 2012, pp. 69–73. ACM, New York (2012)
18. Uden, L., Damiani, E., Gianini, G., Ceravolo, P.: Activity theory for oss ecosystems. In: Digital EcoSystems and Technologies Conference, DEST 2007, Inaugural IEEE-IES, pp. 223–228, February 2007
19. Schultis, K.B., Elsner, C., Lohmann, D.: Architecture challenges for internal software ecosystems: a large-scale industry case study. In: Proceedings of the 22nd ACM SIGSOFT International Symposium on Foundations of Software Engineering, FSE 2014, pp. 542–552. ACM, New York (2014)
20. Serebrenik, A., Mens, T.: Challenges in software ecosystems research. In: Proceedings of the 2015 European Conference on Software Architecture Workshops, ECSAW 2015, pp. 40:1–40:6. ACM, New York (2015)
21. Jansen, S.: How quality attributes of software platform architectures influence software ecosystems. In: Proceedings of the 2013 International Workshop on Ecosystem Architectures, WEA 2013, pp. 6–10. ACM, New York (2013)
22. Janner, T., Schroth, C., Schmid, B.: Modelling service systems for collaborative innovation in the enterprise software industry - the st. gallen media reference model applied. In: IEEE International Conference on Services Computing, SCC 2008, vol. 2, pp. 145–152, July 2008

23. Boucharas, V., Jansen, S., Brinkkemper, S.: Formalizing software ecosystem modeling. In: Proceedings of the 1st International Workshop on Open Component Ecosystems, IWOCE 2009, pp. 41–50. ACM, New York (2009)
24. Sadi, M., Yu, E.: Analyzing the evolution of software development: from creative chaos to software ecosystems. In: 2014 IEEE Eighth International Conference on Research Challenges in Information Science (RCIS), pp. 1–11, May 2014
25. Fontana, F.A., Braione, P., Roveda, R., Zanoni, M.: A context-aware style of software design. In: Proceedings of the Second International Workshop on Context for Software Development, CSD 2015, pp. 15–19. IEEE Press, Piscataway (2015)
26. Monteith, J.Y., McGregor, J.D., Ingram, J.E.: Hadoop and its evolving ecosystem. In: Proceedings of the 5th International Workshop on Software Ecosystems, Potsdam, Germany, 11 June 2013, pp. 57–68 (2013)
27. Taylor, R.N.: The role of architectural styles in successful software ecosystems. In: Proceedings of the 17th International Software Product Line Conference, SPLC 2013, pp. 2–4. ACM, New York (2013)
28. Syeed, M.M.M., Lokhman, A., Mikkonen, T., Hammouda, I.: Pluggable systems as architectural pattern: an ecosystemability perspective. In: Proceedings of the 2015 European Conference on Software Architecture Workshops, ECSAW 2015, pp. 42: 1–42: 6. ACM, New York (2015)
29. Eichelberger, H., El-Sharkawy, S., Kröher, C., Schmid, K.: Easy-producer: product line development for variant-rich ecosystems. In: Proceedings of the 18th International Software Product Line Conference: Companion Volume for Workshops, Demonstrations and Tools, SPLC 2014, vol. 2, pp. 133–137. ACM, New York (2014)
30. Lungu, M., Lanza, M., Grba, T., Robbes, R.: The small project observatory: visualizing software ecosystems. Sci. Comput. Programm. **75**(4), 264–275 (2010). Experimental Software and Toolkits (EST 3): A special issue of the Workshop on Academic Software Development Tools and Techniques, WASDeTT (2008)
31. Musil, J., Musil, A., Weyns, D., Biffl, S.: An architecture framework for collective intelligence systems. In: 2015 12th Working IEEE/IFIP Conference on Software Architecture (WICSA), pp. 21–30, May 2015
32. Ruokolainen, T., Kutvonen, L.: An architecture framework for facilitating sustainability in open service ecosystems. In: 2012 IEEE 16th International Enterprise Distributed Object Computing Conference Workshops (EDOCW), pp. 84–93, September 2012
33. Pettersson, O., Gil, D.: On the issue of reusability and adaptability in m-learning systems. In: 2010 6th IEEE International Conference on Wireless, Mobile and Ubiquitous Technologies in Education (WMUTE), pp. 161–165, April 2010
34. Axelsson, J., Papatheocharous, E., Andersson, J.: Characteristics of software ecosystems for federated embedded systems: a case study. Inf. Softw. Technol. **56**(11), 1457–1475 (2014). Special issue on Software Ecosystems
35. Pettersson, O., Svensson, M., Gil, D., Andersson, J., Milrad, M.: On the role of software process modeling in software ecosystem design. In: Proceedings of the Fourth European Conference on Software Architecture: Companion Volume, ECSA 2010, pp. 103–110. ACM, New York (2010)

The Impact of Internet of Things on Software Business Models

Krzysztof Wnuk(✉) and Bhanu Teja Murari

Department of Software Engineering, Blekinge Insitute of Technology, Karlskrona, Sweden
Krzysztof.Wnuk@bth.se, bhmu14@student.bth.se
http://www.bth.se

Abstract. Context. Internet of Things (IoT) technology is significantly impacting software business. Several contributions were made in the literature regarding IoT. However, the importance of various business model elements for IoT and the impact of IoT on requirements engineering activities remains greatly unexplored. This paper focuses on the impact of IoT on software business models and requirements engineering. The objectives for this research include: (1) summarizing the current business models for IoT, (2) analyzing the impact of IoT on software business models (3) analyzing the impact of IoT on requirements engineering. We conducted a systematic snowballing literature review, followed by an industrial survey. We identified 21 peer reviewed papers which were analyzed in relation to their rigor and relevance and received 56 survey responses. The results of the literature review indicate 9 business model elements that IoT literature focus on. Morevoer, 4 business model aspects were described with respect to the business model structure, context and governance. The industrial survey results highlighted that value proposition, followed by customer segmentation and revenue streams were the most important business model elements for IoT. Moreover, the survey results suggest that requirement management, requirement prioritization and requirement modeling and analysis are highly impacted by IoT.

Keywords: Internet of Things · Software business models · Software development · Requirement engineering

1 Introduction

A world where the physical objects are connected with each other using a network is not a distant future anymore [1,2]. These objects interact with people, systems or other objects in a so called Internet of Things (IoT). IoT is on the edge of a huge market explosion, where the number of machines that are connected to the internet has increased by three times and resulting in over 12 billion of connected devices, according to Cisco [3]. Furthermore, Cisco predicted that the international market for IoT would achieve $15 trillion of profit over the next decade [4].

A. Maglyas and A.-L. Lamprecht (Eds.): ICSOB 2016, LNBIP 240, pp. 94–108, 2016.
DOI: 10.1007/978-3-319-40515-5_7

According to the recent survey regarding IoT based business, 46 % of respondents believe the existing business model will change due to IoT, 30 % respondents believe IoT will unlock new revenue opportunities from the existing product or services and 29 % believe that IoT will inspire new business process [5]. Therefore, many business models [6–11] are created for the IoT. IoT is also going to unravel the new revenues for the current products that will change the existing business model. Despite the growing importance of IoT, no study has yet primarily focused on the impact of IoT on business model canvas elements and requirements engineering. For example, Zhuming Bi [12] investigated the impact of IoT on enterprises, but not on software business model elements.

This paper focuses on the impact of IoT on business models and requirements engineering. The following research questions are investigated in this work:

RQ1: What are the publication trends in IoT business models research?
RQ2: What is the impact of IoT on business model canvas elements?
RQ3: What is the impact of IoT on requirements engineering?

This paper is structured as follows: Sect. 2 presents background and related work while Sect. 3 outlines selected research methods. Section 4 presents and discusses literature review findings while Sect. 5 presents and discusses survey findings. Section 6 concludes the paper.

2 Background and Related Work

Kevin Ashton, was the first who used the word Internet of Things in 2002 and the first conference about IoT was held in 2005 [13]. Nowadays, IoT devices are very affordable and offer acceptable performance and small size. According to Cisco, the number of connected devices by 2050 will increases to 50 billion [14]. Figure 1 depicts the Gartner's hype cycle indicating that IoT for emerging technologies is at peak position.

Business Models. Zott *et al.* [16] gave a synopsis of definitions of business models. The most recent definition by Teece [17] defines a business model as the model that express the logic, data and other information that supports the value proposition for the customer and usable structure of revenue and expenditure for the enterprise that delivers this value. Osterwalder [18] defined the business model as a tool that has a set of elements and relationships and allows to explicit the business logic of an organization in order to generate a profitable and sustainable revenue streams [19].

The Osterwalder's business model canvas [19] consists of nine blocks: customer segmentation, value proposition, channels, customer relationships, revenue stream, key resources, key partnerships and cost structure. In this paper, these blocks are referred as 'elements'. The archetypal business model description divides the business model into "Who (customers), what (value proposition), how (value delivered to the customer) and why (essential model for capturing

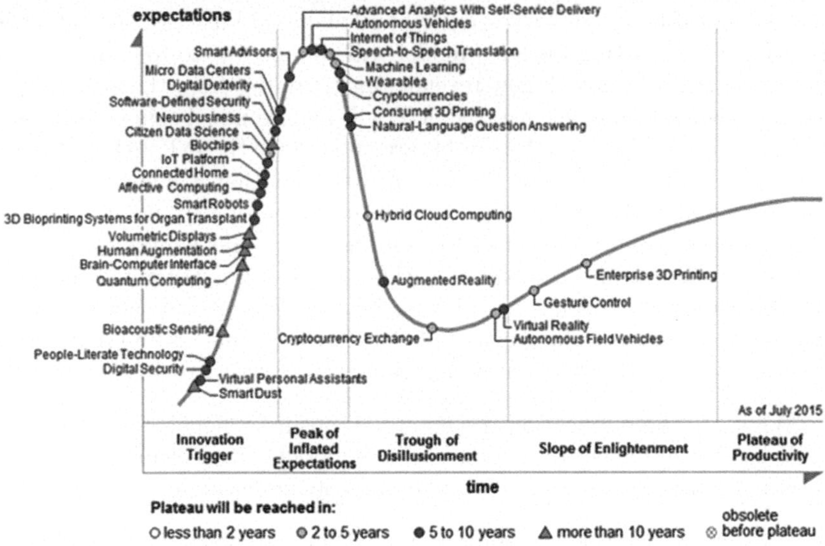

Fig. 1. Gartner's 2015 Hype Cycle [15]

the value)" [20]. In this work, we use Osterwalder's business model (canvas) elements [19] for describing IoT business models as they describe all the significant elements of the business and are widely used and cited in the literature.

Several authors focused on the business models associated with IoT [6–11,21–24]. Turber [6] suggested a framework for IoT business models that includes value network, value creation and benefits and conducted 34 case studies which concluded that this framework is able to represent the business model for IoT. Liu [7] used value proposition and revenue streams to identify how value is created and exchanged between the actors. Fan and Zhou [8] and Glova *et al.* used e3-value methodology for describing value proposition [8] or creating sustainable business models for IoT applications [10]. Berkers *et al.* [9] used value net analysis for creating an IoT business model for a vehicle traffic concept. Bucherer and Uckelmann [22] used value proposition for creating value and revenue in IoT. Finally, Shi [21] proposed a strategy for IoT business models that includes: (1) focusing on improvement of high-quality network for IoT, (2) establishing the value proposition, (3) building key partnerships and (4) launching the IoT products.

3 Research Methods

In this paper we conducted a systematic literature review using the snowballing search method suggested by Wohlin [25] and an industrial survey.

3.1 Literature Review

The snowballing procedure contains two steps: (1) acquiring the start set papers and (2) performing iteration in backward and forward snowballing [25]. The reason for not choosing the database search approach was because it is both complex and difficult to accurately identify the search terms for cross-domain reviews across various databases [25,26].

Start Set Identification. The initial keywords were identified from the research questions and related work, see Sect. 2, and expanded by the vocabulary or synonyms. The following search string was used to derive the start set:

(Internet of Things OR IoT OR Web of Things OR Industrial Internet OR Internet of Everything) AND (Business Models)- we obtained 191 articles

Finding a good start set is similar to the challenges in finding the search string in database search. We used the Engineering Village database for selecting the start set of papers [27]. Google scholar was not used here because our study implies one term, that should be expanded by synonyms such as Web of things or Internet for everything and business models. This indicates that our study requires flexibility and findings relevant papers that required more hence we did not use Google scholar. We used the following inclusion criteria to screen the database results:

- IC1: Papers that are published from 2010–2015 and are peer-reviewed.
- IC2: Papers that are only related to IoT and business models.
- IC3: Articles that are available in full text.
- IC4: Papers which are written in English.
- IC5: Studies that are related to software engineering or requirements engineering, excluding the studies that are related to hardware, system programming etc.

The search string execution resulted in 191 records, after applying IC1 we received 176 candidates. After applying IC2 and IC3 we received 121 candidates and included 62 after title and abstract screening. 30 papers remained after introduction and conclusions reading and 10 after reading the full paper. From the start set of 10 papers (P1 [8], P2 [6], P3 [28], P4 [10], P5 [29], P6 [9], P7 [30], P8 [31], P9 [23], P10 [24]), we performed three snowballing iterations[1].

First Iteration. 253 references were fully examined and evaluated, 71 were removed on basis of publication type, 13 were removed due to language, 108 were removed based on titles and 16 were duplicates. 40 references were removed based on abstract and full text screening. 5 papers were extracted (P11 [32], P12 [33], P13 [22], P14 [34], P15 [21]). 60 citations were screened from the start set: 10 were removed based on language, 27 were removed based on title screening, 5 were duplicates, 16 were removed based on the abstract and full text read. Lastly, 4 papers were included for the next phase (P16 [35], P17 [36], P18 [24] and P19 [30]).

[1] For improved readability we provide the mapping between paper IDs (P1, P2 etc.) and references only here and use paper IDs when presenting literature review results.

Second Iteration. 298 references were examined and evaluated, 129 were removed based on the publication type, 116 were removed based on title screening and 9 were duplicates and 43 were removed after abstract or full text read. Only one paper was (P20 [37]). 232 citations were analyzed, 101 were screened based on the title, 62 based on the publication type, 23 based on the language, 10 were duplicates and finally 35 were removed based on the abstract or full text. One paper was extracted from forward snowballing in this iteration (P21 [38]).

Third Iteration. 44 reverences were examined and evaluated, in which 22 were removed based on title, 17 were removed based on paper type, 2 were removed based on the language, and 3 were removed based on the abstract or full text. 8 citation were examined thoroughly examined, among which 3 were found duplicates, 4 were screened based on the title and one were removed based on the full text. No new papers were identified in this iteration and thus the snowballing has ended.

The extracted data was analyzed using narrative analysis according to the guidelines suggested by Cruzes et al. [39]. We also used the qualitative comparative technique to compare the likeliness between the entities and the types of techniques used by the researchers [40].

3.2 Industrial Survey

The survey questions were based on the literature review and identified related work. The first survey question considered the involvement in IoT software development or sales. Respondents who are or were involved in IoT projects answer additional demographics questions about their role in the IoT project, the domain that the IoT project was targeted at, the size and age of their organization. Next, the importance of business model canvas elements for IoT was measured using a five point Likert scale with a "Don't know" option to be selected if respondents were unsure about the impact. Finally, the impact of IoT on various requirements engineering phases and activities was estimated, followed by open questions about possible improvements for IoT business models[2].

Survey Distribution. The survey was made using the online survey tool "Survio"[3]. A pilot study was conducted beforehand to identify potential issues and mitigate them. The updated survey was distributed in various online groups (LinkeIn, MeetUp, Facebook, mailing lists) related to IoT that had expressed interest in business models or business aspects of IoT. We assumed that all participants of these groups have good understanding of IoT and the challenges that it brings to business modeling. The survey took on average 8 min to complete.

[2] The survey questionnaire is available at this link http://serg.cs.lth.se/fileadmin/serg/IoTBusinessModelsSurveyQuestions.pdf.

[3] www.survio.com.

Statistical Analysis. The survey results were statistically analyzed [41] using Chi-square test to find statistical difference between the obtained answers and demographics and the Cramer's V score for the strength of relationship among two variables [42].

3.3 Validity Threats

We discuss the validity threats following Wohlin *et al.* [43].

Construct validity covers potential issues in establishing appropriate methods and measures for the studied phenomenon. In our case, we used systematic literature review as input to industrial survey. Using two sources of evidence helped us to better understand the studied phenomenon. The way how survey questions are phrased remains a threat to construct validity as they could have been differently interpreted. During survey pilots, we identified and eliminated potential sources of question misinterpretations. Moreover, a risk remains that we generalized from experience that could be based on biased opinions [44]. Finally, the search string was iteratively developed and discussed between the two authors to avoid possible construct validity threats.

Internal validity is concerned with unknown or uncontrolled confounding factors that may affect the studied causal relationships. In this work, we focused on business model canvas and requirements engineering phases as factors that may impact IoT. Therefore a threat remains that other significant factors may impact successful IoT software development. Considering the literature review part of the study, all steps were discussed between the two authors and any disagreements were discussed and resolved.

External Validity is considered as a potential to generalize the results. In this study, most of the identified papers received high rigor and relevance scores and represent industrial contexts. Therefore, the final outcomes are generalizable and are appropriate to the industry. The fact that we obtained over 50 answers in the survey also straightens external validity.

Reliability is concerned with the degree of repeatability of the study. During the literature review, we documented each step to enable replication[4]. Paper screening and analysis procedures were defined beforehand and rigidly followed. Quality assessment based on the rigor and relevance scores was based on the guidelines suggested by Ivarsson and Gorschek [45]. The survey questions are available online to enable replications and further studies. Finally, the characteristics of the population that answered the survey are also outlined.

4 Results and Analysis

4.1 Literature Review Results and Analysis

The identified papers were classified based on the research methodology (survey, case study, experiment etc.) and type of study (evaluation, proposal, solution

[4] The details of the process can be obtained upon request.

etc. [46]), see Fig. 2. 7 papers were classified as framework proposals [P6, P10, P11, P14, P16, P17, P19] and these papers have followed the Osterwalder's [19] business model elements for proposing IoT frameworks. 3 papers [P9, P13, P20] proposed business modeling framework solutions evaluated in industry at IBM [P9], SAP [P13] and RFID identification for logistics [P20]. All three contexts are large and involve millions of potential devices even in the smallest scale, thus emphasizing the challenges that business modeling brings for IoT in terms of creating sustainable solutions that can easily scale up.

6 papers were categorized as case studies - evaluations [P1, P2, P4, P7, P8, P15] in postal logistics [P1], in heating, home security, smart lighting, mobility, smart city [P2], healthcare [P4], Amazon as the evaluation object [P8] or machine to machine communication [P15]. This indicates that although IoT is a new concept it has penetrated several business domains.

Five papers were categorized as survey evaluations [P3, P5, P12, P18, P21] in selecting the business model elements that are used for IoT business models. Paper P3 also studies business model canvas elements for IoT with over 70 respondents. Paper P5 provides an interview survey at Ericsson and Tele2 regarding Smart Grid while paper P18 focuses on smart thermostat technology or supply chain management [P21].

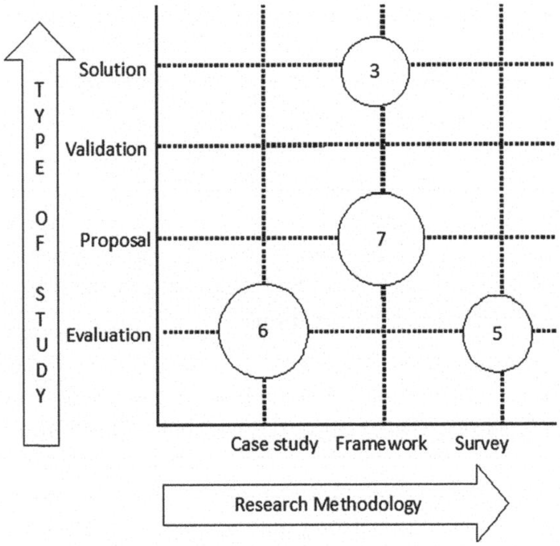

Fig. 2. Classification of papers

The papers were categorized into four quadrants (A, B, C and D) according to the rigor and relevance scores assessment suggested by Ivarsson and Gorschek [47], see Fig. 3. 7 papers were found with high rigor and relevance, 6 papers are found with high relevance and low rigor, 5 papers were found with high rigor and low relevance, 3 papers were found with low rigor and low relevance.

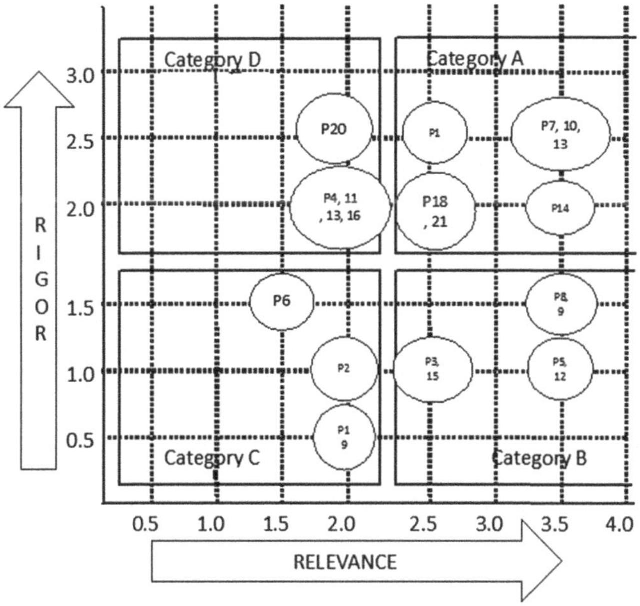

Fig. 3. Quality assessment based on rigor and relevance

Aspects of Value Creation in IoT. We analyzed the value creation aspects in IoT following the four dimensions introduced by Amit and Zott for e-business [48], namely: efficiency, complementaries, lock-in and novelty.

Efficiency is the efficiency of the transaction that the business creates [48]. In the IoT case it includes the values appropriated by each party involved in the transaction. 9 papers [P2, P5, P6, P8, P11, P14, P16, P18, P20] discussed efficiency. Among the papers with high rigor and relevance scores, paper P20 designed a framework for IoT business models for machine to machine communications and smart energy contexts of IoT while paper P14 provided a tool for designing the business model for the IoT that improves the transaction speed and simplicity. Both papers highlight the importance of dynamic adaptations to rapidly changing situation in the IoT business landscape and therefore put the emphasis on efficiency. Paper P5 proposed a combination of offline and online transactions IoT-based healthcare services. This approach enables cross selling between the participants and the IoT product. Interestingly, high efficiency is required for regulated domains, e.g. healthcare or energy. This is a clear indication of the disruption potential of IoT in heavily regulated domains.

Among the papers that were classified in the B quadrant for rigor and relevance, two papers (P2 and P6) focused on reducing the transaction asymmetry for improved efficiency and sustainability of IoT business models. This is important for IoT as they offer new opportunities for devices that used to be passive receivers of commands or data. Three studies P11, P16 (both B category) P18

(C category) focused on value capturing for IoT. The suggested business models reduce information asymmetry and increase the transparency in the flow of information. Finally, paper P8 (C category) focused on business model information flow transparency by identifying the value network for the collaborating partners. They proposed a new model where efficiency is supported by information transparency.

Complementarities represent the situation when a bundle of goods or services represents more value than the individual elements [48]. Brandenburger *et al.* [49] identified that complimentarities are also the source of value creation in IoT software business. Gulati *et al.* [50] stressed that if the customer is satisfied they purchase the complements and increase revenue. Three papers [P13, P19, P20] focused on complementarities for IoT product and services. Papers P13 and P19 (both in category B for rigor and relevance) focused on the benefits for IoT products and the customers satisfaction when offering complimentary services. As IoT offers access to extensive network of devices, there is a significant potential in providing dynamic complementary services that can answer rapidly changing demands. In paper P20, the importance of richness in the virtual market for large scale industries in the context of IoT is stressed.

Lock-in is a mechanism to engage the customer in repeat transactions and prevent them from migrating to competitors [51]. Lock-in creates positive effect on efficiency and complementarities and greatly supports value creation [48]. Five papers [P2, P5, P8, P15, P17] focused on lock-in for IoT business models. Two papers received high rigor and relevance scores. Paper P5 designed a IoT business model that includes strategic lock-in while Paper P17 compared several successful IoT business models and analyzed lock-in mechanisms. Paper P2 (category B) suggested that the customers should be able to compare and select the most relevant IoT features and in this way ensure lock-in. In papers P8 and P15, lock-in was introduced by following customers' preferences and flexibility in the feature offering and context variables.

Novelty strengthens the potential for value creation. Five papers [P4, P7, P8, P9, P11] looked into novel ways for value creation in IoT. In papers P4, P8, P11, the authors have proposed business model framework tools which enable novel capabilities for new IoT business models. The authors have also addressed innovative solutions through this tool which expands the business market. In papers P7 and P9, the authors focused on novel value creation techniques originating from the interactions between the IoT business context players.

Business Model Canvas Elements. We classified the identified studies according to the business model canvas elements suggested by Ostewalder and Pigneur [19]. The classification was reused for the survey part of the study and is presented in Table 1. Value proposition was discussed in 13 studies while revenue streams were discussed in 11 studies. Customer segmentation was discussed in 9 studies while all remaining business model canvas were discussed in five studies each. This indicates that IoT offers new ways to create and deliver value to

Table 1. Business model elements, adapted from [19]

Business model elements	Description	Papers
Customer Segmentation	The value that is offered by the company to segments of the customers.	P1, P3, P6, P7, P10, P11, P13, P15, P20
Value proposition	Complete view of the companys products and services.	P1, P2, P3, P4, P6, P7, P10, P11, P12, P13, P15, P20, P21
Channels	Numerous ways of company to get in touch with the customers	P3, P6, P10, P13, P20
Customer Relationships	Different types of relationship between a company and different segments of customers.	P1, P3, P6, P10, P13, P15, P20
Revenue streams	The ways a company can make money through revenue flows	P1, P3, P4, P6, P7, P10, P13, P11, P15, P20, P21
Key Resources	Adjustment of activities and resources.	P3, P6, P10, P13, P20
Key Activities	Necessary flow to execute the companys business model	P3, P6, P10, P13, P20
Key Partnerships	Agreement with other companies to offer and degrade the value	P3, P6, P10, P13, P20
Cost Structure	Describes the cost structure of business models.	P3, P6, P10, P13, P20

potential customers. What appears to be surprising is that channels and key partnerships were mentioned only in five studies each. This may suggest that companies who are entering IoT business can, to a large degree, reuse the existing partnership networks and channels to bring successful IoT products. At the same time, our results confirm the strategic importance of defining the relevant value elements and perspectives for successful product development [52].

5 Survey Results and Analysis

The survey received 61 responses, 5 respondents had no experience in IoT, so they were removed and the remaining 56 responses were analyzed. The completion rate of the survey is 92 % as per Kitchenham et al. [53] this is sufficient. 10 respondents were software developers, 9 were project managers, 7 were product managers, 7 were hardware suppliers, 9 worked with services, 4 were customer developer, 4 worked with support and 3 with logistics, and three with other roles. Next, questionnaire question 3 aimed to identify the department which

Table 2. The importance of business model canvas elements for IoT. Bold text indicates the most commonly selected option.

	Strongly disagree	Disagree	Neutral	Agree	Strongly agree
Customer Segmentation	0	0	0	24	**32**
Value proposition	0	0	6	17	**33**
Channels	0	0	13	**43**	0
Customer Relationship	0	0	3	**34**	19
Revenue Streams	0	0	10	19	**27**
Key Resources	0	0	9	**28**	19
Key Activities	0	0	15	**24**	18
Key Partnership	0	0	20	**21**	17
Cost Structure	0	0	**22**	**22**	12

their IoT project is targeted at. The following applications were mentioned by our respondents: smart cities (12), smart home and buildings (10), automotive (8), education (6), telecom (5), manufacturing (5), supply chain management (4), security (3), logistics (2) and other(1).

The level of involvement in IoT project was measured in survey questions 1.1 and 2.5[5]. 34 % of respondents how reported any involvement in IoT has 0-1 years of involvement, 28 % respondent has 1–3 years of involvement, 38 % respondent has more than 3 years. Furthermore, 38 % of respondent had 0-1 years of experience in IoT projects, 30 % had 1–3 years of experience and 32 % had over three years. 44.6 % of the respondents worked for large scale organizations (>100), 37.4 % worked for medium scale organizations and 18 % worked for small scale organizations.

The level of importance of the business model canvas elements for IoT was measured among the survey respondents (question 3.1), see Table 2. Value proposition received mean rank of 5.78, followed by customer segmentation (mean rank 5.26), customer relationship (mean rank: 4.89) and revenue streams (mean rank: 4.94). This result confirms the literature review results about the importance of value proposition for IoT, e.g. Gloze [10] emphasized that value proposition is crucial in the business model canvas for IoT business models for e-health care. The cost structures received the most neutral answers indicating that this aspect does not change significantly in IoT. Moreover, key partnerships received less importance according to our respondents indicating that companies that enter the IoT business can put less emphasis on making strategic partnerships and more dynamically make or change them based on changing demands.

Impact of IoT on Requirement Engineering. The respondents were asked to grade the impact of IoT on requirements engineering, see Table 3. 54 % of respondents who had worked with IoT identified that IoT has high impact on requirement management, 52 % of respondents identified that IoT has high

[5] http://serg.cs.lth.se/fileadmin/serg/IoTBusinessModelsSurveyQuestions.pdf.

Table 3. Heat map for Impact of IoT on requirement engineering

	Low	Medium	High
Requirement Elicitation	9	**26**	21
Requirement Modeling & analysis	7	23	**29**
Requirement Specification	8	22	**26**
Requirement Validation	8	21	**27**
Requirement Management	6	19	**31**
Requirement Prioritization	10	16	**30**
Release planning	5	24	**27**

impact on requirement prioritization while 51 % of respondents indicates that IoT impacts requirements modeling (we allowed mulitple answers to this question). The Chi-square test results indicated no significant relation between respondents' experience and the impact of IoT on requirements engineering. This indicates that companies who develop IoT products should focus on both value propositions and requirements prioritization and keep track of product requirements by utilizing robust requirements management methods.

6 Conclusions and Future Work

With rapid increase in the IoT technology, software organizations need to better understand and utilize its potential in creating business opportunities. Business model tools, e.g. business model canvas, help IoT organizations create value for customers [22]. This paper focuses on exploring the current IoT business models in the literature and industrial practice. We also focus on the impact of IoT on business model canvas elements and requirements engineering.

Answering **research question RQ1** frameworks and case studies dominated among the identified papers. Moreover, only three identified papers received low rigor and relevance scores, indicating that the studies were mostly rigorously conducted and the results are relevant and creditable. Efficiency of the transactions that the business creates was the most commonly studied aspect among the identified papers. Lock-in mechanisms for IoT and novelty were also often considered, followed by complementarities.

Answering **research question RQ2** our investigations uncovered that value proposition and revenue streams are the most commonly mentioned business model canvas elements in the surveyed literature. The survey respondents confirmed the importance of these two aspects, however customer segmentation and relationships were also considered as important.

Answering **research question RQ3** requirements management and prioritization are highly impacted by IoT. Interestingly, IoT has less impact on requirements elicitation and release planning according to the survey respondents.

The main limitation of this work is that it explored IoT only through the lens of business model canvas and requirements engineering. We are aware the IoT is much richer than its business model and impacts other software development and product management activities. Thus, we plan to expand the understanding provided in this paper in future research activities. We also plan to conduct case studies at IoT companies to better understand how requirements engineering activities impact business modeling and realization and if any patterns can be identified. We would also like to explore possible improvements to requirements engineering practice that could better support IoT.

References

1. Atzori, L., Iera, A., Morabito, G.: The internet of things: a survey. Comput. Netw. **54**(15), 2787–2805 (2010)
2. Steen, G., Robinson, J., Dwyer, R., Brown, G.: Intel's APAC internet ofthings day event report (2013). http://www.digitimes.com/supply_chain_window/story.asp?datepublish=2013/12/04&pages=PR&seq=202. Accessed February 5, 2016
3. Bradley, J.: Cisco's internet of everything (ioe) (2013). https://www.cisco.com/web/about/business-insights/docs/ioe-value-index-top-10-insights.pdf. Accessed 2016
4. Bort, J.: Cisco's john chambers (2013). http://www.businessinsider.com/ciscos-john-chambers-has-found-a-new-14-trillion-market-2013-5?IR=T. Accessed Feb 5, 2016
5. E. I. U. report, The internet of things business index (2013). http://www.economistinsights.com/analysis/internet-things-business-index. Accessed February 5, 2016
6. Turber, S., vom Brocke, J., Gassmann, O., Fleisch, E.: Designing business models in the era of internet of things. In: Tremblay, M.C., VanderMeer, D., Rothenberger, M., Gupta, A., Yoon, V. (eds.) DESRIST 2014. LNCS, vol. 8463, pp. 17–31. Springer, Heidelberg (2014)
7. Liu, L., Jia, W.: Business model for drug supply chain based on the internet of things. In: 2010 2nd IEEE InternationalConference on Network Infrastructure and Digital Content, pp. 982–986 (2010)
8. Fan, P.-F., Zhou, G.-Z.: Analysis of the business model innovation of the technology of internet of things in postal logistics. In: 2011 IEEE 18th International Conference on Industrial Engineering and Engineering Management (IE&EM), pp. 532–536. IEEE (2011)
9. Berkers, F., Roelands, M., Bomhof, F., Bachet, T., Van Rijn, M., Koers, W.: Constructing a multi-sided business model for a smart horizontal iot service platform. In: 17th International Conference on Intelligence in Next Generation Networks, ICIN 2013, October 2013, Venice, pp. 126–132 (2013)
10. Glova, J., Sabol, T., Vajda, V.: Business models for the internet of things environment. Procedia Econ. Finance **15**, 1122–1129 (2014)
11. Meyer, S., Ruppen, A., Magerkurth, C.: Internet of things-aware process modeling: integrating IoT devices as business process resources. In: Salinesi, C., Norrie, M.C., Pastor, Ó. (eds.) CAiSE 2013. LNCS, vol. 7908, pp. 84–98. Springer, Heidelberg (2013)
12. Bi, Z., Da Xu, L., Wang, C.: Internet of things for enterprise systems of modern manufacturing. IEEE Trans. Ind. Inf. **10**(2), 1537–1546 (2014)
13. Mattern, F., Floerkemeier, C.: From the internet of computers to the internet of things. In: Sachs, K., Petrov, I., Guerrero, P. (eds.) Buchmann Festschrift. LNCS, vol. 6462, pp. 242–259. Springer, Heidelberg (2010)

14. Cisco: Cisco's connections counter: The internet of everything in motion (2013). http://newsroom.cisco.com/feature-content?articleId=1208342. Accessed Feb 5, 2016
15. G. A. 2015: Gartner's 2015 Hype Cycle for emerging technologies identifiesthe computing innovations that organizations should monitor (2015). http://www.gartner.com/newsroom/id/3114217. Accessed Feb. 2016
16. Zott, C., Amit, R., Massa, L.: The business model: recent developments and future research. J. Manag. **37**(4), 1019–1042 (2011)
17. Teece, D.J.: Business models, business strategy and innovation. Long Range Plann. **43**(2), 172–194 (2010)
18. Osterwalder, A.: The business model ontology: A proposition in a design science approach (2004)
19. Osterwalder, A., Pigneur, Y., Tucci, C.L.: Clarifying business models: Origins, present, and future of the concept. Commun. Assoc. Inf. Syst. **16**(1), 1 (2005)
20. Gassmann, O., Frankenberger, K., Csik, M.: Revolutionizing the business model. In: Gassmann, O., Schweitzer, F. (eds.) Management of the Fuzzy Front End of Innovation, pp. 89–97. Springer, New York (2014)
21. Shi, X.: A research on internet-of-things-based business model of china mobile. In: International Conference on Logistics Engineering, Management and Computer Science (LEMCS 2014). Atlantis Press (2014)
22. Bucherer, E., Uckelmann, D.: Business models for the internet of things. In: Uckelmann, D., Harrison, M., Michahelles, F. (eds.) Architecting the Internet of Things, pp. 253–277. Springer, Heidelberg (2011)
23. He, M., Ren, C., Wang, Q., Shao, B., Dong, J.: The internet of things as an enabler to supply chain innovation. In: 2010 IEEE 7th International Conference on e-Business Engineering (ICEBE), pp. 326–331. IEEE (2010)
24. Leminen, S., Westerlund, M., Rajahonka, M., Siuruainen, R.: Towards IOT ecosystems and business models. In: Andreev, S., Balandin, S., Koucheryavy, Y. (eds.) NEW2AN/ruSMART 2012. LNCS, vol. 7469, pp. 15–26. Springer, Heidelberg (2012)
25. Wohlin, C.: Guidelines for snowballing in systematic literature studies and a replication in software engineering. In: Proceedings of the 18th International Conference on Evaluation and Assessment in Software Engineering, p. 38. ACM (2014)
26. Kitchenham, B., Brereton, O.P., Budgen, D., Turner, M., Bailey, J., Linkman, S.: Systematic literature reviews in software engineering-a systematic literature review. Inf. Soft. Technol. **51**(1), 7–15 (2009)
27. Charles, K.I.K., Knisely, W.: Engineering communication (2015). http://www.wadsworthmedia.com/marketing/sample_chapters/2013/9781133114703_ch02.pdf. Accessed Feb. 2016
28. Dijkman, R., Sprenkels, B., Peeters, T., Janssen, A.: Business models for the internet of things. Int. J. Inf. Manag. **35**(6), 672–678 (2015)
29. Alvarez, O., Ghanbari, A., Markendahl, J.: Smart energy: Competitive landscape and collaborative business models. In: 2015 18th International Conference on Intelligence in Next Generation Networks (ICIN), pp. 114–120. IEEE (2015)
30. Westerlund, M., Leminen, S., Rajahonka, M.: Designing business models for the internet of things. Techn. Innov. Manag. Rev. **4**(7), 5–14 (2014)
31. Keskin, T., Kennedy, D.: Strategies in smart service systems enabled multi-sided markets: Business models for the internet of things. In: 48th Hawaii International Conference on System Sciences, pp. 1443–1452. IEEE (2015)
32. Haller, S., Karnouskos, S., Schroth, C.: The Internet of Things in an Enterprise Context. Springer, New York (2009)

33. Mejtoft, T.: Internet of things and co-creation of value. In: Internet of Things (iThings/CPSCom), 2011 International Conference on and 4th International Conference on Cyber, Physical and Social Computing, pp. 672–677. IEEE (2011)
34. Mazhelis, O., Luoma, E., Warma, H.: Defining an internet-of-things ecosystem. In: Andreev, S., Balandin, S., Koucheryavy, Y. (eds.) NEW2AN/ruSMART 2012. LNCS, vol. 7469, pp. 1–14. Springer, Heidelberg (2012)
35. Chan, H.C.: Internet of things business models. J. Serv. Sci. Manag. **8**(04), 552 (2015)
36. Blythe, C.: Business models for value generation in the internet of things. Data-and Value-Driven Software Engineering with Deep Customer Insight, p. 8
37. Sun, Y., Yan, H., Lu, C., Bie, R., Thomas, P.: A holistic approach to visualizing business models for the internet of things. Commun. Mobile Comput. **1**(1), 1–7 (2012)
38. Wagenaar, J.: The impact of the internet of things on revenue in supply chains. In: 17th Twente Student Conference on IT, Netherlands (2012)
39. Cruzes, D.S., Dybå, T.: Research synthesis in software engineering: A tertiary study. Inf. Soft. Technol. **53**(5), 440–455 (2011)
40. Spitzlinger, R.: Mixed method research-qualitative comparative analysis (2006)
41. Little, R.J., Rubin, D.B.: Statistical Analysis with Missing Data. Wiley, New York (2014)
42. Rea, L.M., Parker, R.A.: Designing and Conducting Survey Research: A Comprehensive Guide. Wiley, New York (2014)
43. Wohlin, C., Runeson, P., Höst, M., Ohlsson, M.C., Regnell, B., Wesslén, A.: Experimentation in Software Engineering. Springer Science & Business Media, New York (2012)
44. Siegmund, J., Kästner, C., Liebig, J., Apel, S., Hanenberg, S.: Measuring and modeling programming experience. Emp. Soft. Eng. **19**(5), 1299–1334 (2013)
45. Ivarsson, M., Gorschek, T.: A method for evaluating rigor and industrial relevance of technology evaluations. Emp. Softw. Eng. **16**(3), 365–395 (2011)
46. Wieringa, R., Maiden, N., Mead, N., Rolland, C.: Requirements engineering paper classification and evaluation criteria: a proposal and a discussion. Requir. Eng. **11**(1), 102–107 (2006)
47. Ivarsson, M., Gorschek, T.: A method for evaluating rigor and industrial relevance of technology evaluations. Emp. Soft. Eng. **16**(3), 365–395 (2011)
48. Amit, R., Zott, C.: Value creation in e-business. INSEAD (2000)
49. Brandenburger, A.M., Stuart, H.W.: Value-based business strategy. J. Econ. Manag. Strategy **5**, 5–24 (1996)
50. Gulati, R., et al.: Network location and learning: The influence of network resources and firm capabilities on alliance formation. Strateg. Manag. J. **20**(5), 397–420 (1999)
51. Williamsson, O.: Markets and hierarchies, analysis and antitrust implications: A study in the economics of internal organization (1975)
52. Khurum, M., Gorschek, T., Wilson, M.: The software value map an exhaustive collection of value aspects for the development of software intensive products. J. Softw. Evol. Process **25**(7), 711–741 (2013)
53. Kitchenham, B., Pfleeger, S.L.: Principles of survey research: part 5: populations and samples. ACM Soft. Eng. Notes **27**(5), 17–20 (2002)

Leveraging Bitcoin Blockchain Technology to Modernize Security Perfection Under the Uniform Commercial Code

David S. Gerstl(✉)

Department of Computer Systems, School of Business,
Farmingdale State College, The State University of New York,
2350 Broadhollow Road, Farmingdale, NY 11735, USA
GERSTLD@farmingdale.edu

Abstract. The states of the United States operate parallel registration systems under the rules of the Uniform Commercial Code to provide notice of existing security interests in collateral to lenders. The current system is primarily a paper-based system more suited to the 19th than the 21st century. While the states have implemented varying degrees of computerization and modernization, dealing with fifty separate registration databases has made it difficult for banks and their attorneys to automate their processes, leading to errors and loss. The system could be modernized by storing the records for all 50 states in a single shared database with external electronic access. In this paper, we propose an implementation of a distributed, replicated database utilizing a variation on the Bitcoin blockchain for data storage and validation.

Keywords: Uniform Commercial Code · Secured transactions · UCC Filing · Bitcoin · Blockchain · Distributed databases · Government records

1 Introduction

Commercial and industrial loans not tied to real estate are big business for US banks, with outstanding balances of about US$1.8 trillion [1]. A key enabler of the large indebtedness is the notion of a **secured loan**, a loan where after a default the lenders have recourse to a specific set of assets, called **collateral**, in preference to other creditors. In cases of bankruptcy, where the existing assets are insufficient to cover all obligations, the effectiveness of agreements for preferential treatment and for creation of tiers of creditors with respect to collateral are vital to increasing loan availability by reducing risk and therefore reducing the expense of commercial loans.

In the United States, the laws governing most classes of collateral are state laws, not U.S. federal laws. A long standing effort to harmonize state laws on commercial transactions has resulted in all states having broadly similar laws

A. Maglyas and A.-L. Lamprecht (Eds.): ICSOB 2016, LNBIP 240, pp. 109–123, 2016.
DOI: 10.1007/978-3-319-40515-5_8

for **secured loans** (those with collateral) based upon **Article 9** of the Uniform Commercial Code (**UCC**, hereafter). The fundamental rule in priority of **security interests** (interests in collateral by a lender) is that a borrower can effectively designate an object as collateral by contract and be bound by that designation. This designation, however, has limited effectiveness against competing claims by third parties unless the lender takes steps to give others actual or constructive notice of the status of collateral in accord with specific statutorily defined steps, a process known as **perfection**. For most types of collateral, registration of the security interest with the state serves this purpose. Other potential lenders can then query the state and receive copies of the registration.

States maintain independent perfection databases. In many states the parties and their attorneys interface with the state through paper or facsimile forms and signatures, not electronic access. Without a unified system, the standard procedure on the termination of the loan requires the attorney for the lender to perform searches for security interests tied to the borrower's legal name, filter them manually by lender and deal, and then to draft forms to terminate the relevant security interests. In a recent case in New York [2], in the process of a loan payoff by General Motors, Chase Manhattan Bank released three security interests, one of which was related to a different loan, not in payoff. The third security interest, with a value of over $1.5 Billion, was released soon before the bankruptcy of General Motors, leaving the lenders **unsecured creditors** with a much lower priority and no special access to the collateral. While one would like to claim that a number of safeguards failed in this case, in fact few safeguards exist. The current system is almost entirely dependent on ad-hoc processes at law firms and banks, and on multiple sets of eyes checking documents to ensure that the registration of a security interest is filed in the correct state, with the correct name of the borrower, is manually renewed at exactly the required time, and that the proper liens are released upon loan payoff.

While unified electronic registration system would not solve all of these problems, it would make technological and process solutions to the problem much easier, and likely lead to increased penetration of commercial and proprietary software to manage loans and file electronically. There is already a standard for electronic interface for collateral filings, but requirements that dictate different filing locations and uneven implementation have meant that most banks and law firms have felt reduced urgency to move their in-house systems to directly file.

The questions of distributed databases, distributed authority, and record integrity have been well explored in the realm of cryptocurrencies. The current darling of cryptocurrencies, the Bitcoin protocol, uses an innovated design called the blockchain to record and protect the integrity of transaction information. The blockchain is well suited to storing small amounts of public data in a tamper resistant distributed database. In this paper we show how the blockchain algorithm can be adapted to form the basis for a multi-state system that distributes and duplicates collateral registration data.

Prior work connecting the UCC with Bitcoin has been almost entirely concerned with the status of Bitcoin itself as either a currency or an asset when creating a security interest on Bitcoin [3]. The work presented here is more akin to companies advocating using a new Blockchain as a data storage medium [4], although much of the commercial activity in this area is utilizing the existing Bitcoin blockchain as an unwilling medium for storing hashes to prove data existed at a point in time [5].

While UCC filings are made at various levels of government in the United States, from the U.S. Federal Government down, for the purposes of clarity in exposition, we use the term **state** to refer to any entity able to receive UCC filings, including but not limited to the 50 states of the United States as well as to other entities similarly situated with respect to property records. We refer to the party that grants collateral as the **debtor** and the party with recourse to the collateral as a **lender** or a **secured party**.

Section 2 discusses the Uniform Commercial Code, the legal framework that defines the rights of a creditor to collateral. Section 3 discusses the Bitcoin Blockchain algorithm. Section 4 describes a method of using some of the technical aspects of the Bitcoin Blockchain as the basis for a distributed database to store Uniform Commercial Code records. Finally, Sect. 5 discusses the barriers to implementation.

2 Secured Transactions and the UCC

In granting a loan, a financial institution looks at a number of factors that bear on the ability and willingness of the borrower to repay the loan as well as well as the damage should the loan not be repaid in full. One key tool to reduce the risk to the bank is to use collateral, assets to which the holder of a loan can resort should the debtor default on the associated loan obligation. A specific debtor may have a number of secured and unsecured lenders. A particular piece of property may be collateral for a number of obligations. The typical commercial credit agreement contains a **cross default provision** that puts every loan containing the provision in default when any loan to the borrower is in default [6]. The result is that when a default occurs on one loan, often all loans to that borrower go into default, and all lenders may start trying to claim the assets forming collateral. The commercial loan world thus requires a mechanism to determine the priority of competing claims on the collateralized assets of a debtor. Article 9 of the Uniform Commercial Code serves this purpose.

Article 9 is written to encourage lending by making it easier and cheaper to create and enforce contractual arrangements involving collateral, but must balance the rights of a secured creditor against those of other secured and unsecured creditors in the event of a default. The method the UCC uses to prioritize creditors makes it easy to make an asset collateral (called **attachment**) but limits the effect of attachment alone on **third parties** (those other than the specific secured party and debtor) without an additional step called **perfection**. The steps required to perfect a security interest vary somewhat with the nature of the collateral, but a major goal is to provide actual or constructive notice to subsequent lenders, informing them that there may be an existing security interest on this collateral (see e.g., note 7 of the official comments to UCC §9-301) [9]. The effect of perfection is that, absent an explicit inter-creditor agreement, priority on an item of collateral is in order of perfection.

Article 9 has a complex set of rules for deciding on the government entity with which registration must be made. For most collateral, the **place of business** of the debtor governs. The place of business, defined in UCC §9-307, is not always clear. In fact the official comments to the UCC advocate perfection in multiple places when the secured party is unclear as to where the filing should take place (see, e.g., note 2 of the official comments to UCC §9-307 [9]). The result may be a significant number of unnecessary filings as well as follow-on legal work to maintain and terminate the filings. In about three quarters of states [7], notice is given by filing a standardized UCC Financing Statement form (**UCC1** hereafter) either directly with the state or with an independent service provider authorized by that state. The form itself requires the debtors legal name, and a textual description of the collateral [8]. Subsequent potential lenders (secured and unsecured) can then file an information request form (**UCC11**) and the state will return UCC1s as well as any amendments, changes, or **continuations** (renewals) (**UCC3** form) where the debtor name matches exactly. The registration of a security interest will be ineffective if a search by a potential lender with the correct name of the debtor would not find the UCC as filed, putting the onus on the lender to get it exactly correct in the registration. Many states also offer additional services returning unofficial results that use non-standard *enhanced search logic* to return variants on the debtor name. allowing for a UCC1 to slightly vary from the correct name and still be correct.

3 The Bitcoin Protocol and the Blockchain

As internet commerce has become ubiquitous, the inadequacies of credit cards and electronic bank transfers for some transactions has become evident. Credit cards are widely accepted on the internet, but expose the buyer's identity (much to the chagrin of recent users of the Ashley Madison dating site) and have high transaction fees that impact minimum practical transaction size. Bank transfers have lower transaction fees, but are just as identifying. The identification associated with these payment methods is not an unintended side effect. Bank transfers and credit cards are reversible, so identification gives the vendor recourse should the buyer try to reverse the transactions after goods are delivered. In face-to-face transactions, cash provides a non-reversible anonymous alternative. Electronic cash, and Bitcoin [9] in particular are efforts to create an electronic currency that has the advantages of cash and coins, the ability to be spent with virtual anonymity, but with protections for the seller to ensure that they get paid by making the transactions irreversible.

3.1 The Problem of Double Spending

The name Bitcoin is itself somewhat of a misnomer. An important feature of coins [and cash] is that they are hard to duplicate well, and therefore once a party spends them the buyer cannot simply spend another copy of the same coin. With electronic currency, the bits are easily duplicated, so a pure electronic coin is subject to counterfeiting. One solution to the double spending problem is to create a ledger, in which every grant of money and transaction is recorded. The problem is that a ledger usually implies a bookkeeper, and thus requires a trusted bookkeeping party and a loss of anonymity.

The Bitcoin protocol retains anonymity without trust by introducing a distributed ledger called the **blockchain** and a peer-to-peer network of untrusted computers, called **nodes**, to administer it. The distributed ledger is designed in such a way that tampering with records in the ledger is self evident unless the tampering party is willing to allocate significant computational resources. The network of nodes, as a group, decides on the canonical version of the blockchain by 'voting with their feet', choosing to accept or reject blocks added to the blockchain, and building upon the blocks they accept. The protocol has been designed so that the verification of other's work is relatively easy and the incentives are for parties to verify each work. Thus even untrusted nodes can form the network as long as most nodes are not colluding as a single group.

3.2 The Blockchain and Proof of Work

We presume that the reader is familiar with public key encryption [10], authentication and digital signatures [11], and with one-way hash functions [12].

A typical bitcoin transaction records the transfer of some [fractional or whole] number of bitcoin from one party to another. For example if a party B (buyer) is shopping with S (seller) and B transfers bitcoin to S, the transaction is recorded as shown in the right side of Fig. 1. The ability of B to transfer the bitcoin is validated in three ways. First, examining the prior history of valid transactions, a node should find the record encoding that the coin was transferred to B[1] (the left side of Fig. 1). Second, the node can verify that B has not spent that bitcoin in the interim using the history (blockchain). Finally, in the original transaction that granted B the coin, B's public key was recorded as the recipient. As part of the transaction process for this sale, B takes the prior block and takes S's public key, hashes both and signs the hash. A node checking the transaction can validate B's signature (on the right side of Fig. 1) using the public key recorded in the transfer of the coin to B (on the left side).

While B could use a well known public/private key combination, there is actually no need for this, just that a matching pair of keys is used to acquire and to transfer the bitcoin. Therefore, a certification authority is unnecessary, and B is free to generate a new key combination every time it acquires new bitcoin, frustrating efforts to connect different transactions and get a picture of B's activity using its public key.

When a transaction is completed, the previous owner releases the transaction to the network. Nodes receive these transactions and construct **blocks**, which

[1] To simplify this explanation, we omit the cases where only a fraction of a Bitcoin or only part of a grant of Bitcoin is spent. We briefly discuss coin creation below.

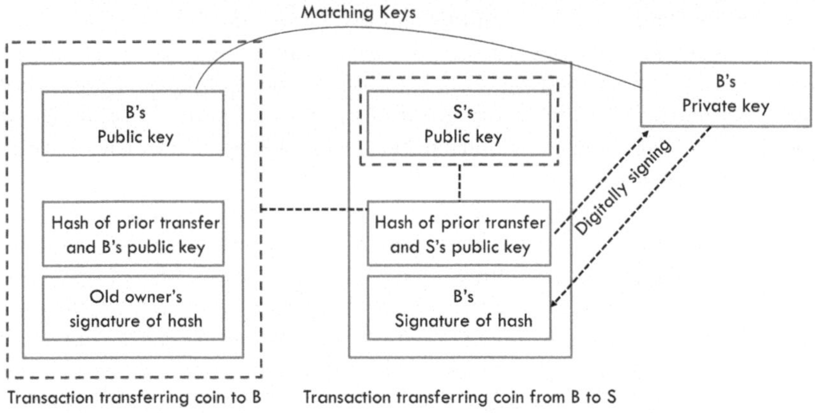

Fig. 1. Signing a bitcoin transfer (adapted from [9])

are packaged groups of possibly unrelated transactions. A node's goal is to create a block that is accepted by the peer-to-peer network as each constructed block is currently associated with a payment that accrues to the creator (mining). Additional fees may accrue to the block creator from transactions paying a transaction fee, incentivizing nodes to include that transaction in their blocks.

The Bitcoin network is calibrated to produce an average of one block every 10 min. In addition to housekeeping fields and the transactions, the block contains a filler field called a **nonce**. The content of the nonce is not itself meaningful, but the nonce is used as part of the mechanism to pace the production of new blocks and to require CPU cycles to create a block. In order to maintain the 10 min pace, the network has a **difficulty** value that represents a threshold above which it will not accept a block's hash. The difficulty value is adjusted to maintain a 10 min pace.

Since the hash is one-way, the mining node cannot analytically determine the value for the nonce that will yield a hash below the threshold. Thus all the nodes, many with a slightly different set or order of transactions, will be trying various values for the nonce that result in a hash to an acceptable value. The average duration of the process can be statistically determined, but the process itself is entirely by chance, and is akin to a lottery game where the odds of winning are in proportion to the number of tickets bought. Here the odds of successfully finding an acceptable value for the nonce are roughly proportional to the fraction of the network's computational resources working on behalf of this node. Once a node finds a valid nonce, it publishes the block. Since the average frequency is set, this scheme is zero-sum. Nodes have an incentive to validate blocks that claim to be correct. Once other nodes validate the block, they then start building new blocks on it, expressing their 'vote' that the block should be added to the blockchain. In the event two valid blocks are found simultaneously, the nodes will accept the block representing the most computational difficulty. In the case there is a tie, the network will fork into partitions working on one chain or the other, but the chains will reunite eventually when one chain grows longer. In this manner, the entire network eventually agrees on a specific order and list of valid transactions, a form of **eventual consistency**.

This scheme makes altering old blocks computationally difficult or impossible. If B wishes to transfer bitcoins to D that it already paid to S some time ago, B must manage to remove the payment to S from the block that contained it and then create a subsequent sequence of blocks longer than the current blockchain in order to be accepted by the network. As finding each nonce takes time, and as the remainder of the network is also moving forward, it becomes increasingly unlikely that B can find the correct nonce values and overtake the current blockchain unless B controls a significant amount of processing power relative to the remainder of the network [9].

4 Using the Blockchain for Security Registration

The current Article 9 is an imperfect system that has had trouble with incorrect debtor names [13], with clerical errors [14], with mistaken releases of significant size collateral, and with unauthorized filings [2]. Additionally, the current system relies on a single state to hold the canonical version of all security interest records recorded in that state. While the records themselves are generally public, implying that a breach and publication is not a major problem, a hacker unhappy with the banking system could do significant damage by altering or destroying records and creating temporary uncertainty as to collateral. Given the frequency with which businesses need loans for working capital, this may prove fatal to businesses unable to refinance promptly.

As early as 1996 the authors of the UCC addressed the possibility of electronic filing, noting that nothing in the UCC prevents states from adopting this technology [15]. An XML specification for an Article 9 filing interface has existed since at least 2001, and was most recently revised in 2013 [16]. Yet it was only in 2012 that Colorado became the first state to require electronic filing, followed by New Jersey (2015), Delaware (2015), and North Dakota (2016) [17]. Delaware is an instructive case, as it's a major destination for filings due to the favorable tax, legal, and business climate that has seen 65 % of large U.S. public corporations incorporate in the state [18]. Despite transitioning to electronic filing, the state still has a list of authorized service companies to perform the filing on behalf of customers and is explicit that they continue to accept paper forms [19].

Properly implemented electronic filings fixes some but not all issues with the current UCC. The mistaken release of collateral relating to different loans by the same parties, as in [2], can be eliminated with software that clearly relates loans to filing numbers for UCC1s and files the UCC3 terminations, rather than relying on a manual process. A unified database would allow electronic filing, even for states that do not maintain that capability. It would also allow the filing in only one jurisdiction in cases where the secured party is not clear about the correct venue. A single national system would have security and financial implications. If the states could distribute the database, duplicate it in each state, and make the database tamper evident, the problem of database hacking is reduced. Instead of relying on a system that merely converts the current scheme into a unified electronic doppelganger, we suggest an overhaul of the way that notifications are processed and stored based upon the blockchain, with some differences in distributed consensus.

4.1 Replacing Names with Public Keys

The current identification system in the UCC is based upon the legal corporate name of the debtor. The standard UCC1 form instructions admonish the user to enter debtor's "exact full legal name" (emphasis in original) [8], recognizing that instances of variants and trade names have caused ineffective perfection in the past. Unfortunately, even with this warning, names are imperfect identifiers. Filers continue to have problems using the full legal name and this continues to cause ineffective perfection (e.g., [13]). Names are also not unique, especially with smaller companies that might not hold a U.S. federal trademark.

If the blockchain is to be used, every company will require at least one public/private key combination. In the Bitcoin protocol the public keys may be anonymous. In most uses other than Bitcoin, however, the public key is published with identity information and can be used to verify both the integrity of messages as well as the identity of the counterparty using digital signatures [11]. Anonymity of both parties is a valued commodity in cash transactions. In the case of a security interest, however, anonymity of the debtor makes no sense. For notice to function as intended, subsequent lenders must be able to search on the debtor and find all filed UCC1s. Thus the debtor in a UCC filing must be identifiable. A Bitcoin adapted protocol already requires a public key which can be used for identification. The risk of accidentally changing a key and having it match another debtor should be less than that of having a key collision, which is known to be vanishingly small [20].

While anonymity of the borrower makes no sense in recording secured transactions, anonymity of the secured parties might be desirable for some lenders. A secured party could theoretically generate a public/private key pair for each loan or item of collateral and remain anonymous, at least to the government and third parties. This turns the loan into something like a bearer instrument, where anyone who holds the private key can release the collateral, prove to a court that they own the loan and should collect payment, or be entitled to the collateral. This also raises the real possibility that a lender could lose the private key associated with a loan and thus the borrower would need to wait 5 years for it to expire (UCC §9-515). We leave to law reviews and politicians the public policy implications of lenders that are anonymous to even the government.

4.2 Building Records and Blocks

A Bitcoin analogue could be used to encode the UCC records with some minor differences driven by known identity of the nodes in the UCC context. The UCC system has three fundamental types of transactions: establishing a security interest (UCC1), modifying, continuing (renewing), or deleting a security interest (UCC3) and querying a security interest (UCC11). Only the first two produce transaction records within the database. UCC transaction records would be encapsulated into blocks which would be attached to a blockchain.

While the UCC is explicitly exempted from the coverage by the two US Federal laws covering electronic signatures, the UCC has provisions for allowing for electronic signatures to evidence consent to the filing of a UCC1 [21]. Under the current UCC (§9-509) permission of the debtor is necessary to file a UCC1, but the permission may be in another document, not filed with the government. In the event of a possibly unauthorized UCC filing, the question of whether the filing is authorized would be dealt with in litigation. The current XML standard for Article 9 filings has a `Document` element, for filings, that contains a field `FileSignature` and a `Names` element, for filers or debtors, that contains a field `Mark`. Both are apparently placeholders to enable digital signatures, but are marked as "not used" and "not currently ... implemented" [16]. Implementing these would allow the current XML standard to be used with digitally signed UCC records.

For the UCC blockchain, provisions for digital signatures would be made, but per UCC §9-509 the record cannot be required to be signed by the debtor. Another potential lender, finding the absence of a borrower's signature on a filing, would have inquiry notice and would be presumed to have sufficient suspicions that they should inquire about the situation. If a debtor's signature is evident, the nodes creating blocks will validate the signature against the debtor's public key, which can be done without reference to an outside directory as the public key is also being used to identify the debtor in the record. The UCC1 must be signed by the secured party, and should contain a one-time or permanent public key. For a UCC3 modifying, renewing or terminating the security interest, the UCC3 should be signed using the corresponding private key so authorization for the UCC3 can be checked against the original UCC1. Thus, presumably, the field `FileSignature` would be required in a version of the XML specification that is modified to interface with any new systems using digital signatures on filings (as we have here) while the `Mark` element would remain optional.

A fundamental characteristic of the Bitcoin protocol is that the past is sacrosanct. Once a transaction has been recorded in a block and the block added to the blockchain, the only way to modify the transaction is to supersede the block and all subsequent blocks in the blockchain with a longer chain, a rare occurrence. For legal records, such as UCC records, this is exactly the behavior expected. Old records are never deleted, just amended or superseded. To handle the inevitable litigation, courts would require their own well known public/private key combination with the power to remove or modify security interests on court order, and to record a report of a lost or stolen private key to prevent subsequent signatures with the same key [11].

There are two search modes for UCC records on the standard UCC11 form [8]. A UCC search is either requesting a specific record by number or [more frequently] requesting information relating to a specific debtor. The mixed blocks of UCC transaction records are essentially a log file. Each security interest is a series of records that will be linked directly in a list from the first filing (UCC1) to the final filing, just as an database transaction log would contain undo and redo log entries linked by transaction. Since records cannot be modified once the nonce for their block has been computed, the chain must start at the most recent record and point backwards, forming a linked list by referencing the date and unique ID of the preceding filing record relating to that security interest. An index structure, for example using a B+ trees, can be used to find records. Since the chain of pointers to related records moves backwards, the index need only point to the latest record for each security interest chain. A similar chain and structure can be used to index debtors, pointing only to the latest record relating to that debtor, with each record pointing to the prior debtor record, whether or not that record is in reference to the same security interest. A representative tail end of a UCC blockchain with associated indices is illustrated in Fig. 2. Additional functionality could be added to link and search by secured party in a straightforward manner, although the current UCC11 form lacks this capability.

4.3 Assembling a UCC Blockchain

After blocks are created they can be added to the blockchain. While it would be possible for each state to have its own blockchain, this would eliminate many of the benefits of a distributed database and each state would only have incentive to verify its own transactions. A single national blockchain has a few major advantages. Significant redundancy is introduced by having multiple copies of every UCC record. In the event of a system failure or hack in one state, a live backup exists and UCC processing can continue. Additionally, if the incentives are well designed, multiple states will examine each UCC filing while trying to create blocks and while verifying other's blocks, ensuring the prompt discovery of invalid filings.

The advantages of a distributed blockchain also accrue for customers. A lender searching for UCC records need no longer access multiple states or guess as to the location of the records. Every state will have a duplicate of the entire blockchain and searches can be made from any state. Every state should theoretically have the ability to accept UCC1 registrations and perhaps UCC3 modifications/terminations, ameliorating some filing location ambiguities.

Differences in Distributed Consensus. There are a few aspects of the UCC blockchain that will be very different than those in Bitcoin. The Bitcoin network, composed of anonymous and untrusted nodes, uses CPU cycles as a proxy for investment. Voting on the correct blockchain is on this basis, under the assumption that most of the investment will be among nodes that are, if not honest, at least are not colluding, and so are unlikely to reach a distributed consensus on acceptable blocks that does not satisfy the protocol. The nonce serves dual purposes, as proof of [computational] work and to randomize the distribution of rewards in rough proportion to that computational work. With the UCC, the

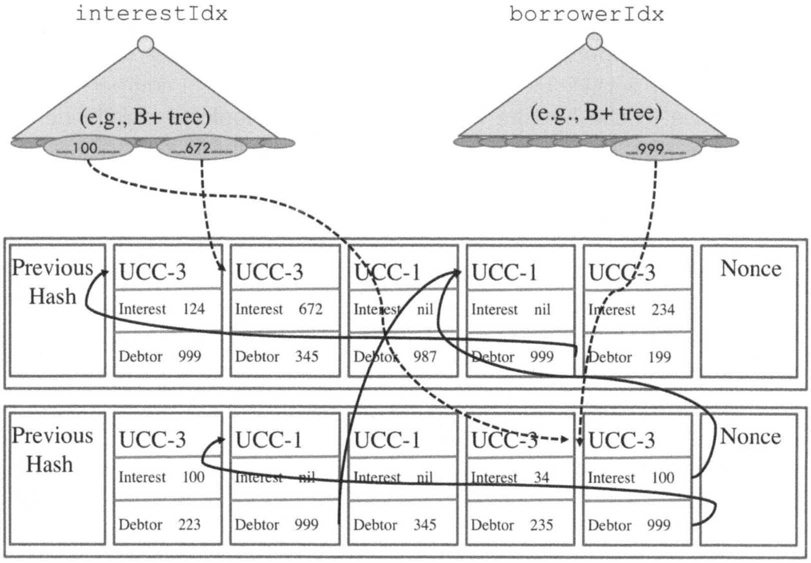

Fig. 2. A representative UCC Blockchain Tail Fragment

States are known [and somewhat trusted] parties. The nonce is not needed as proof of work, as voting on the correct blockchains will have to be on the basis of one state, one vote to avoid disenfranchising almost all states from the oligopoly of Delaware, New York, California, D.C., and few other jurisdictions.

Without compensation for creating a block, no state has an incentive to do the work to create blocks. With a nonce providing some randomness, each state has an opportunity to create an accepted block. States cannot create blocks containing only their own transactions, as a network so dominated by major producers of UCC records will be quickly abandoned by the smaller states unable to record their filings, risking the entire enterprise. Rather states will form consortia which share UCC transactions with each other and place each other's transactions in their own blocks. A maximum market share for each consortium can be assured by restricting each consortium to only contain one member of the aforementioned oligopoly and to limit the total percentage of UCC filings accounted for by any consortium. The filing state will offer revenue sharing on the record to the state who completes the block, much as transaction fees operate in Bitcoin. Thus even those states outside a consortium might choose to include another state's filings to reap the financial benefits. Other jurisdictions with very small filing volume may choose to forgo their own recording system, and rely on peer states. Since the effectiveness of a UCC filing is dependent on recognition in the law of the state where the filing would take place under the current system, and since a state could restrict the effectiveness depending on where the UCC1 is filed, revenue sharing with that state is also likely to emerge.

In contrast to registrations, states have no pricing power on lookups. Unless one state has a monopoly on a particular technical or process innovation that makes their lookup service far better than others, states will compete on lookup price and a race to the bottom will ensue. Instead, lookups should be free or almost free, and fees should be shifted to filings. Enhanced lookup services, for example monitoring of other security interests to your borrowers, can be offered by private service providers

The Bitcoin algorithm is designed to produce a block every 10 min. Finding a valid nonce, however, is a random process and the actual distribution of solution times likely follows a Poisson distribution with significant variability. While response times for UCC filings are on the order of a day, a target of a block per day would be exceedingly dangerous as the variability will result in periods of multiple days without a block. The actual target rate, and the periods when blocks are produced is likely to require at least high granularity data on filing frequency. Thus far New York and Delaware have been unable or unwilling to provide the author with even aggregate statistics, and thus we omit an analytical determination of even an initial rate. Likely an initial target of 10 min per block would be reasonable.

In Bitcoin, the system is optimized for eventual consistency, allowing for a temporary fork (partition) of the network until eventual agreement is reached on the blockchain. It's rare that the partition lasts any significant period of time. The single exception, when in 2013 the blockchain was split for 24 blocks before returning to consistency was the result of a software error [22]. In a system using proof of work such as Bitcoin, the appearance of a longer blockchain is evidence of computational expenditure greater than that incurred building the older blockchain. In Bitcoin the magnitude of computation required for this is suggestive that the shorter blockchain only existed on a small partition of the network. With the UCC, the parties are known. A partition of the network would be evident relatively quickly. Without the possibility of a sustained partition, the introduction of a new, longer blockchain is suggestive of nothing more than a state's node being hacked and a new, false, blockchain introduced. Given the aggregate CPU cycles expected to be devoted to the UCC by the states is likely to be a fraction of that devoted to Bitcoin, blockchain decisions should become more or less permanent after a fixed period, perhaps 24 h or even less.

Truncating the UCC Blockchain. UCC §9-515 sets the maximum duration of most UCC1 financing statements at 5 years and the longest duration of effectiveness at 30 years. After this time, a financing statement without a UCC3 continuation expires and will not be reported in a UCC11 search and cannot be continued by a later UCC3. Thus the blockchain used in active searches can be truncated after 30 years of records, but only if the integrity of the blockchain can be protected by ensuring that the hashes on old transactions cannot be changed. To facilitate the discarding of old records while ensuring the integrity of the blockchain, the Bitcoin algorithm uses a Merkle tree [11]. The same method should work here. The actual records will need to be stored forever as government records, but need not be available on a live system.

Creating the Links Within a Block. Pseudo code to link a new UCC3 record (termination, modification or continuance) record `rcd` just prior to adding it to a block `blk` under construction to create the structure in Fig. 2 is as follows:

```
ucc3Link(blk: UCCBlock, rcd: UCC3Record) {
   // If this borrower already appears in this block
   rcd.lastBorrower = blk.findLast(rcd.borrower)
   // If that didn't work, then check existing blockchain
   if nil == rcd.lastBorrower
       rcd.lastBorrower = borrowerIdx.lookup(rcd.borrower)
   // Same process for the chain of this security interest
   rcd.lastInterest = blk.findLast(rcd.interest)
   if nil == rcd.lastInterest
      rcd.lastInterest = interestIdx.lookup(rcd.interest)
}
```

Linking UCC1 records is a straightforward extension with the caveat that the borrower might not exist and the security interest should not exist in the index.

Adjusting the Indices. If the block is successfully added to the blockchain, the implication is that every node accepting this new block has an identical blockchain, and thus the links created above will be correct. After a block has been added to the blockchain, the local index itself can be adjusted for each entry in the new block:

```
adjustIndices(blk: UCCBlock) {
    foreach rcd in blk { // starts at beginning
        // Set index for rcd.borrower to rcd
        borrowerIdx.update(rcd, rcd.borrower)
        interestIdx.update(rcd, rcd.interest)
    }
}
```

Finally, should it be necessary to remove a block because it was superseded by a longer/more difficult block, the block is read in reverse, using the links in the block to point the index to the prior value for the index (essentially undo log processing:

```
removeAdjustedIndices(blk: UCCBlock) {
    foreach_reverse rcd in blk {
        // This starts at the end in case borrower appears >1x
        // in block. Set index for rcd.borrower to prior value
        borrowerIdx.update(rcd.lastBorrower, rcd.borrower)
        interestIdx.update(rcd.lastInterest, rcd.interest)
    }
}
```

5 Barriers to Implementation

As was demonstrated here, the technological barriers to implementation of a national distributed UCC security interest registration system are surmountable. The main barriers to implementation will be the entrenched interests, of which there are three, states, lawyers, and service companies.

States have pricing power over registrations since it is state law that gives them effectiveness, so the states are unlikely to object as long as they continue to reap filing fees roughly equivalent to their current revenues. While the current system encourages filing in multiple locations, the use of a standardized identifier based on the public key should allow a directory of corporations and their principal places of business for the purpose of determining the location of legal effectiveness and revenue sharing. Thus filing fees could be increased under the assumption that filing need only occur once. The current inconsistencies in state laws, including the single state giving 10 years of effectiveness to a UCC1 [23] and the two states requiring non-public information in UCC filings [23] may be a bigger barrier, as these are evidence of state legislatures picking and choosing among the provisions of "uniform" laws. While both of these differences can be dealt with, the possibility of future inconsistencies makes it difficult to commit to a system that may cease to work if the inconsistencies grow. Some sort of a-priori agreement would be required of the states before transitioning to a unified system. In an era of the ascendancy of the philosophy of "states' rights", this may remain a problem.

The attorneys that prepare UCC filing might be seen as opposing changes to their cash cow. The authors think this unlikely. The major job of the attorneys working on deals requiring UCC filings is not the filing of the rote paperwork, but in committing the [often bespoke] agreements of the parties to writing. The UCC filings themselves are often delegated to support staff (as is illustrated in the court record in [2] which contains the disclosure that the original paperwork error on the $1.5 billion release was that of a paralegal). Unifying the registration databases will have little or no effect on the content of the filings, only the processes and forms.

Finally, the service providers may be opposed to these changes because they will adversely effect their revenue streams. While service providers may be able to make up some of this revenue loss with search revenue, the authors assume they will still be opposed to the change in the status quo. As the vast majority of the stakeholders are attorneys and not service providers, this change should be able to overcome their objections.

References

1. Federal Deposit Insurance Corporation (USA): Quarterly banking profile: Third quarter 2015 (2015). https://www.fdic.gov/bank/analytical/quarterly/2015_vol9_4/FDIC_3Q2015_v9n4_QBP.pdf
2. United States Court of Appeals for the 2nd Circuit: In re motors liquidation co. 2015 U.S. App. Lexis 859

3. Schroeder, J.L.: Bitcoin and the uniform commercial code. Available at SSRN 2649441 (2015)
4. Wilkinson, S., Boshevski, T., Brandoff, J., Buterin, V.: Storj: A peer-to-peer cloud storage network (2014). http://storj.io/storj.pdf
5. Kirk, J.: Could the bitcoin network be used as an ultrasecure notary service?, May 2013. http://www.computerworld.com/article/2498077/desktop-apps/could-the-bitcoin-network-be-used-as-an-ultrasecure-notary-service-.html
6. Wight, R., Cooke, W., Gray, R.: The LSTA's Complete Credit Agreement Guide. McGraw Hill Professional, New York (2009)
7. Duncan, R.F., Lyons, W.H., Wilson, C.L.: The Law and Practice of Secured Transactions: Working with Article 9. Law Journal Press, New York (2015)
8. International Association of Commercial Administrators: UCC Forms. https://www.iaca.org/secured-transactions/forms/
9. Nakamoto, S.: Bitcoin: A peer-to-peer electronic cash system (2008). https://bitcoin.org/bitcoin.pdf
10. Diffie, W., Hellman, M.E.: New directions in cryptography. IEEE Trans. Inf. Theory **22**(6), 644–654 (1976)
11. Merkle, R.C.: Protocols for public key cryptosystems. In: Proceedings of the IEEE Symposium on Security and Privacy, pp. 122–133. IEEE (1980)
12. Rogaway, P., Shrimpton, T.: Cryptographic hash-function basics: definitions, implications, and separations for preimage resistance, second-preimage resistance, and collision resistance. In: Roy, B., Meier, W. (eds.) FSE 2004. LNCS, vol. 3017, pp. 371–388. Springer, Heidelberg (2004)
13. US Bankruptcy Court, E.D. Virginia: In re tyringham holdings inc. (2006)
14. Minnesota Supreme Court: Borg Warner Accept. v. ITT Diversified Credit (1984)
15. Permanent Editorial Board for the Uniform Commercial Code: PEB Commentary No. 15 ((electronic filing under Article 9) (1996)
16. Ose, T.M.: XML Technical Specifications For Uniform Commercial Code Revised Article 9. Technical report, International Association of Commercial Administrators, May 2013
17. National Corporate Research: North dakota to require electronic UCC filing: Review of requirements for all e-filing only states, February 2016. http://info.nationalcorp.com/blog
18. State of Delaware, Division of CorporationsD: Delaware Division of Corporations 2014 Annual Report (2015). https://corp.delaware.gov/Corporations_2014AnnualReport.pdf
19. State of Delaware: UCC Authorized Filers. http://corp.delaware.gov/uccauthfilers.shtml
20. Lenstra, A., Hughes, J.P., Augier, M., Bos, J.W., Kleinjung, T., Wachter, C.: Ron was wrong, whit is right. Technical report, IACR (2012). https://eprint.iacr.org/2012/064.pdf
21. Tank, M., Emley, S., Whitakey, R.D.: A brief guide to using electronic signatures in security transactions. Practical Compliance and Risk Management for the Securities Industry, pp. 23–34, July-August 2013
22. Buterin, V.: Bitcoin network shaken by blockchain fork (2013). https://bitcoinmagazine.com/articles/bitcoin-network-shaken-by-blockchain-fork-1363144448
23. National Corporate Research: UCC article 9 filing and searching info. http://www.nationalcorp.com/ncr/resources/UCC-Resources/UCC-Article-9-Filing-and-Searching-Info

To Network or not to Network? Analysis of the Finnish Software Industry – A Networking Approach

Katariina Yrjönkoski(✉), Nina Helander, and Hannu Jaakkola

Tampere University of Technology, Tampere, Finland
katariina.yrjonkoski@tut.fi

Abstract. The purpose of this paper is to study the role of networking in the development and present situation of Finnish software companies. Although the target of interest of this study is Finland, the conclusions can also to some extent be applied to other countries with mature software industries. In Finland there is uniquely wide longitudinal material on the software business available; the software industry survey is an annual study targeted for the branch, which has already been repeated for 18 consecutive years. The study shows that networking has been a key trend in the industry and also a driver for internationalization, but as it has not been identified very well in networking literature concerning the software industry, there is a clear need for further examination of software industry networks.

Keywords: Networks · Software business

1 Introduction

This paper focuses on the development curve of the Finnish software business during the last ten years (2005–2015). Finland is an interesting target for examination because the development of the Finnish software industry represents an example of the establishing and maturing of the industry into one of the world's most high-quality software countries. ICT has also long been one of the central elements of the national strategy in Finland. Uniquely longitudinal research data is also available in Finland; the software industry survey is an annual study targeting the branch, which has been repeated for 18 consecutive years, starting from 1997. This paper aims to give an initial understanding of the development of the Finnish software industry and the role and state of networking within the industry, based on these annual Finnish Software Industry Survey reports.

The role of the software industry has become critical in modern society, as software plays a key role in many contemporary activities, services, and devices, and overall its secondary impact on the remainder of the economy is disproportionate (Jansen et al. 2013; Popp 2011). It is argued that the software business differs from other business sectors due to the following special characteristics: software differs from information as an economic good as software is valued for what it does; substantial economies of scale are much greater than in material goods, leading to the law of increasing returns;

A. Maglyas and A.-L. Lamprecht (Eds.): ICSOB 2016, LNBIP 240, pp. 124–134, 2016.
DOI: 10.1007/978-3-319-40515-5_9

development of software is expensive, but reproducing and distribution are cheap; shorter technology cycles than in many other industries and partly due to this, the first mover advantages are not always as clear, as there are schedule and bug challenges. However, usually the trust in market leaders facilitates the buying decision and the lock-in effects can be great for several reasons, like personal switching costs that increase over time. (See e.g. Cusumano 2008; Messerschmitt and Szyperski 2005) Earlier literature on the software business has also brought up the importance of networking (including ecosystems, alliances, and business networks) in the industry (Jansen et al. 2013). In particular, in order to sustain growth and to support internationalization, networking has been seen as a prerequisite for small and medium-sized (SME) software companies (Ojala and Tyrväinen 2006).

In the present study, the aim is to take a closer look at the networking phenomenon, as well as its role and importance in software industry development. We have chosen the Finnish software industry as the context of this study, as the annual software industry offers the possibility to follow the development curve of this interesting sector and the networking phenomenon in the industry. For the purposes of this study, we have chosen to analyze the results of the annual software industry survey systematically for a ten-year time period, from 2005 to 2015. In this way the present study is able to take an overall look at the development of the Finnish software industry, especially from the networking perspective. The research questions of the present study are:

1) How has the Finnish software industry developed in the last ten years?
2) How does networking manifest itself in the Finnish software industry?

The objective is to identify networking indicators from the previous ten-year history of the Finnish software industry. Systematically collected longitudinal data (The Finnish Software Industry Survey) is used as material. The study offers exceptional data because its history is long and the collecting method repeated consistently in a similar manner. The paper proceeds as follows: in the first phase, the longitudinal research material based on annual software industry survey reports is explored (Sect. 2, "Recent 10 Years in the Finnish Software Industry Development"). The second phase consists of an examination of networking structures based on selected theoretical frameworks (Sects. 3, "A networking framework" and 4, "Challenges and Opportunities of Networking"). Finally, in the third part, the theoretical framework is applied to the analysis material covering the development of the software industry (Sect. 5, "Answers to Research Questions and Conclusions").

2 Recent 10 Years in the Finnish Software Industry Development

It is justified to concentrate on examining the time period of the last 10 years for various reasons. Even though the software industry has existed since the 1980s in Finland, the industry has taken shape during the last ten years and has become established at international level. In the first half of the 2000s, the software business was only starting to form and find its own role in the field of Finnish industry. By the latter half of the 2010s, the Finnish software business has become a stable business and has also been ranked high in global comparisons. The business is consolidating more and more all the time, and growth forecasts have settled to a conservative level, while still remaining positive. (Kuitunen et al. 2005; Rönkkö and Peltonen 2012; Peltonen et al. 2013; Luoma and Rönkkö 2014).

It is significant that the definition and borders of the industry are somewhat ambiguous in industry surveys and other literature. At the beginning of the present century, particularly the product business was considered of interest and worthy of research. With the development of the field, the need for software-related services has also increased. The services have gradually become an independent sector, with a turnover that already accounts for more than half of the total turnover of the industry.

The growth of the industry branch in Finland has followed the international growth trend. In a European comparison, the growth rate of the Finnish software industry represents the middle level. The growth of the branch in Finland has been about 47 % (from 2,077 b€ to 3,053 b€) in the period of this examination, depending on the industry definition. The estimate cited above includes both Finnish and foreign companies operating in the Finnish software market. The annual growth rate has been between 3 – 10 %, with the exception of 2009, when there was a decrease of about 9 % in the business, due to the worldwide economic recession. The economic downturn caused a downswing in the growth of the branch and in the profitability of the companies – but nevertheless, the effect of the recession on the software field was smaller than in many other industries. After the recession, growth has continued to be more moderate, staying under 10 %. During the whole ten-year examination period, growth has occurred mainly in small and medium-sized companies. (Kuitunen et al. 2005; Lassila et al. 2006; Rönkkö et al. 2007; 2008; 2009, 2010; 2011; Rönkkö and Peltonen 2012; Peltonen et al. 2013; Luoma and Rönkkö 2014; Luoma and Kinnunen 2015). In 2013, the growth curve turned upwards a little more with 11.6 % and as much as 20.4 % growth in 2014 (Luoma and Rönkkö 2014; Luoma and Kinnunen 2015).

Attention must be paid to the fact that along with the development of the industry, its definition in the literature has also varied. In the middle of the 2000s, the software business was mainly studied as a product business; a traditional way to sell packaged software products and the services related to them, like installation, maintenance, and customer training. Nowadays, software is an organic part of a growing group of products. This makes the definition of the borders of the industry challenging. The Internet has changed the environment of the field, affecting all the central functions hugely. As it has become more common, it has offered a base for quite new products and services, like SaaS, ASP, and later, cloud services. It has also partly replaced the traditional sales and distribution channels. The biggest change in the share of revenue has taken place in packaged software license sales; in 2005 license sales provided 49 % of total revenue, but had fallen to 15 % by 2008. ASP and SaaS were first identified in the Software Industry Survey in 2009, and then accounted for about 10 % of the total revenue. However, the growth of SaaS has not been quite as expected and revenues have accumulated more slowly than first thought. (Kuitunen et al. 2005; Lassila et al. 2006; Rönkkö et al. 2007; 2008; 2009, 2010; 2011; Rönkkö and Peltonen 2012; Peltonen et al. 2013; Luoma and Rönkkö 2014; Luoma and Kinnunen 2015).

The majority of Finnish software companies are small – there are even companies that employ only a few persons. In 2005, 40 % of the companies achieved a turnover of less than one million euros. Only in 28 % of the companies did turn over exceed three million euros. The number of small firms is increasing; for example, in 2011 over 70 % of all companies had a total revenue of less than 1 m€ (Rönkkö et al. 2008). However, regarding this result, the expanded definition of the branch should also be taken into account. During the "IT bubble" in the 1990s, the company birth rate was momentarily exceptionally high. Although the software business has been growing slowly but steadily ever since, there is a continuous public debate on entrepreneurship, willingness to establish a company, and supporting entrepreneurship and growth. Committing to entrepreneurship does not seem to be attractive enough. With a majority of companies, there does not seem to be a desire for aggressive growth and internationalization. One reason for this may be the limited access to capital, which is a challenge in the Finnish business field. Especially start-ups and small companies experience difficulties with financing. Despite these challenges, many of the crucial success factors are at least at a moderate level in Finland; availability of skilled labor is good, the pass rate of university exams in math and sciences is high, and ICT is valued highly in both national and European Union level strategies. Although technological capability in Finland is at a good level, sales, marketing, and productization skills are also needed to run a successful national or global business. All three were identified as targets for development during the last ten-year period. (Kuitunen et al. 2005; Lassila et al. 2006; Rönkkö et al. 2007; 2008; 2009, 2010; 2011; Rönkkö and Peltonen 2012; Peltonen et al. 2013; Luoma and Rönkkö 2014; Luoma and Kinnunen 2015).

3 A Networking Framework

Networking as a phenomenon can be examined through different frameworks, for example:

- Network taxonomies based on the identification of different network types. Taxonomy takes into account organization borders and location aspects (e.g. Jaakkola et al. 2015)
- The IMP approach to networks: a network approach based on several base/background theories, e.g. the so-called interaction approach, which has emerged from the research of business dyads (See e.g. Håkansson 1992)
- Networks as a strategic value adding system (see e.g. Möller et al. 2004; Jarillo 1988): networks appear as a system to add value. They consist of the value functions commanded by the companies and by other actors, in other words of those activities and activity chains through which things and services are refined from different raw materials, materials and knowledge reserves to the customers. The model differs from the IMP model by perceiving networks as meaningfully established and strategically managed objects.

In the present study, a closer look is taken at both the distribution taxonomy of Jaakkola et al. (2015) and the IMP network approach.

Networking is based on the organizations' need to distribute their activities. It is an organized, in most cases contract-based, collaboration model that cultivates a productive relationship between the parties. The networking emphasizes the importance of

Table 1. Organizational distribution taxonomy (Jaakkola et al. 2015)

	Intraorganizational		Interorganizational		Outside	
	One activity	Several activities	One activity	Several activities	One activity	Several activities
National	One site (N1)	Multiple sites (N2)	Outsourcing (N3) Rightsourcing	Multisourcing (N4) Cosourcing	Broker outsourcing (N5) Rightsourcing	Broker multisourcing (N6) Broker cosourcing
International	Offshoring (I1) Nearshoring	Offshoring (I2) Nearshoring	Offshore outsourcing / nearsourcing (I3) Offshore rightsourcing	Offshore multisourcing (I4) Offshore cosourcing	Broker offshore outsourcing (I5) Broker offshore rightsourcing	Broker offshore multisourcing (I6) Broker offshore cosourcing
	Insource		Outsource			

the communication and the need for the exchange of information between the parties. This is especially suitable in the software business, which is characterized by close collaboration and communication between individual developers and teams. (Jaakkola et al. 2015).

Table 1 introduces the taxonomy of the complex phenomenon of organizational distribution defined by Jaakkola et al. (2015). The term "networking" has aspects related to both organizational and location. In the discussion below, networking refers to the organizational dimension - how activities are organized in the network. The term "decentralization" or "distribution," on the other hand, refers to a location and to geographical distance. The third concept, which it is important to identify in this context, is globalization. It refers to the distribution of activities over geographical or cultural borders.

In the row dimension, the table covers two categories, national (networking parties are located in one country, following the same legal rules, adopting more or less the same business environment) and international (referring to global, multicultural collaboration). The three main columns refer to the organizational complexity of the distribution – intraorganizational (parties inside one legal unit; also called "insourcing"), interorganizational (parties belong to different legal units), and outside (subcontracting, based on a loose level of collaboration and reasonably high independence between parties). Outsourcing covers the transfer of work related to one activity outside one's own organization to an external contractor. Rightsourcing means the transfer of activities related to one activity to several external contractors, and multisourcing the transfer of several activities outsourced to several contractors. Co-sourcing describes the situation in which several organizations have a permanent collaboration network to implement several related activities. The broker role indicates the situation in which the work is outsourced to independent external contractors that have loose connections to the "activity owner." All distribution types provide different benefits and challenges. (Jaakkola et al. 2015).

In taxonomies based on structure, a network may appear as an object controlled by a single strong company. In that kind of stereotype, a network might be seen only as a group of companies working together for a certain project. However, these types are generally the picture of a network as seen from a particular perspective or those held by a particular company. However, these same networks are of a different type if seen from a different perspective. The IMP approach represents the opposite school of thought: it does not involve identifying any "types" or taxonomies of networks. According to the IMP approach, it is important to emphasize that there are no absolute or objective network types. All networks consist of actors, relationships, and activities. Actors are a large number of active and heterogeneous companies, each interacting with others and seeking solutions to their different problems. However, networks have different elements, characteristics, and possibilities when seen from different perspectives or when parts of the network outside their considerations of any one company are included. There is no single, objective network, "correct" definition, or specific owner of the network. Also, the outcomes of the actions of any company in the network cannot just be related to that single company – many of them will be more or less collective. (Ford et al. 2003).

However, all the different network approaches have at least one thing in common: networking is seen as based on mutual communication. Communication has three dimensions that can cause challenges: the type of distribution (Table 1), the amount of collaboration (needed to conduct activities; partially included in Table 1, depends on the independence between activities), and cultural diversity. In multicultural collaboration, the parties have to take into account the differences that have their root in national cultures. Multicultural collaboration is a natural part of the globalized work context, but also has a growing role in all organizations as a consequence of the free mobility of labor. (Hofstede et al. 2010; 2016; Lewis 2011; 2016).

Internationalization is a special case of networking. It is based on the openness of economic and societal systems. It implies the opening of local and nationalistic perspectives to a broader outlook of an interconnected and interdependent world with free transfer of capital, goods, and services across national frontiers. From the individual company or organization point of view, globalization is driven by several forces, including:

- the ambition towards bigger business units and the need to connect activities after corporate acquisition and mergers;
- the need for networking and specialization;
- the need to operate (geographically) close to clients;
- the need for skilled personnel or other scant key resources;
- the costs of the strategic business factors (work, office space, etc.);
- the importance of operating in different time zones (to guarantee a 24/7 operation level);
- the desire to extend the market;
- the desire to be located closer to the sources of innovations;
- the recognized differences between and gaps in the skill profiles in different locations.

It is also worth noticing that the same driving forces fit the distribution of activities on local (national) level. To summarize and simplify – the motivation factors may be both organizational and economic. In many cases, globalization is also seen as a path to growth (of business and company size/value). (Hofstede et al. 2010; 2016) In the Finnish software industry, internationalization has progressed in waves. The outsourcing progress has roots in the late 1990s and early 2000s. The first wave was targeted at China and India; the main driving force was the availability and low cost (<50 % of the Finnish level) of the skilled workforce. Some companies also moved their activities close to the key client – the production industry operating in those areas. Partially simultaneously and somewhat later, the second internationalization wave started with the target of Russia, the Baltic countries (Estonia, Latvia, Lithuania), and the former socialist bloc countries (Hungary, Poland, Romania, Czech Republic, Belarus) – in the form of nearshoring/offshoring. The third wave of internationalization had its target in new/fast-growing economies, like Vietnam, Indonesia, Brazil, and Mexico. Throughout this time, additional global level operations were being implemented as a part of normal business progress in Scandinavia, Western Europe, Japan, and the USA. The main factors for outsourcing were economic and the availability of a skilled workforce. Simultaneously to the "outbound" direction, there was also some "inbound" outsourcing – e.g. Indian and Chinese companies bought Finnish software companies or established their own branch organizations in Finland. (Jaakkola 2009; 2012; Jaakkola et al. 2011).

4 Challenges and Opportunities of Networking

Networking with other companies is a significant way to improve one's competitive advantage. The advantages of networking may be for example achieving resource flexibility, expanding one's market area in either domestic or global markets, increasing marketing and sales force, boosting competence, or developing new technologies and offerings. Successful networking can enhance the interfaces between companies and thereby also decrease transaction costs. It may also allow a company to focus on its own core competencies while someone else in the network takes care of the parts outside of the core business. (Valkokari et al. 2006; Möller et al. 2004) In some cases, networking is necessary in order to gain credibility among customers and/or investors. Networks are also a way to expand business for many SME enterprises (Senik et al. 2011).

Software projects, for example, always require good communication in the network for success. However, software projects quite often fail. When the reasons behind software project failures have been examined, bad or deficient communication between the parties is often found, especially at the initial stage of the project. The most typical mistakes caused by defective communication between parties that have led to failure include deficient specifications, changing and non-fixed requirements, unclear expectations, or unrealistic schedule expectations. (Elzamly and Hussin 2014; Savolainen 2011) To reduce these risks, all the parties must commit themselves to the cooperation and must consider the partnership as so important that it is motivating to reserve time and resources for the work and communication that takes place at the company interface.

According to the CHAOS report published by Standish Group, the reality is dark; in the American software project business as many as 31.1 % of projects are uncompleted. About 52 % of the projects exceed their costs by nearly 90 %. According to the Standish Group estimate, failed projects cost American software companies 81 billion dollars annually. Only 16.2 % of all projects are successful. (Standish Group 2014) The findings of the report are also partly applicable to Finland's conditions in which the software industry is at a similar, stable level. One can estimate that the costs of unsuccessful software projects will be of the order of at least half a billion euros, which is a great deal when proportioned to the total industry size. (Standish Group 2014).

Networking often adds transaction costs, compared to the arranging of the same function internally with the company's own resources. Networked companies also often become dependent on each other to some extent. According to resource dependency theories, this in particular pushes companies towards interaction with each other. Small companies often have limited resources, and networking has to be done in order to survive. If the advantages of networking are examined merely through the immediate economic advantages, actors may start to behave opportunistically and will not persevere in their commitment to the network, its common goals, or to other actors in the network. (See e.g. Mittilä 2006).

5 Answers to Research Questions and Conclusions

In answer to the research question "How has the Finnish software industry developed in the last ten years?" it can be stated that, during a ten-year examination period, the Finnish software industry has established its place as a mature and nationally significant sector. During the period in question the industry has diversified. In the middle of the 2000s, the focus was on a packaged, licensed software product. After ten years the field has been taken over by the Internet, mobile platforms, SaaS and cloud services, leaving traditional licensing models behind. In addition, the consumerization of software has appeared during the last ten years. The use of different software is part of the everyday life of ordinary consumers through personal computers, tablets, smartphones, and the numerous applications that are used in them.

The major finding of this study is that although a number of articles have been published during the last ten years studying the Finnish software industry from different business aspects (e.g. Helander and Ulkuniemi 2012; Luoma et al. 2012; Harison and Koski 2010; Sainio and Marjakoski 2009; Rajala and Westerlund 2008; Ojala and Tyrväinen 2006), and even specifically on the networking aspect of the software industry (e.g. Ojala and Helander 2014; Jansen et al. 2013; 2007), there is still a lack of studies that look at the overall development of software industry from the viewpoint of networking, its state and its role in software business development. In the longitudinal material used in the present study, networking is considered to be crucial to the success of small companies in particular, and it has been identified as a target for development, year after year. However, there are still no statistics or even a single case study covering the state of networking among software companies. Networking theories are mainly developed within the context of the manufacturing industry, which does not allow software industry specific questions to be covered.

There have been some successful networking stories in the history of the Finnish ICT and software industry – like the cell phone manufacturer Nokia. Nokia built a global, strategic product development and production network, which was more flexible and cost-effective than the affiliate company structures used by Nokia's competitors (Mittilä 2006). However, these kinds of cases are examples of networks with a single, powerful company, whose goals and strategies the rest of the actors serve. The model does not represent a balanced network with common goals.

In answer to the research question "How does networking manifest itself in the Finnish software industry?" it can be generally stated that networking has been a key trend in the industry year after year, and it has also been a driver for internationalization. However, at the same time, networking has not been covered very widely in previous literature. Networking capabilities have been identified as a success factor in every industry field including the software industry. However, there is little material examining the network from all the parties' point of view. In forthcoming studies the examination of networks should concentrate on the network as balanced entities in which the interaction and advantages works both ways.

Internationalization can be regarded as closely connected to networking, and this would be worthy of its own study. Internationalization seems to have already lived through a full cycle with a rise and fall; lately there have even been reverses of the globalization decisions made some years ago. For example, Helsingin Sanomat (10.2.2016) reports cases in which operations have been relocated from China back to Finland – not to be done by humans but by various automated solutions and robotics. The current trend is to return functions to Finland and to close down activities abroad. The reasons may be manifold and not reported in public. One of the main reasons seems to be cost erosion - in "cheap labor" countries, the wage level has risen close to that of Finland. Additionally, due to the recession, the need for labor has diminished.

The present study shows a clear need to examine networks in the context of the software business in more detail. It shows that networking would be a crucial factor among SME software companies, which represent the majority of Finnish software companies, but even the state of networking has not been identified very well. In further studies, the network has to be examined as a balanced object in which all the parties have committed themselves congruently to the objectives of the network and will also receive consistent value-added. The present study will be expanded and complemented by a case study, which examining networking in one or two software companies. The case study will be carried out during the spring and summer of 2016. The main author of the present study will also focus more deeply on the networking theme in the near future. This study will also be followed by a systematic literature review covering network management literature.

References

Cusumano, M.: The changing software business: moving from products to services. Computer **41** (1), 20–27 (2008)

Elzamly, A., Hussin, B.: Identifying and Managing Software project risks with proposed fuzzy regression analysis techniques: maintenance phase. In: 2014 International Conference on Management and Engineering (CME 2014) (2014)

Ford, D., Gadde, L.-E., Håkansson, H., Snehota, I.: Managing networks. http://impgroup.org/uploads/papers/4198.pdf. Accessed 3rd Feb 2016. (A modified version of the paper is to form Chapter 8 of "Managing Business Relationships: A Network Perspective, Second Edition, Chichester, John Wiley (2003))

Harison, E., Koski, H.: Applying open innovation in business strategies: evidence from finnish software firms. Res. Policy **39**(3), 351 (2010)

Helander, N., Ulkuniemi, P.: Customer perceived value in the software business. J. High Technol. Manag. Res. **23**(1), 26–35 (2012)

Håkansson, H.: Evolution process in industrial networks. In: Axelsson, B., Easton, G. (eds.) Industrial Network: A New View of Reality, pp. 28–34. Routledge, London (1992)

Hofstede, G., Hofstede, G.J., Minkow, M.: Cultures and Organizations: Software of the Mind: Intercultural Cooperation and its Importance for Survival. McGraw-Hill, New York (2010)

Hofstede, G.: Geert Hofstede Resource Pages (2016). http://www.geert-hofstede.com. Accessed 7th Jan 2016

Jaakkola, H.: Culture sensitive aspects in software engineering. In: Düsterhöft, A., Klettke, M., Schewe, K.-D. (eds.) Conceptual Modelling and its Theoretical Foundations. LNCS, vol. 7260, pp. 291–315. Springer, Heidelberg (2012)

Jaakkola, H.: towards a globalized software industry. Acta Polytech. Hung. **6**(5), 69–84 (2009)

Jaakkola, H., Henno, J., Linna, P.: From local to global - path towards multicultural software engineering. Int. J. Knowl. Learn. (IJKL) **7**(1/2), 5–24 (2011)

Jaakkola, H., Henno, J., Thalheim, B., Mäkelä, J.: Collaboration, Distribution and Culture – Challenges for Communication. In: Biljanovic, P. (eds.) Proceedings of the MIPRO 2015 Conference, Opatija, pp. 758–765. Mipro and IEEE (2015)

Jansen, S., Cusumano, M.A., Brinkkemper, S. (eds.): Software Ecosystems: Analyzing and Managing Business Networks in the Software Industry. Edward Elgar Publishing, Cheltenham (2013)

Jansen, S., Brinkkemper, S., Finkelstein, A.: Providing transparency in the business of software: a modeling technique for software supply networks. In: Camarinha-Matos, L.M., Afsarmanesh, H., Novais, P., Analide, C. (eds.) Establishing the Foundation of Collaborative Networks. IFIP, vol. 243, pp. 677–686. Springer, US (2007)

Jarillo, C.: On strategic networks. Strateg. Manag. J. **9**(1), 31–41 (1988)

Kuitunen, H., Jokinen, J.-P., Lassila, A., Mäkelä, M., Huurinainen, P., Maula, M., Ahokas, M., Kontio, J.: Finnish Software Product Business: Results from the National Software Industry Survey. Centre of Expertise for Software Product Business, Espoo (2005)

Lassila, A., Jokinen, J.-P., Nylund, J., Huurinainen, P., Maula, M., Kontio, J.: Finnish Software Product Business: Results of the National Software Industry Survey. Centre of Expertise for Software Product Business, Espoo (2006)

Lewis, R.D.: When Cultures Collide. Leading Across Cultures, 3rd edn. Nicholas Brealey International, London (2011)

Lewis, R.D.: Richard Lewis Resource Pages-Cross-culture (2016). http://www.crossculture.com/services/cross-culture/ and http://www.cultureactive.com. Accessed 7th Jan, 2016

Luoma, E., Kinnunen, H.: Software Industry Survey, Overview of the Finnish Software and IT Services Sector (2015)

Luoma, E., Rönkkö, M.: Software Industry Survey, Summary of Results (2014)

Luoma, E., Rönkkö, M., Tyrväinen, P.: Current software-as-a-service business models: evidence from Finland. In: Cusumano, M.A., Iyer, B., Venkatraman, N. (eds.) ICSOB 2012. LNBIP, vol. 114, pp. 181–194. Springer, Heidelberg (2012)

Messerschmitt, D.G., Szyperski, C.: Software Ecosystem: Understanding an Indispensable Technology and Industry. MIT Press Books, Massachusetts (2005)

Mittilä, T.: Verkosto-osaaminen – liiketoimintaosaamisen uusi mantra. "Liiketoimintaosaaminen kilpailukykymme keskiössä". Kauppatieteellinen yhdistys (2006)

Möller, K., Rajala, A., Svahn, S.: Tulevaisuutena liiketoimintaverkot. Johtaminen ja arvonluonti. Helsinki: Teknologiateollisuuden julkaisuja 11/2004 (2004)

Ojala A., Helander, N.: Value creation and evolution of a value network: a longitudinal case study on a Platform-as-a-Service provider. In: 2014 47th Hawaii International Conference on System Sciences (HICSS), pp. 975–984. IEEE (2014)

Ojala, A., Tyrväinen, P.: Business models and market entry mode choice of small software firms. J. Int. Entrepreneurship **4**(2–3), 69–81 (2006)

Peltonen, J., Rönkkö, M., Mutanen, O.-P.: Growth Forum 2013. Summary Report. Aalto University, School of Science (2013)

Popp, K.: Software industry business models. IEEE Softw. **28**(4), 26 (2011)

Rajala, R., Westerlund, M.: Capability perspective of business model innovation: analysis in the software industry. Int. J. Bus. Innov. Res. **2**(1), 71–89 (2008)

Rönkkö, M., Eloranta, E., Mustaniemi, H., Mutanen, O.-P., Kontio, J.: Finnish Software Product Business: Results of the National Software Industry Survey. Helsinki University of Technology (2007)

Rönkkö, M., Mutanen, O.-P., Koivisto, N., Ylitalo, J., Peltonen, J., Touru, A.-M., Hyrynsalmi, S., Poikonen, P., Junna, O. Ali-Yrkkö, J., Valtakoski, A., Huang, Y., Kantola, J.: National Software Industry Survey 2008: The Finnish Software Industry on 2007. Helsinki University of Technology (2008)

Rönkkö, M., Peltonen, J.: Software Industry Survey 2012. Aalto University, School of Science (2012)

Rönkkö, M., Peltonen, J., Pärnänen, D.: Software Industry Survey 2011. Aalto University, School of Science (2011)

Rönkkö, M., Ylitalo, J., Peltonen, J., Koivisto, N., Mutanen, O.-P., Autere, J., Valtakoski, A., Pentikäinen, P.: National Software Industry Survey 2009. Helsinki University of Technology (2009)

Rönkkö, M., Ylitalo, J., Peltonen, J., Parkkila, K., Valtakoski, A., Koivisto, N., Alanen, L., Mutanen, O.-P.: Software Industry Survey 2010. Aalto University, School of Science and Technology (2010)

Sainio, L.M., Marjakoski, E.: The logic of revenue logic? Strategic and operational levels of pricing in the context of software business. Technovation **29**(5), 368–378 (2009)

Savolainen, P.: Why do software projects fail? Emphasising the Supplier's Perspective and the Project Start-up. Doctoral dissertation. University of Jyväskylä (2011)

Senik, S.C., Scott-Lad, B., Entrekin, L., Adham, K.A.: Networking and internationalization of SMEs in emerging economies. J. Int. Entrepreneurship **9**(4), 259–281 (2011)

The Standish Group: Report CHAOS (2014)

Valkokari, K., Airola, M., Hakanen, T., Hyötyläinen, R., Ilomäki, S.-K., Salkari, I.: Yritysverkoston strateginen kehittäminen. VTT:n tiedotteita 2348 (2006)

A Dynamic Pricing Model for Software Products Incorporating Human Experiences

Andrey Saltan[1,2(✉)], Uolevi Nikula[1], Ahmed Seffah[1], and Alexander Yurkov[2]

[1] Department of Software and Innovation, Lappeenranta University of Technology, Skinnarilankatu 34, 53851 Lappeenranta, Finland
{uolevi.nikula, ahmed.seffah}@lut.fi

[2] Department of Information Systems in Economics, St. Petersburg State University, 7/9 Universitetskaya nab., 199034 St. Petersburg, Russia
{a.saltan, a.yurkov}@spbu.ru

Abstract. At the age of software as a service (SasS) and cloud computing as compared to what is used to be earlier, designing product strategies is a challenging concern for software product management researchers. Comparative statics models are considered to identify software market characteristics while assessing the managerial decisions during the software product strategy design. However, their applicability in dynamic market analysis is rather limited. Important concerns in dynamic market such as dynamic pricing cannot be fully estimated. This motivated the development of a simulation-based dynamic model to evaluate the efficiency and effectiveness of using different pricing models. The proposed (simulation) approach given in details in this paper can be used in conducting complex analysis of software product strategy that involves consideration of product strategy as a portfolio of interrelated solutions rather than a set of independent managerial decisions.

Keywords: Software product strategy · Software market · Decision making · Pricing model · Simulation model

1 Introduction

The ever changing software markets make it difficult for software development companies, big and small ones, to improve and package their products as well as to customize it to the diverse markets and consumer needs. They also have to look for other discontinuous innovation or disruptive technology that will revolutionize their industry or require heavy reengineering and re-packing of their software products. Furthermore, the rapid change that characterizes software industry today results in high instability and uncertainty, which may make product strategy development meaningless. In reality, the inverse proves to be true, and in this case product strategy becomes even more crucial than in other industries due to the nature of high-tech markets [5].

Two decades ago, the software companies' product strategies were slightly different from the strategies of any other goods. Software products were sold as physical

A. Maglyas and A.-L. Lamprecht (Eds.): ICSOB 2016, LNBIP 240, pp. 135–144, 2016.
DOI: 10.1007/978-3-319-40515-5_10

products on a CD or a floppy disc. Most often, they are packaged in two or three versions (e.g. professional/domestic, beginner/advanced, etc.). Nowadays, software as a service, mobile, web-service and the future services for the Internet of things are making software very different from other goods. We see them as indestructibility, transmutability, and reproducibility [9]. The evolution of the Internet has challenged the company to reconstruct their product strategy.

From scientific point of view, product strategy lies in the intersection of product design and development, marketing and sales, strategy and business. There is no universal product strategy, neither a unifying theory is. Each company has its own strategy that takes into account the software product specifications, the market segment characteristics as well as the consumers' experiences, needs and expectations. Various models have tried to address these notions concerning product strategy.

The traditional comparative statics models were introduced first to identify software market characteristics and qualitatively assess factors determining its development. Software market and software product characteristics being identified offer unprecedented opportunities to companies. However, the application scope of these models as a tool for qualitative and dynamic market analysis are very limited. The development of simulation-based models to design a product strategy based on the dynamic presentation of software users' experiences seems to be potentially an efficient approach. The mentioned task has both theoretical and practical effect on development of informational economy since business models and product strategies of todays market participants – the software companies – up to now are being developed intuitively, and later being corrected according to cut-and-try method. With this economic viability and effectiveness of business models can be tested by their approbation at the real market, while companies have no instruments for their justification in advance.

In this paper, we investigate one specific model for evaluating the potential of the dynamic pricing strategy. The main objective of this paper is not only to develop a practical model that industry can use. This is a long-term objective that requires years of research. More precisely the key objective is to develop a ground for studying market analysis at the research level. Still, possibility of carrying out complex analysis of software product strategy based on the proposed model is discussed.

2 Background and Works Related

Our research is based on the previous investigations on software economics in general and pricing aspects of product strategy in particular. Studying the existing academic papers and analytical research reveals the following software market determinants describing the fundamental characteristics of software as digital goods:

1. The software markets are determined by network effect. Direct network effect or the so-called Demand Side Economies of Scale results in the fact that potential consumers' value and willingness to buy software correlates with total amount of users existing. Indirect network effect or the so-called Supply Side Economies of Scale create the situation in which the increase in sales of the original software results in rising sales of complementary goods, which in turn increases the value of the original product for users [10, 14].

2. Economies of scale and network effect cause non-stop price pressure for the companies operating on software markets and make for the establishment of monopolies and oligopolies on these markets [13].
3. In addition to the network effect, the important property of software being a digital good is the possibility of being copied easily without significant loss in quality. This results in unauthorized use or piracy. The practice shows that piracy being on high level on a specific regional market prevents companies from reducing it by their own. This makes companies design their product strategy taking piracy as one of market characteristics and trying to minimize their financial losses or even improving their non-financial indicators [3, 4, 12].
4. Extremely low costs of reproducing software results in the situation in which companies have a structure of expenses with high fixed expenses for software development and incomparably small variable expenses [1].

Under the name of a software company, we mean companies dealing with R&D, distribution and maintenance of general software products aimed at the wide range of consumers. Software consumers are natural persons who buy produced software products for their own purposes.

The above mentioned software products and software markets characteristics result in an extremely diverse list of options available for designing software product strategy. While offering value to the consumers at the right price is the prime aim of software companies, versioning and pricing plays a key role in most software companies' product strategies [10]. Monopolistic competition market and costs structure let software companies to establish any pricing policy they need. Its inadequacy, though, will soon result in serious financial problems.

Recently, several studies [6, 8, 9] have examined the structure of the pricing policy. Despite different approaches all the above mentioned studies identified dynamic pricing as one of the key options in designing the pricing strategy supported by price bundling and price discrimination. As far as we know, the problem of choosing the optimal dynamic pricing model has not been tackled in the literature, especially with the uncertainty in consumer valuation, network effect, and piracy. We believe it to be the result of lack of opportunity to carry out such analysis by means of microeconomic modeling. At the same time, the dynamic modification of existing models gives us a chance to estimate efficiency of different methods of dynamic pricing in relation to various market factors.

Traditionally, according to [6, 11] the dynamic pricing has been based on the following four policies:

- **Penetration pricing.** Penetration strategy sees using of low prices in order to maximize market penetration as its main objective. This is especially important for software companies when entering the market if alternative software already have a large installed base. Later on it will be possible to rise prices. This strategy is widely used in the software industry due to low variable costs and network effect.
- **Skimming pricing.** Companies utilizing skimming strategy set rather high starting prices to reduce them in the course of time. The aim is to skim consumers with high willingness to pay first and then move to consumers with lower willingness to pay and offer them lower prices.

- **Long-term real price.** The long-term real price strategy involves keeping the product launch level price within the sustained period of time. So prices are not adjusted as a predetermined part of the strategy.
- **Free-pricing.** In case of the follow-the-free strategy, consumers receive a product for free. The software company's objective is to create a lock-in effect on the consumers' side in order to generate revenues later on by means of complementary products or premium versions.

Harmon et al. [6] indicate some possibilities for hybrid dynamic pricing associated with bundling or versioning, but these options are out of scope of this study.

3 The Small Picture: Dynamic Pricing Model

Figure 1 demonstrates the proposed model for dynamic pricing. It differs substantially from the microeconomic models that are most cited and used. We propose a dynamic model that poses the properties allowing to solve the managerial problem of choosing one out of three types of dynamic pricing: Penetration, Skimming or Long-term real price. We've excluded Free-pricing because the assumptions behind this model do not allow us to demonstrate possible attractiveness of this strategy for a particular type of software products.

Fig. 1. Approach for developing Dynamic Pricing Model

3.1 Basic Assumptions on Software Market Structure

The software market structure model is based on the following assumptions:

1. In this model we consider software market that consist of a certain number of potential users for newly developed software product. Information about the new product spreads according to the theory of diffusion and can be expressed by the following equation:

$$m_i = m_{i-1} + (a + bm_{i-1})(m_G - m_{i-1}), \quad (1)$$

where m_G – total number of potential consumers on the software market, m_i – number of potential consumers who are informed about the new product by time period t_i, $i = 0,..,T$, T – quantity of time periods when software will be available for the consumers, a, b – parameters reflecting the speed of information spreading.

2. In addition to the original version provided by a software company, pirated version is also available for consumers on the market. Consumers do not pay for pirated version, but they bear costs of finding appropriate ones. These costs can be estimated in monetary terms. Suppose that costs expected for obtaining pirated version are the same for all consumers and equal to c.
3. Every time a consumer uses the product he/she gets some value out of it. This short-term value can be estimated in monetary terms by a consumer and includes two components both internal and network ones. The internal component is defined as the value resulting from using the software in the situation when no one but the user uses it. The network component is known as the benefit depending on the total number of users of this software and is the same for all its users.
4. Let us assume that there is a complete awareness of all potential users that concerns all major market parameters. Besides this, every consumer can calculate long-term value over original and pirated versions and makes rational surplus-maximizing decision on the necessity of using either the original or the pirated one. Consumer's rationality and awareness are traditional simplifications for economic models taking into account consumers behavior. Consumers' bounded rationality can still be considered later and requires preliminary investigations connected with studying the degree of users' rationality in decision-making on software using which have not been carried out.
5. Both software development and sales are considered by the company as investment project. We shall assume that the software development costs are fixed and do not depend on demand, while variable costs per software copy are equal to zero. The software company needs to determine dynamic pricing strategy for its original product that will maximize discounted revenue from selling the original version within the given time horizon.

All the suggested market assumptions are traditional for economic models used for both modelling and investigating markets for durable goods. Taking into account the network effect as well as the availability of pirated versions and the opportunity of different pricing policies is only possible through using simulation modelling.

3.2 Modelling Software Consumer Behavior

The market consists of surplus-maximizing potential consumers. Consumers are heterogeneous in their valuation of the above mentioned software product. Let's index every individual consumer by k. The values for original and pirated versions for the consumer k within the time period t_i will be denoted by $V^O_{k,i}$ and $V^P_{k,i}$ respectively. We define the log-normal distribution for the initial internal value ($i = 0$) of both product versions for all consumers. We simulate internal consumer value for both original and pirate versions within time period t_i as the sum of both internal value within the previous period of time and random variable η_O and η_P respectively. We believe these random variable η_O and η_P to be independent and distributed identically according to normal distribution with zero mean and variance σ for original version and mean -μ and variance σ for the pirated. The assumption of diminishing utility of pirated version takes place because of the fact that pirated product user does not receive software updating service from the company. He also faces the risk that the program may be suspended or the initial installation will lead to its being infected by a computer virus.

The network component of the software product value is defined as a non-decreasing function of the total number of users. To make it simple lets consider the linear type of this function: $f(n_i) = e \cdot n_i$, where parameter e – the power of network effect.

The consumer calculates the expected total value of using software for the original ($\mathbf{E}[V_k^O]$) and pirated ($\mathbf{E}[V_k^P]$) versions by integrating over all the paths of valuations and makes the decision either on buying, or using pirated version, or rejecting to use the product according to rational and surplus-maximizing rules presented in Table 1.

Table 1. Decision-making rules

DECISION	RULE
BUY ORIGINAL VERSION	$\begin{cases} \mathbf{E}[V_k^O] - p_i + f(n_i) \geq 0 \\ \mathbf{E}[V_k^O] - p_i \geq \mathbf{E}[V_k^P] - c \end{cases}$
USE PIRATED VERSION	$\begin{cases} \mathbf{E}[V_k^P] - c + f(n_i) \geq 0 \\ \mathbf{E}[V_k^O] - p_i < \mathbf{E}[V_k^P] - c \end{cases}$
DO NOT USE	$\begin{cases} \mathbf{E}[V_k^O] - p_i + f(n_i) < 0 \\ \mathbf{E}[V_k^P] - c + f(n_i) < 0 \end{cases}$

3.3 Optimization Problem for Software Company

As is was discussed earlier, all market parameters and distribution of valuations across consumers are well known by the software company. Still, the company knows nothing about its particular consumer. The company should define dynamic pricing policy by selecting one of these options:

- Using long-term real pricing;
- Using penetration pricing;
- Using skimming pricing.

According to our pricing model, we believe that the company denotes a "fair" price for its product with p. This price is determined by two factors: current prices for similar products as well as consumers' willingness to pay for this product. Using long-term real price strategy requires the company's selling software at the given price over the given time horizon. Using penetration pricing presupposes that the company should initially offer its consumers the 50 % discount and then sequentially raises the price and in the last period it sells software with the 50 % premium to the price considered "fair". The skimming pricing is completely opposite to the penetration pricing: the company consistently drops the price over the given time horizon from a 50 % premium to a 50 % discount.

The company is trying to maximize discounted revenue over the given time horizon from selling the original version in respect to demand restrictions associated with their consumer's rational behavior and availability of pirated version on the market:

$$\pi = \sum_{i=0}^{T} \frac{p_i \cdot d_i(p_i)}{(1+r)^i} \to max,$$
$$\begin{cases} d_i(p_i) = \left| \left\{ k \in M_i \backslash N_i : \begin{cases} \boldsymbol{E}\left[V_k^O\right] - p_i + f\left(\sum_{j=0}^{i-1}(d_j + q_j)\right) \geq 0 \\ \boldsymbol{E}\left[V_k^O\right] - p_i \geq \boldsymbol{E}\left[V_k^P\right] - c \end{cases} \right\} \right|, \\ q_i(p_i) = \left| \left\{ k \in M_i \backslash N_i : \begin{cases} \boldsymbol{E}\left[V_k^P\right] - c + f\left(\sum_{j=0}^{i-1}(d_j + q_j)\right) \geq 0 \\ \boldsymbol{E}\left[V_k^O\right] - p_i < \boldsymbol{E}\left[V_k^P\right] - c \end{cases} \right\} \right|. \end{cases} \tag{2}$$

To solve this maximization problem, methods of iteration searching, approximation on a constant-pitch grid and simulation modeling are used.

3.4 Results

Figure 2 represents distribution of dynamic pricing strategies that the software company should follow depending on the strength of the network effect and expenses for searching a pirated version. As Fig. 2 shows, dynamic pricing can result in increase of revenue of software company.

The economic explanation of result given above is as follows: when the costs of obtaining pirated version are low, the only option for the company is to decrease the initial price to rise it only later when the network effect increases the consumers' value

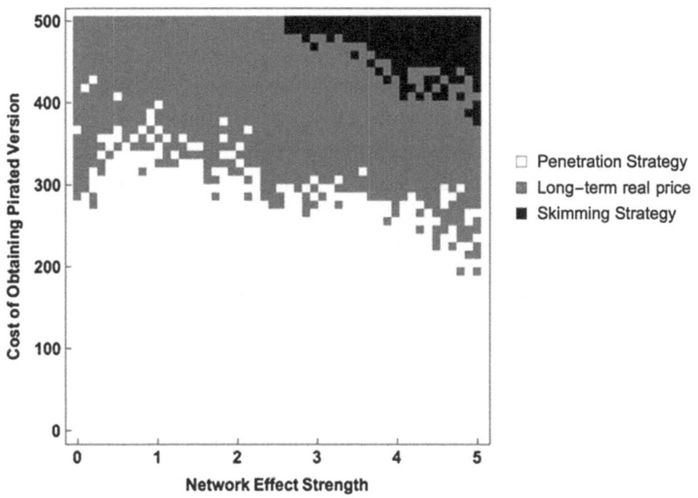

Fig. 2. Distribution of dynamic pricing strategies

and their willingness to pay. This is exactly what penetration strategy means, so with costs being low companies should use penetration pricing.

In case of high searching costs for pirated versions the company may avoid focusing on fighting the piracy and it may set a "fair" price from the very beginning. This will bring to the increased revenue due to the time value of money. In addition, with the network effect being strong, the company may even try to use skimming strategy: we can always find people with high internal value. Even if the number of such people is small, they will create network effect and attract other people to follow their way.

4 The Big Picture: Software Product Strategy Design

Software pricing is a key issue that not only influences the commercial success of any software product, but it is also an important activity in the software product strategy design. Further we shall highlight and discuss the importance of the proposed model as part of the big picture of the software product strategy design.

The issue of designing software product strategy is a matter of detailed study in the sphere of information technologies. This resulted in the emergence of a whole stream of academic research dealing with analyzing the software product strategy.

The proposed approach and the simulation model based on it can be easily adapted to analyzing other managerial decisions with regard to product strategy design. However, the product strategy mentioned is an aggregate portfolio of managerial decisions similar to the discussed in the previous sections. The analysis of this product strategy requires the portfolio approach.

There is no unified and conventional approach to determining the product strategy. Still, a large variety of product strategy definitions and concepts can be found in the economic literature. The restrained point of view suggests to focus exclusively on marketing issues while the wider one doesn't make distinction between product and business strategies. The former approach is more typical for past year papers, when it was believed that sales and marketing could be separated from development and other business issues. The latter approach on software product strategy can be found in papers on start-ups and entrepreneurship. In case of start-ups it can be difficult to distinguish between product and business strategies mainly since the same people are in charge of making all managerial decisions for different areas of business process.

Nowadays product strategy is believed to lie at the intersection of three business functions: sales and marketing, strategy and finances, development and design. Buxmann [2] suggests making a distinction between product design strategy, communication strategy, distribution strategy, and pricing strategy. Buxmann separates the product strategy component associated with software development. In line with the proposed integration idea, though, it seems logical to rewrite the offered software product strategy as follows: Communication and Promotion, Sales and Distribution, Upgrade and Support, Versioning and Pricing.

Pricing decision is one of the most crucial decisions which a company can make when planning the launch of any new software product. Comprehensive taxonomy of pricing models for durable goods has been proposed by Iveroth [7] who also defines pricing models as systems of price-related characteristics of the agreement between buyer and seller. Price models are described with the help of 5 dimensions listed without priority of anyone: Scope, Base, Influence, Formula, Temporal Rights. The framework is called the SBIFT model that is the abbreviation of the dimensions mentioned above. Laatikainen et al. [8] evaluated and adapted SBIFT model to by applied in the sphere of cloud services. As a result, they suggested a 7-dimensional pricing framework that added two more characteristics (Degree of discrimination and Dynamic pricing strategy) to the five existing dimensions (SBIFT).

Another pricing framework was proposed by Lehmann and Buxmann [9] with the following pricing parameters: Price formation, Structure of payment flow, Assessment base, Price bundling, Price discrimination and Dynamic pricing strategies.

The described classification of options available for software companies in designing product strategy demonstrates the importance of carrying out complex analysis of software product strategy. This analysis involves taking product strategy as a portfolio of interrelated solutions, rather than as a set of independent managerial decisions.

5 Concluding Remarks

This paper is devoted to the matters of importance and challenges facing software industry in designing software products strategy and, more precisely, in pricing. The dynamic model for market analysis was developed through illustrating how it works and how the model can be used. The proposed model as well as underlying theoretical framework seem interesting and highly promising. The next important step demands a large and wide empirical research to test and confirm the above mentioned theoretical positions. So, this research will prove the applicability of the above mentioned approach to the software product strategy design by real companies.

References

1. Bontis, N., Chung, H.: The evolution of software pricing: from box licenses to application service provider models. Internet Res. **10**(3), 246–255 (2000)
2. Buxmann, P.: Network effects on standard software markets: a simulation model to examine pricing strategies. In: 2001 2nd IEEE Conference Standardization and Innovation in Information Technology, pp. 229–240. IEEE (2001)
3. Chellappa, R.K., Shivendu, S.: Managing piracy: Pricing and sampling strategies for digital experience goods in vertically segmented markets. Inf. Syst. Res. **16**(4), 400–417 (2005)
4. Conner, K., Rumelt, R.P.: Software piracy: An analysis of protection strategies. Manage. Sci. **37**(2), 125–139 (1991)
5. Cusumano, M.A.: The changing software business: Moving from products to services. Computer **41**(1), 20–27 (2008)
6. Harmon, R., Raffo, D., Faulk, S.: Pricing strategies for information technology services: A value-based approach. In: 42nd Hawaii International Conference on System Sciences, HICSS 2009, pp. 1–10. IEEE (2009)

7. Iveroth, E., Westelius, A., Petri, C.-J., Olve, N.-G., Cöster, M., Nilsson, F.: How to differentiate by price: Proposal for a five-dimensional model. Eur. Manag. J. **31**(2), 109–123 (2013)
8. Laatikainen, G., Ojala, A., Mazhelis, O.: Cloud services pricing models. In: Herzwurm, G., Margaria, T. (eds.) ICSOB 2013. LNBIP, vol. 150, pp. 117–129. Springer, Heidelberg (2013)
9. Lehmann, D.-W.-I.S., Buxmann, P.D.P.: Pricing strategies of software vendors. Bus. Inf. Syst. Eng. **1**(6), 452–462 (2009)
10. Shapiro, C., Varian, H.R.: Information Rules: A Strategic Guide to the Network Economy. Harvard Business Press, Boston (1999)
11. Shipley, D., Jobber, D.: Integrative pricing via the pricing wheel. Ind. Mark. Manage. **30**(3), 301–314 (2001)
12. Soloviev, V.: Mathematical modeling of strategic commitments and piracy in Windows/Linux competition. In: 15th Annual Conference Proceedings., International Conference on Management Science and Engineering, ICMSE 2008, pp. 10–12. IEEE (2008)
13. Varian, H.R.: High-technology industries and market structure. University of California, Berkeley. 33 (2001)
14. Weitzel, T., Wendt, O., von Westarp, F.G., Konig, W.: Network effects and diffusion theory: Network analysis in economics. Int. J. IT Stan. Stand. Res. (IJITSR) **1**(2), 1–21 (2003)

A Case Study of the Health of an Augmented Reality Software Ecosystem: Vuforia

Lamia Soussi, Zeena Spijkerman, and Slinger Jansen(✉)

Utrecht University, Utrecht, The Netherlands
{l.soussi,z.spijkerman}@students.uu.nl, slinger.jansen@uu.nl

Abstract. Augmented Reality is becoming increasingly popular. The success of a platform is typically observed by measuring the health of the software ecosystem surrounding it. In this paper, we take a closer look at the Vuforia ecosystem's health by mining the Vuforia platform application repository. It is observed that the developer ecosystem is the strength of the platform. We also determine that Vuforia could be the biggest player in the market if they lay its focus on specific types of app development.

1 Introduction

Software ecosystems (SECOs) are sets of businesses functioning as a unit and interacting with a shared market for software and services, together with the relationships among them. The inability to function in a software ecosystem has already led to the demise of many software vendors, leading to loss of competition, intellectual property, and eventually jobs in the software industry [1].

Vuforia is a platform for Augmented Reality (AR) that provides Application Programming Interfaces (API) in C++, Java, Objective-C, and the .Net languages through an extension to the Unity game engine. With the use of 2D and 3D targets, AR gives a new way to perceive the environment around combining virtual to real. Vuforia was introduced by Qualcomm five years ago and has become an industry-leading platform that has been supported by a global ecosystem of developers. Vuforia was sold to PTC Inc. in 2015 and supported a global ecosystem of 175,000+ registered developers and has powered 20,000+ apps with more than 200 million app installs worldwide [2].

The research question we try to answer is *"Can Vuforia improve its position in the market of AR platforms?"* To that end the focus is on the involvement of the developers and the analysis on the categories, maturity and ratings will show us the position of Vuforia in the AR mobile app market. For instance if the developers seem to be active, then Vuforia should focus on other parts to improve the health of their ecosystem to get a better position in the market, for example their marketing approach or their position in the mobile ecosystem.

2 Research Method

To measure the longevity and propensity for growth, as we define software ecosystem health, of Vuforia a combined qualitative and quantitative research

A. Maglyas and A.-L. Lamprecht (Eds.): ICSOB 2016, LNBIP 240, pp. 145–152, 2016.
DOI: 10.1007/978-3-319-40515-5_11

is performed. The developer's website is the main source of information for this study. Forums on the developer network page provide information about Vuforia's developer ecosystem. These forums are important to get an insight on the developer's point of view on the ecosystem they shape and their opinion on the changes between Qualcomm and PTC.

A study from 2013 by Chen et al. [3] introduces the maturity ratings by both app providers, App Store and Google Play. With some minor differences the maturity rating defined by minimum age is more regulated with the App Store than Google Play. It provides a maturity rating based on the content of the app with a minimum age of "4+", "9+","12+", or "17+". In accordance, the health measurement of the Vuforia applications is conducted within the AppStore only. The apps are extracted manually in a table by name, category, customer rating, maturity rating (rating based on minimum age), and provider. We expect that AR will mostly be used for gaming. We state the following hypothesis:

- H1: Less serious categories get more ratings.
- H2: Apps with immature content get lower rates.
- H3: Apps with mature content are paid over apps with immature content.

We use Import.io [4], a Web Data Platform and free Web Scraping Tool, to extract the needed data. With the tool's feature "*bulk extract*", which runs the extraction method into multiple links at the same time, it is possible to extract all data into tables from all paginations of the forum. The extracted data which includes the discussed topics, the developer's name, the number of views and replies provides also an insight into the time line of the Vuforia platform since 2011.

3 Analysis and Results

3.1 The Developers Network and Applications

The extracted data from the forum of the website helps to determine how many actual active actors there are among the developers. Currently the website is changing as new topics are being added every day. Measurement on SPSS is conducted in the data gathered previously from the forum. From the data it has been determined that 4,803 different developers have created one topic or more in the forum. And the first five most active users have respectively posted between 125 and 61 topics. The first actor started being active in 2012, the second in 2010, the third in 2011, the fourth and the fifth in 2013.

The data mining tool import.io has been used for extracting the topics discussed in the forum webpage, the number of replies and views, the name of the active developer who posted the subject and the date of posting. The forum consists of 11,248 topics, 63,353 posts and 184,289 users (developers) [5]. Within the forum three topics have been created: News & Announcements, FAQ and the AR Technical Discussion. The AR Technical Discussion consists itself of a range of topics which have been added by developers.

The analyzed apps are extracted from the marketing website of Vuforia [2]. The app data was collected and listed manually in a table with name, category, satisfaction rating, maturity rating and the provider. After extracting only the apps available in the EU App store, and only the apps of which the wanted information was available, 848 apps have been analyzed.

Figure 1 shows the rating of the apps which varies from 1 to 5 stars in the App Store. Most of the apps did not have enough ratings to calculate an average. We can also see that the apps that have been rated, received a high rating, around 4 and 4.5 stars.

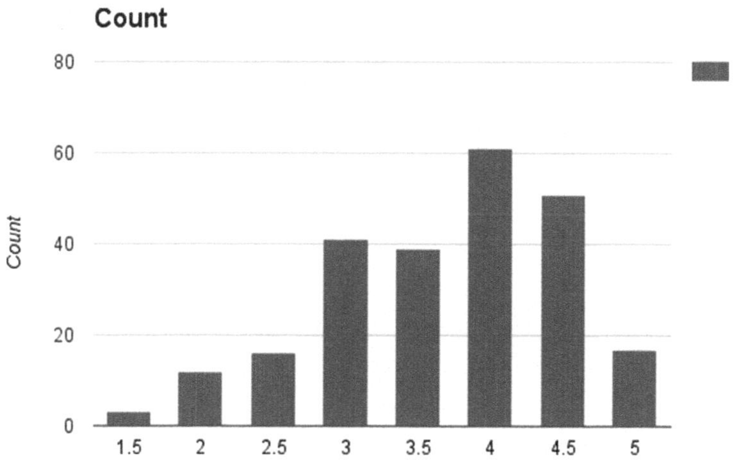

Fig. 1. Counted customer ratings of Vuforia's Apps

To see if the apps that use Vuforia make profit on sales, the data on the price of the apps have been collected. The percentage of free apps and paid apps is considerably different. 97.4 % of the analyzed apps are free and the rest of the apps have a price range from $1,99 to $3,99.

The apps were also divided across 18 categories, as shown on the website [2]. The maturity rating of the apps, can be respectively ages 4+, 9+, 12+ or 17+. These age ratings are based on the content of the apps and shows if Vuforia is mostly used for apps with a low or high minimum age for use. Most of the apps (84.8 %) are suitable for persons of 4 years and older. The rest of the maturity ratings are almost equally divided.

The categories : Advertising, Apparel, Architecture, Art, Automotive, Education, Electronics, Politics, Publishing, Retail/Etail, Sports, Tourism and Toys which scored an average age maturity equal or lower than 5 were placed as less serious categories. The categories Entreprise, Entertainment, Food & Beverage,Gaming and Health which received an age maturity average higher than 5 were placed as serious categories. Figure 2 details the different categories with the less serious categories in green and serious categories in blue.

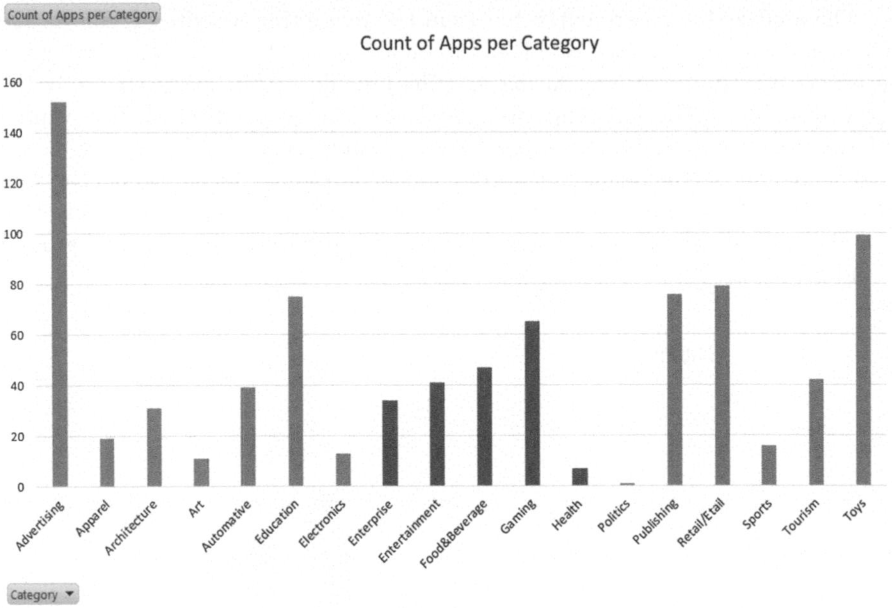

Fig. 2. Number of apps per category (Color figure online)

With the average age maturity of every category, a regression on the app categories could be performed, therefore 2 groups were conducted: Group 1 are the less serious apps and Group 2 are the serious apps. Three hypotheses have been conducted to measure the correlations between the ratings, maturity ratings and app categories.

- H1: Less serious categories get more ratings.

The Pearson correlation test gives us significance of 0,004 which means that we are not able to reject hypothesis H1. There is a correlation between the category of the apps and the number of ratings they get.

- H2: Apps with immature content get lower rates.

The test result from the Pearson correlation is 0,628 which is higher than the significance level so we have to reject H2.

- H3: Apps with mature content are paid over apps with immature content.

The correlation test on the third hypothesis shows us that the apps with mature content are not paid over apps with immature since the outcome is 0,939 on a significance level of 0,05.

3.2 The Software Network of Augmented Reality SDKs

The software components that are part of Vuforia could be interacting and connecting with other components outside Vuforia's own ecosystem like other AR SDKs, together forming the software network [6]. A comparison of several AR SDKs is made to find out where the other platforms of the software ecosystem are placed in the overall AR SDK market, and which one is the best to use for developers.

D. Amin and S. Govilkar [7] did an extensive comparison on the differences between AR SDKs. Metaio [8] has recently stopped selling their products and subscriptions because it was sold to Apple in 2015 [9]. It is not clear what Apple's plans are with the SDK therefore Metaio will not be taken into account in the comparison.

The first point in the comparison made by Amin & Govilkar [7] is based on the license type the mentioned companies use. As we can see in Table 1 only ARToolkit provides an open source license, and is also available for free as for commercial. The rest of the SDKs are available for free or can be bought as a commercial version.

Table 1. Comparison based on license type and supported platform [7]

AR SDK Type		Vuforia	Metaio	Wikitude	ARToolKit	D'Fusion	ARmedia
License	Open Source	x	x	x	v	x	x
	Free	v	v	v	v	v	v
	Commercial	v	v	v	v	v	v
	iOS	x	v	x	v	v	v
	Android	v	v	v	v	v	v
	Windows	v	v	v	v	v	v

The second point in the comparison is the platform which the SDKs support, the possibilities have been narrowed down to iOS, Android or Windows. Only Vuforia and Wikitude are an exception because their SDKs does not support iOS. The rest of the SDKs support every platform.

3.3 The Orchestrator: From Qualcomm to PTC

The first orchestrator of the Vuforia ecosystem was the company Qualcomm, founded in July 1985 in San Diego (U.S.), which focuses on a variety of industries. In an official statement on November 3rd Qualcomm presented the sale of Vuforia to PTC Inc. PTC is a global provider of technology platforms and solutions and is like Qualcomm also focusing on IoT, Smart Homes, and is deployed in 28,000 other businesses.

On the news page of PTC's website [10] they state that PTC commits to not only the continued growth of Vuforia technology, but also to the community, and the Vuforia ecosystem. According to Qualcomm, the current apps will remain unchanged and developers will continue to have the same level of support from the Vuforia team [2]. PTC's plan is to combine Vuforia more with the IoT: *"Vuforia has also captured the attention of industry leaders who envision the potential for augmented reality to transform work."*

4 Discussion

4.1 The Developers Network and Applications

Within the research on the Vuforia SECO, the individual actors are the developers. According to Manikas and Hansen [6] it is important to look at the health of the individual actors because they influence the overall health of the ecosystem (p. 32).*"The active participation and engagement of actors brings value to the ecosystem, while the actor's robustness increases the probability that the actor exists and remains involved in the ecosystem activity in the future."* This statement can be proved according to the findings of this study. With the 5 most active users we notice an important number of contributions in the forum with publications from 129 topics to 61 topics. These topics generate other responses from other actors in the ecosystem, making the network actors connecting between each other. As noticed that those top actors are active already for several years from 2010 up until now.

According to the data extracted the number of active developers posting in the forum is important with 4.803 developers, although the website states a bigger number the assumption is made that this number includes all the registered developers in the website.

The network of actors and their interaction within an ecosystem play an important role in the SECO health of Vuforia and any other platform [6]. As an addition to this, Manikas and Hansen state that the individual actor health can be weighted according to the role of the actor in the network. The active developers are more likely to make improved apps since they are more involved in the ecosystem. If the developers feel confident in posting articles and information on the developer portal, they will feel confident in the network. We have seen that the network of actors is quite large with 184289 users and 63353 posts.

This research looked into the apps of Vuforia, the categories, the customer ratings, the maturity ratings based on the content of each app and if it is a free or paid app. This is done to see if it is interesting for Vuforia to invest in apps with more mature content according to the number of ratings they get. This is also interesting for the developers since they know if their apps with the use of Vuforia make them successful or what kind of apps are most rated. The correlation tests in SPSS showed us that there is a correlation between categories and the customer rating, and between the app categories and the app ratings.

The conclusion from the first hypothesis is that less serious categories get more ratings. This could be because of the number of users per category. Another possible reason is because the less serious category contain more apps than the serious ones (98 apps in category toys against 6 apps in the category health).

The third hypothesis showed us that apps with more mature content are not paid over apps appropriate for users with a lower minimum age, this means that the apps with immature content can generate the same revenue as apps with mature content. The developers will not gain more money with apps that contain mature content and Vuforia does not really have to focus more on the developers that make more serious app.

We noticed that after the release note of a new component or new version of the SDK the publications about questions and tutorials on how to use them gets higher. The library prepares a mention of frequently asked questions followed by a detailed answer to it. Links to tutorials are provided to understand how to use some features of the SDK. Adding to it a whole page following step by step how to start a work space for beginners. All these subject are related effectively with all the details and videos that explain the use of the tool and how to fix some errors for example.

4.2 The Orchestrator: From Qualcomm to PTC

According to Syed and Jansen [11]: "*SECO orchestrators can develop strategies to keep a SECO vibrant and profitable for other organizations in the SECO*". Manikas and Hansen [6] refer to the orchestrator as the one that can monitor the health of the ecosystem and take measures to promote ecosystem health if necessary. To monitor the health, the orchestrator needs a good overview of the ecosystem and must consult effective measurements. In the case of PTC this can be hard in the beginning because Qualcomm has already build an ecosystem on its own. Additionally, the orchestrator can act by creating rules and processes for the actors, this is also a point where PTC has to put effort to keep the developers, which are part of the developer community, happy. The change of orchestrator is not yet really visible and might indicate that it will take some time to figure out which orchestrator will make/have made Vuforia a complete and successful ecosystem.

5 Conclusion

This research paper focused on the health of the Vuforia platform ecosystem and tried to answer the research question: **Can Vuforia improve its position in the market of AR platforms?** The analysis on the developers and developer network showed us that the actors of the ecosystem are well connected through the forum in the developer portal.

The network consists of a large number of developers and the active ones seemed to be active already for several years. For the complete ecosystem of Vuforia, the developer network does not need extra attention, but PTC should be aware of the possible changes it brings and should make sure that the developers stay well connected and content. The Vuforia platform is well accessible for developers and non-developers to gain information on the application and the ecosystem.

After analyzing the apps on Qualcomm's website not only a correlation between the categories of the apps and their rating was found but also between the app categories and the maturity ratings. Less serious categories seem to get higher ratings, this means that for the revenue of the company and its position in the market, the focus should be on these app categories. A reason might be that the apps in a less serious category are used for entertainment and are more fun to use in contrary to more serious apps. The actual reason of the outcome could be measured and studied in further research. Less serious apps do not get less or lower rates, and serious apps are not paid over less serious apps.

The comparison between AR SDKs in the software network showed us that no framework is the best and the choice of SDK depends on the choice of the developer. According to PTC, Vuforia is already the biggest player but Metaio has been bought by Apple and could rise to become big competition for Vuforia.

References

1. Jansen, S., Finkelstein, A., Brinkkemper, S.: A sense of community: a research agenda for software ecosystems. In: 31st International Conference on Software Engineering-Companion Volume, ICSE-Companion 2009, pp. 187–190. IEEE (2009)
2. Qualcomm: Vuforia Augmented Reality for 3D Mobile Content. https://www.qualcomm.com/products/vuforia
3. Chen, Y., Xu, H., Zhou, Y., Zhu, S.: Is this app. safe for children?: a comparison study of maturity ratings on android and ios applications. In: Proceedings of the 22nd International Conference on World Wide Web, pp. 201–212. International World Wide Web Conferences Steering Committee (2013)
4. Import.io: Web Data Platform and Free Web Scraping Tool. https://www.import.io/
5. Forums–Vuforia Developer Portal. https://developer.vuforia.com/forum
6. Manikas, K., Hansen, K.M.: Reviewing the health of software ecosystems-a conceptual framework proposal. In: IWSECO@ ICSOB, pp. 33–44. Citeseer (2013)
7. Amin, D., Govilkar, S.: Comparative study of augmented reality SDKs. Int. J. Comput. Sci. Appl. (IJCSA) **5**, 11–26 (2015)
8. Metaio: Metaio Product Support. https://www.metaio.com/product_support.html
9. Miller, J., Constine, J.: Apple Acquires Augmented Reality Company Metaio – TechCrunch, 28 May 2015
10. PTC to Acquire Augmented Reality Leader Vuforia from Qualcomm – PTC. http://www.ptc.com/news/2015/ptc-to-acquire-vuforia-from-qualcomm#sthash.3orEg4XO.dpuf
11. Syed, S., Jansen, S.: On clusters in open source ecosystems. In: IWSECO@ ICSOB, pp. 19–32. Citeseer (2013)

Towards 'Human/System Synergistic Development': How Emergent System Characteristics Change Software Development

Helena Holmström Olsson[1(✉)] and Jan Bosch[2]

[1] Faculty of Technology and Society, Malmö University, Nordenskiöldsgatan 1, 211 19 Malmö, Sweden
helena.holmstrom.olsson@mah.se

[2] Department of Computer Science & Engineering, Chalmers University of Technology, Hörselgången 11, 412 96 Gothenburg, Sweden
jan.bosch@chalmers.se

Abstract. With recent and rapid advances in areas such as online games, embedded systems and Internet of Things, the traditional notion of what constitutes a system, as well as how a system is typically developed, is fundamentally changing. Instead of systems that are specified upfront, and for which there are pre-defined purposes and tasks, we are increasingly experiencing a situation in which interconnectivity and emergent configurations of systems allow dynamic system capabilities that evolve and adjust over time. Regarded as the new digital business paradigm, these types of systems offer fundamentally new ways for software development companies in their service- and value creation. At the same time, they present challenges in these organizations. In this paper, and based on multiple case study research in three different domains, we identify emergent system characteristics that pose new challenges on software development. We present a model that outlines the transition from traditional development towards 'Human/System Synergistic Development' (HuSySD), in which software development is a joint effort between software development teams and intelligent systems.

Keywords: Online games · Embedded systems · Internet of Things · Self-learning systems · Self-actuation · Decentralized control · 'Human/System Synergistic Development'

1 Introduction

With recent advances in software technology, we are experiencing a fundamental shift in how people interact with software-intense systems and what is expected from these systems. In different domains, new types of systems are emerging with characteristics that make them very different from the systems we are used to and that software development organizations have traditionally developed. As one example, and as highlighted in a trend forecast published by Gartner [1], Internet of Things systems offer fundamentally new opportunities for value creation, and are rapidly permeating our everyday lives. These

A. Maglyas and A.-L. Lamprecht (Eds.): ICSOB 2016, LNBIP 240, pp. 153–160, 2016.
DOI: 10.1007/978-3-319-40515-5_12

systems incorporate a number of functions such as e.g. sensing, actuation and control, and they use advanced data collection and analysis mechanisms to initiate actions and to make decisions in a predictive or adaptive manner [2, 3]. As a result, these systems foster new user behaviors and allow new forms of user interaction, they enable new service- and value creation and they allow innovative business models and opportunities. However, while these new types of systems offer a wide range of opportunities, they also pose significant challenges to the organizations developing these. Instead of being systems that are specified upfront, and for which there are pre-defined purposes and tasks, these systems are interconnected systems in which emergent configurations allow for dynamic system capabilities that evolve and adjust over time, and in which advanced data collection and analysis mechanisms allow continuous and automated optimization of system functionality. For most software development companies, these characteristics make the systems we see emerge very different from the systems that they have traditionally developed.

In this paper, and based on multiple case study research in three different domains, we identify emergent system characteristics that pose new challenges on software development. We present a model that outlines the transition that software development companies experience when moving from traditional development towards what we term 'Human/System Synergistic Development' (HuSySD). In this development approach, software development is no longer only a human effort conducted by software development teams, but instead a joint effort in which human development teams and autonomous intelligent systems share effort and responsibility in development of continuously evolving systems.

2 Background

Due to rapid advances in technology, new types of systems are emerging with characteristics and capabilities that we didn't experience up until now. With physical objects becoming connected to the Internet, data revealing users' behaviors being collected and shared, and systems with computational power beyond what we can imagine and abilities to learn, adjust and take action [4, 5], the potential of future software systems and services is stunning. As a consequence, the ways in which software systems are developed, and the ways in which development organizations and teams traditionally work, are being disrupted. At the same time as these new types of systems allow tremendous opportunities, they pose great challenges on current software development practices. Below, we discuss some of the characteristics that distinguish these systems from other systems, and that pose new challenges on current software development practices.

First, today's systems are becoming increasingly powerful with advanced data collection and analysis mechanisms. They collect data continuously, they efficiently process vast amounts of data, and they response to queries during run-time [6, 7]. For instance, and as a well-established practice in the web and software-as-a-service industry, companies increasingly adopt A/B testing techniques [8] as a way to continuously learn from the data they collect, and to have this data inform experiments with different aspects of their systems. Also, and with increasingly intelligent systems, there is the potential to have the systems experiment with different behaviors and learn from these experiments to more rapidly adjust according to e.g. user preferences. With rapid developments in the areas of embedded intelligence and adaptive systems [5, 9], we will have systems that can experiment within boundaries set by development teams, and perform automated and frequent validation of functionality in relation to requests from these teams [10].

Second, as a means to accelerate the development of new innovative services, systems are becoming increasingly interconnected [11–13]. Interconnectivity implies having a multitude of heterogeneous systems dynamically discover one another, and seamlessly interconnect at runtime. Typically, this is achieved by having mediators [14], mediating adapters [15], or converters [16] perform the necessary coordination and translation that allow applications to interoperate despite the heterogeneity of their data models and interaction protocols. Given the huge heterogeneity and dynamism characterizing these systems, automated solutions are used to achieve interoperability timely and with the needed level of flexibility [17]. As a result, interconnected systems can increasingly learn from each other and start to autonomously adapt, adjust and predict actions [18, 19] based on the collective knowledge generated in the network.

Third, the concept of systems that adapt and improve over time has been a topic of interest in the artificial intelligence and machine learning communities for a long time. The basic premise is a software system that learns to reconfigure or adapt itself to new or changing inputs [3, 9], and that take decisions based on continuous data collection. In contrast to traditional systems, an adaptive system with embedded intelligence is the one initiating action [9]. As a result, systems with adaptive characteristics require less user interaction the more they learn about the user.

3 Research Methodology

3.1 Case Companies

The research presented in this paper builds on close collaboration with software development companies in the online gaming, the embedded systems and the Internet of Things domain. In Table 1, we describe the case companies that were involved in our study, the domain in which they operate and the systems they produce.

3.2 Case Study Design

The research reported in this paper is based on longitudinal multi case study research [20] in fourteen companies in three different domains: online games, embedded systems and Internet of Things. Our research is based on close collaboration and frequent meetings with these companies over a period of more than five years. In each company, we conducted interview studies, group interviews workshops, observations and validation sessions with people representing the software development teams, the release organization, project and product management and sales and marketing. In this paper, we present a summary of our learnings from the different domains, with a special focus on how new types of systems, and emergent system characteristics, pose fundamentally new challenges on software development.

Table 1. Case companies in three domains.

Case company	Domain	System
Company A	Embedded systems	Developer of navigational information, operations management and optimization solutions for the world's largest aerospace company
Company B	Embedded systems	Producer of circular pumps for heating and air conditioning, as well as pumps for water supply
Company C	Embedded systems	Developer of network cameras, video encoders and camera applications for professional IP video surveillance
Company D	Embedded systems	Manufacturer and supplier of transport solutions for commercial use
Company E	Embedded systems	A premium automobile manufacturer
Company F	Embedded systems	Provider of telecommunication systems and equipment for mobile and fixed network operators
Company G	Online gaming	Developer of mobile games
Company H	Online gaming	Developer of mobile games and online entertainment
Company I	Online gaming	Developer of IT solutions for businesses, developers, individuals and children
Company J	Internet of Things	Provider of services in the heating and 'smart energy' domain
Company K	Internet of Things	Provider of waste monitoring and logistics solutions
Company L	Internet of Things	Developer of mobile phones, tablets, smart wear and associated devices that enhance user experience for consumers and businesses
Company M	Internet of Things	Developer of mesh network technology that enables mobile devices to form instant networks
Company N	Internet of Things	Developer of connected monitoring and alarm solutions and services for smart homes

4 Findings

Online Games. During the last two years, we have engaged with three companies in the online gaming domain. In these companies, data is systematically collected from products in the field, and there are defined metrics that serve different stakeholders and teams in the organization. The companies run continuous experiments with customers and they collect data revealing system performance and operation. There are specialized data analytics teams that serve the organizations by processing requests, creating reports, defining data dashboards and by automating analysis. Typically, management and development teams have identified a set of key metrics that provide insights into how the organization is delivering value to its customers, and there is a close collaboration between management, the development teams and the data analytics team. However, the companies collect far more data than what they use, and they struggle with identifying key indicators that effectively drive the overall business goals.

Embedded Systems. We have studied six companies in the embedded systems domain for the last five years. In all companies, huge amounts of data are collected to help assess product performance and operation. Primarily, this data works as the basis for troubleshooting and support activities, and as input for understanding any misbehavior or deviation in the system. However, although there are significant advances in data collection and use, there is no systematic analysis and use of the data. Often, ad hoc practices emerge in relation to individual or team needs or based on specific requests from a customer. Analysis is not fully automated and some of the companies report on tedious work for individuals when shifting through large sets of data to answer a query.

Internet of Things. We studied five companies developing Internet of Things systems during the last two years. These companies experience an explosion in the amounts of data that is generated from their systems, and they are in the midst of trying to understand how to make effective use of this data in relation to systems that interconnect and interact with other systems in larger networks. The processing of the data needs to become much quicker as the company feels that innovative value propositions and interesting business cases might otherwise be lost.

In Table 2, we summarize the challenges we identify in the case companies.

To summarize our empirical findings, we see that the companies we studied are experiencing major shifts in the types of systems they develop. To manage this transition,

Table 2. Summary of challenges identified in the case companies.

Area of concern:	Challenges:
R&D process	• The transition from development of standardized systems, towards dynamic systems that continuously evolve • The transition from long-term planning and pre-defined milestones, towards continuous experimentation and evaluation of hypotheses • The definition of rules, actions and control in decentralized systems consisting of interconnected objects and devices
Data collection and use	• The collection, analysis and visualization of data from multiple sources • The collection of real-time data for dynamic optimization of user interfaces and data presented to the user • The collection of data in systems where user interaction over time decreases due to the intelligence of the system itself • The collection of data revealing user behaviors and preferences in relation to a larger system of which an individual device is only one part
Business and organization	• The alignment of R&D data collection practices and PdM decision-making processes • The interplay between R&D teams/human efforts, and smart systems/automated efforts

there is the need for companies to move beyond current software development practices and adopt new ways-of-working that support development of continuously evolving systems.

5 Towards 'Human/System Synergistic Development'

Based on the case, we see the first beginning of a number of emerging system characteristics. These are: (1) *self-learning systems,* (2) *self-actuation systems,* and (3) *decentralized control.* First, self-learning systems refer to adaptive systems whose operation algorithm improves based on trial and error. Second, self-actuation systems refer to systems that actively initiate actions based on input from the environment in which they operate [9]. Finally, decentralized control refers to systems in which each master in the network has all data. This supports local decision-making and allows for rapid actions to be taken in the network. A key challenge that all companies experience, is how to transition towards new development approaches that cater for the emergent system characteristics they experience. In a number of studies, the transition from traditional development towards agile development has been outlined [22], as well as the move beyond agile development practices [6]. Recently, and due to increasingly intelligent systems [10], we are experiencing a shift towards intelligent systems that experiment and adjust their responses and behaviors. To reflect this synergy between development teams and systems, we coin the term 'Human/System Synergistic Development' (HuSySD) to denote a development approach where the development team provides functionality to the system in the field, and set boundaries within which the system itself can run automatic experiments (Fig. 1).

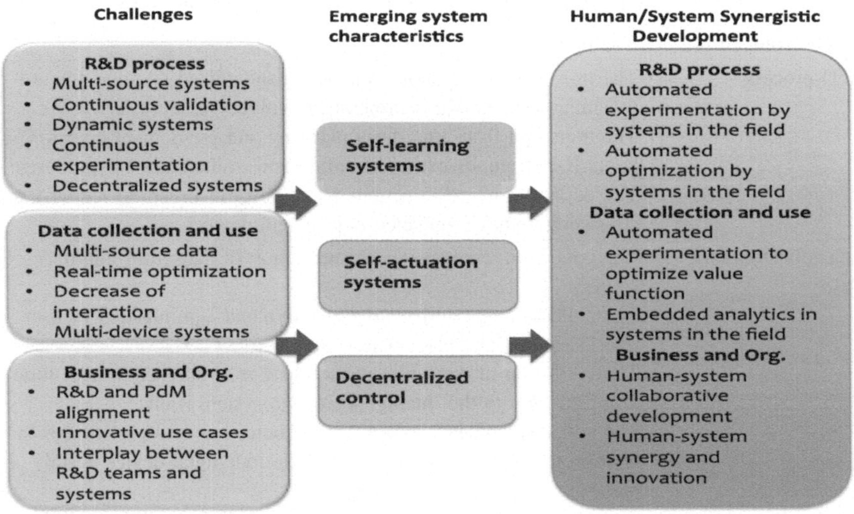

Fig. 1. The challenges and emerging system characteristics influencing current software development practices, and how the new development approach 'Human/System Synergistic Development' (HuSySD) address these.

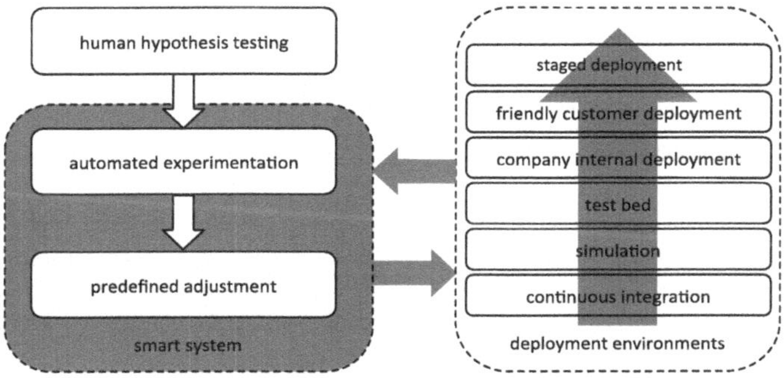

Fig. 2. The 'Human/System Synergistic Development' (HuSySD) model.

In the development approach we describe above, development teams do hypothesis testing while smart systems do automated experimentation and adjust according to the results from these. In Fig. 2, we outline the 'Human/System Synergistic Development' (HuSySD) model with regards to the human and system loops, as well as the steps that can be deployed to confirm system behaviors.

6 Conclusion

In this paper, we identify emergent system characteristics that pose new challenges on software development. We identify these challenges and we present a new development approach in which software development is a joint effort between software development teams and smart systems.

References

1. Levy, H.: What's new in Gartner's Hype cycle for emerging technologies (2015). http://www.gartner.com/smarterwithgartner/whats-new-in-gartners-hype-cycle-for-emerging-technologies-2015/
2. Gubbi, J., Buyya, R., Marusic, S., Palaniswami, M.: Internet of Things (IoT): a vision, architectural elements, and future directions. Future Gener. Comput. Syst. **29**, 1645–1660 (2013)
3. Kinsner, W.: Challenges in the design of adaptive, intelligent and cognitive systems. In: Proceedings of the 6th IEEE International Conference on Cognitive Informatics, 6–8 August, Lake Tahoo, CA, pp. 13–25 (2007)
4. Kranz, M., Holleis, P., Schmidt, A.: Embedded interaction: interacting with the Internet of Things. IEEE Internet Comput. **14**, 46–53 (2010)
5. Chong, C.Y., Kumar, S.P.: Sensor networks: evolution, opportunities, and challenges. Proc. IEEE **91**(8), 1247–1256 (2003)
6. Olsson, H.H., Bosch, J.: From opinions to data-driven software R&D: a multi-case study on how to close the 'Open Loop' problem. In: Proceeding of the 40th Euromicro Conference on Software Engineering and Advanced Applications (SEAA), 27–29 August, Verona, Italy (2014)

7. Deng, A., Xu, Y., Kohavi, R., Walker, T.: Improving the sensitivity of online controlled experiments by utilising pre-experiment data. In: Proceedings of the 6th ACM International Conference on Web Search and Data Mining (WSDM 2013), 4–8 February, Rome, Italy (2013)
8. Kohavi, R., Longbotham, R., Walker, T.: Online experiments: practical lessons. IEEE Comput. **43**(9), 82–85 (2010)
9. Peters, G.: Six necessary qualities of self-learning systems: a short brainstorming. In: Proceedings of the International Conference of Neural Computation Theory and Applications, pp. 358–364 (2015)
10. Bosch, J., Olsson, H.H.: Submitted. data-driven continuous evolution of smart systems. Submitted to an International Workshop on Software Engineering
11. Evans, D.: The Internet of Things: how the next evolution of the internet is changing everything. CISCO White Pap. **1**, 14 (2011)
12. Leminen, S., Westerlund, M., Nyström, A.-G.: Living Labs as open-innovation networks. Technol. Innov. Manag. Rev. **2** (2012)
13. Miorandi, D., Sicari, S., De Pellegrini, F., Chlamtac, I.: Internet of things: Vi-sion, applications and research challenges. Ad Hoc Netw. **10**, 1497–1516 (2012)
14. Wiederhold, G.: Mediators in the architecture of future information systems. IEEE Comput. **25**(3), 38–49 (1992)
15. Yellin, D.M., Strom, R.E.: Protocol specifications and component adaptors. ACM Trans. Prog. Lang. Syst. **19**(2), 292–333 (1997)
16. Calvert, K.L., Lam, S.S.: Formal methods for protocol conversion. IEEE J. Sel. Areas Commun. **8**(1), 127–142 (1990)
17. Di Marco, A., Inverardi, P., Spalazzese, R.: Synthesizing self-adaptive connectors meeting functional and performance concerns. In: Software Engineering for Adaptive and Self-Managing (SEAMS) (2013)
18. Rowland, C., Goodman, E., Charlier, M., Light, A., Lui, A.: Designing Connect-ed Products: UX for the Consumer Internet of Things. O'Reilly Media, Inc., Sebastopol (2015)
19. Liu, Y., Zhou, G.: Key technologies and applications of Internet of Things. In: 2012 Fifth International Conference on Intelligent Computation Technology and Automation (ICICTA), pp. 197–200 (2012)
20. Yin, R.K.: Case Study Research: Design and Methods. Sage Publications, Los Angeles (2009)
21. Tieben, R., Bekker, T., Schouten, B.: Curiosity and interaction: making people curious through interactive systems. In: Proceedings of the 25th BCS Conference on Human-Computer Interaction, pp. 361–370. British Computer Society, Swinton (2011)
22. Olsson, H.H., Alahyari, H., Bosch, J.: Climbing the "Stairway to heaven": a multiple-case study exploring barriers in the transition from agile development towards continuous deployment of software. In: Proceedings of the 38th Euromicro Conference on Software Engineering and Advanced Applications, 5–7 September, Cesme, Izmir, Turkey (2012)

User Dimensions in 'Internet of Things' Systems: The UDIT Model

Helena Holmström Olsson[1(✉)], Jan Bosch[2], and Brian Katumba[1]

[1] Department of Computer Science, Malmö University, Nordenskiöldsgatan 1, 205 06 Malmö, Sweden
{helena.holmstrom.olsson, brian.katumba}@mah.se
[2] Department of Computer Science and Engineering, Chalmers University of Technology, Hörselgången 11, 412 96 Göteborg, Sweden
jan.bosch@chalmers.se

Abstract. 'Internet of Things' (IoT) systems are fundamentally changing the way in which we interact and perceive technology. In this paper, we focus on two dimensions of IoT systems; (1) the IoT user interface and (2) the IoT ecosystem. We develop a model that identifies how data is presented to users and how users interact with the system, and the level at which systems interconnect with, and collects data from, external systems. Companies can use the model to map their systems according to the dimensions in order to: (1) identify current state of their systems, (2) identify desired state and (3) better understand the steps necessary to develop more advanced IoT systems. We evaluate the dimensions in five case companies and provide empirical evidence on the transition towards increasingly advanced IoT systems.

Keywords: Internet of Things · User interface · Ecosystem · User value

1 Introduction

Recently, Gartner published its 'Hype Cycle for Emerging Technologies', which illustrates how a technology, IT method or management discipline stacks up against others in terms of maturity [1]. In this trend forecast, the 'Internet of Things' (IoT) is presented at the peak of the curve with high expectations as the new digital business paradigm that will offer fundamentally new ways for service- and value creation [2, 3]. With technologies allowing interconnectivity of objects, unobtrusive user interfaces and embedded intelligence, IoT applications will rapidly permeate our everyday lives by transforming the way we interact with information technology and our surrounding environment. Already now, we see examples of how IoT technologies change everyday life. From being exceptions rather than the norm, concepts such as e.g. 'smart cities' [4], 'smart homes' [5] and 'smart health [6] are rapidly changing how we interact with, and what we expect from, technology.

In this paper, we identify and explore two of the many dimensions that make IoT systems interesting: (1) the *IoT user interface* and (2) the *IoT ecosystem*. We develop a model in which we: (1) identify the different formats in which data is presented to users

A. Maglyas and A.-L. Lamprecht (Eds.): ICSOB 2016, LNBIP 240, pp. 161–168, 2016.
DOI: 10.1007/978-3-319-40515-5_13

and the ways in which users interact with the system, and (2) the level to which systems interconnect with external systems to allow data collection from multiple sources. We evaluate the two dimensions in the model in five case companies and we outline the typical evolution path that companies take when transitioning towards developing more advanced IoT systems.

2 Background: IoT User Interfaces and Ecosystems

Already in 2000, Kevin Ashton envisioned a world where physical and electronic objects would be networked and interconnected to each other. Currently, it is estimated that by 2020, more than 50 billion devices will be connected to the Internet [7]. When connected, these devices become active participants in business, information and social processes where they are enabled to interact and communicate among themselves, and with the environment, by exchanging data and information [8, 9].

IoT systems offer radically new opportunities in how to present information to users, and how to have users interact with the system [10, 11]. Today, users interact not only by touching, pointing and scanning, but also by audio, video and gestures [12], and as recognized in [13, 14], the desktop metaphor with windows, icons and pointers is quickly being replaced with smartphone user interfaces and touch screen input. An example is a smart home that possesses ambient intelligence and automatic control, and where residents interact with different appliances via touch interfaces, mobile devices, physical screens and gestures. With more advanced IoT systems we see a rapid growth of subtle and smart devices that might not even have a screen, and where remotely controlled, physical and even invisible user interfaces are becoming the norm. Physical user interfaces support active interaction with IoT systems and they are designed with a few buttons, a tiny display and/or some minimal audio output. Finally, some IoT devices are so subtle that we don't notice them at all. As an example, most thermostats and alarms are designed to only demand user attention when there is urgency or when the system recognizes a deviation from the normal state. With more advanced IoT systems that automatically adjust to users' context and goals, no interface might be the best interface. For presentation and visualization of information, IoT systems use formats ranging from static presentation of data to dynamic visualization of data. In static user interfaces, the system presents available data for the user in a standard format without the opportunity for the user to influence the format. Most often, IoT systems for control and monitoring of devices such as e.g. applications for monitoring energy consumption use this format. On the contrary, dynamic user interfaces adjust and adapt continuously, and allow the users to explore and influence the way in which data is presented. As an example, route optimization systems typically use this format.

IoT systems are networks of interconnected objects [15, 16]. In a post from September 2015, Jim Hunter [17] presents a pyramid in which he outlines the different needs of an IoT system. At the very top of the pyramid, "smart" needs are identified, i.e. needs that are realized when multiple systems are connected and when analytics, logic and distributed intelligence allow systems to learn about, and predict, user behaviors. At this level, and when connected to other systems in the ecosystem, IoT systems can collect data from multiple sources, combine and correlate real-time information and merge large data sets to help answer queries by its users. Also, and as the main characteristic, systems can learn from each other and from users and start to autonomously adapt, adjust and predict behaviors [13, 18] based on the collective knowledge generated in the ecosystem.

3 The UDIT Model: 'User Dimension in IoT'

Based on literature, we develop the 'User Dimensions In IoT' (UDIT). The model focuses on two dimensions of IoT systems: (1) the *IoT user interface* dimension and (2) the *IoT ecosystem* dimension. In Fig. 1, we present the model and we define the characteristics of systems in each quadrant. The model can be used to: (1) identify the different formats in which data can be presented and the ways in which users interact with the system, and (2) the level to which systems interconnect with external systems. Also, companies can map their systems to identify their current state and identify the desired state.

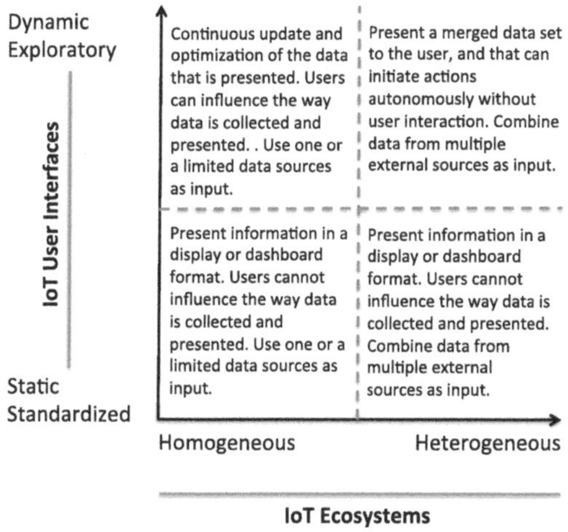

Fig. 1. The UDIT model: User dimensions in IoT.

In being static/standardized, the system presents information in a display/dashboard format, and users cannot influence this. Static/standardized IoT systems are typically reactive and waiting for the user to initiate action. On the other end of the spectrum, 'dynamic/exploratory', refers to interfaces that continuously optimize and where users can influence the way data is presented. The 'IoT ecosystems' dimension pictures the ways in which the system interconnects with external systems. In being 'homogeneous', the system uses data from a single source. In being 'heterogeneous', the system interconnects with external systems to present a merged and synthesized data set.

4 Method

This paper reports on a five-months multi-case study (August–December 2015) in five companies developing IoT systems. In our study, we adopt an exploratory approach [19, 20]. As a research method, case study research is used [20], and a multi-case approach was chosen. For the purpose of this study, we started with conducting a literature review focusing on the 'user interface' and the 'ecosystem' dimensions of IoT systems. Our choice of dimensions was based on the fact that while there is an impressive amount on research focusing on the technological and architectural aspects of IoT, there is less research focusing on the user interaction aspects. Based on our literature review, we developed a model in which we capture the insights from literature and in which we picture the two dimensions. A draft of the model was presented at a cross-company workshop to get feedback from the companies. To further evaluate the model, we conducted expert interviews where we asked the company representatives to map one of their systems according to the two dimensions in the model. As the start for each interview, the interviewees were given the opportunity to select one existing IoT system that they develop, and that they wanted to use as the basis for the discussion. After presenting the model and the different dimensions to the interviewees, we asked the interviewees to map the selected system according to the dimensions we had defined. Also, we asked the interviewees to identify the desired state of the system and how they pictured the transition towards this state. All interviews were carried out face-to-face with 1-3 people in each company, and lasted for 1-1.5 h. After each interview the researchers went through the notes, discussed the main items that had been shared, and confirmed the mapping of the selected system.

4.1 Case Companies

Company A is a supplier of energy and energy related services. The company is providing a mobile application that presents information about your electricity consumption, and that be used remotely on any mobile device. For the purpose of this study, we met with the project manager for business innovation.

Company B develops mobile phones, tablets, smart wear and associated devices that enhance use and experience of information and communications technology for consumers and businesses. For the purpose of this study, we met with one of the senior research managers for technology research and advanced applications.

Company C offers a wide portfolio of IP-based products and solutions for security and video surveillance, network cameras, video encoders, video management software and camera applications for professional video surveillance. For the purpose of this study, we met with two senior people from the core technology group.

Company D offers mesh network technology with a software package that enables mobile devices to form instant networks. For the purpose of this study, we met with two software developers.

Company E develops monitoring and alarm solutions for homes, and it provides connected services for smart homes. For the purpose of this study, we met with three people from the research and development unit.

5 Results

5.1 Current State: Homogeneous and Static IoT Systems

Company A. The application is a monitoring solution that helps users track and reduce energy consumption. Data from two sensors is presented in a mobile app in a dashboard format. Users can view energy consumption in the household and choose what appliances to connect to the system, but they cannot influence how data is presented. Currently, data is collected from a limited number of internal sources.

Company B. The application is an activity tracker application that presents information in the form of 'tiles' via a mobile phone app interface. Users can easily switch from one tile to another in order to monitor different activities, and they can choose what tiles to view. The application is static in the way data is presented. Currently, data is collected primarily from a few internal sources.

Company C. The product is a surveillance camera that streams video data from surveillance systems at airports and grocery stores etc., and stores it for further analysis. Currently, data is collected from one source. The products have standardized interfaces that record and display video streams for the user without any opportunities to interact.

Company D. The company has so far not focused on user interfaces. However, with new applications being under development it is only a matter of time before the user interface will become an area of interest to the company. In providing instant connection to other devices, the system has the opportunity to use data from several external sources.

Company E. The system is a home security and surveillance system that allows the user to keep in contact with the home. Information is presented to the user in a static way and based on a few data sources. Users cannot influence presentation of data and the system does not integrate with external systems.

5.2 Desired State: Heterogeneous and Dynamic IoT Systems

Company A. The goal is to have a heterogeneous system that connects with external systems and collects data from these. The company wants to become an integrated part in a larger ecosystem where several systems provide user value and customized experiences in an increasingly autonomous way.

Company B. The company aims at providing a more dynamic system in which the different tiles base their information on several data sources, and where the presentation of data is continuously updated. If so, the system would require less user interaction and it would act autonomously to satisfy user needs.

Company C. The company views the transition towards more heterogeneous systems as the most important step, and foresees great potential for new and innovative services that combine surveillance with other monitoring tasks.

Company D. The flexibility of the mesh technology gives the company the opportunity to cut across both business and consumer markets. There is a great potential in building applications on top of the network in order to allow dynamic interaction among multiple users, and with an interface that responds dynamically.

Company E. Company E aims at having the system collect data from several sources, and to combine this data to enhance functionality and increase the value of the product.

5.3 The UDIT Model: Mapping of IoT Systems

As part of the interview study, we asked the interviewees to map one of their systems according to the dimensions in the UDIT model (Fig. 2).

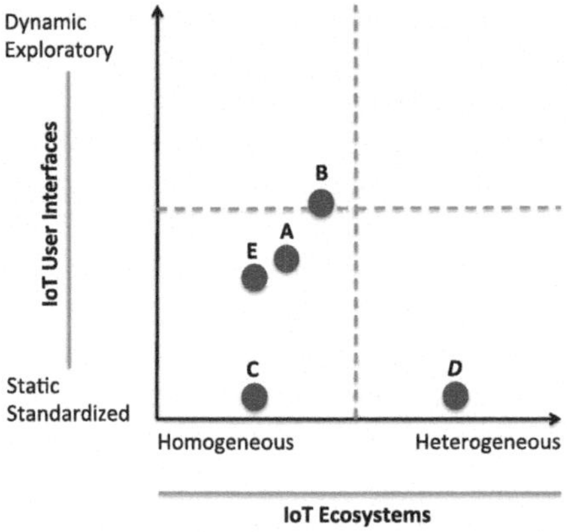

Fig. 2. Mapping of case study IoT systems according to the UDIT model.

As can be seen, the majority of the systems are placed within the lower left quadrant implying that the user interface dimension is static/standardized and that users cannot influence the way data is presented. Also, this quadrant implies that the systems use one or a very limited number of data sources as input.

6 Discussion

Based on our interviews, we see that most of the companies identify the transition towards heterogeneous ecosystems as critical. The main reason for this is the access to multiple data sources that, if connected, could leverage new user value and innovative business opportunities. Also, a heterogeneous ecosystem that connects with, and collects data from, multiple sources would allow increasing system automation [18]. In our case companies, the opportunity to have interconnected systems that learn from each other, and that adjust based on input from each other, is seen as the next step towards autonomous systems. With regard to the user interface dimension, our study reveals that companies strive for increasingly dynamic user interfaces. Although they all agree on that exploratory interfaces are important for improving user experience, they emphasize that with increasingly intelligent systems user interaction will, and should, be reduced over time. Overall, and in similar with what previous research suggests [11–14], the interviewees recognize the way in which information is presented to the user as vital, and with increasingly intelligent systems users should only be exposed to accurate information that help them accomplish a certain task, and with the system being responsible for continuous presentation of the most attractive alternative. Although the companies we studied target different domains, we identify a number of similarities in relation to what drives the transition towards more advanced IoT systems. In Table 1, we outline the drivers for the transition towards *(1)* heterogeneous ecosystems, and towards *(2)* dynamic interfaces.

Table 1. Drivers for transition towards more advanced IoT systems.

Transition:	Definition:	Drivers:
(1) Towards heterogeneous ecosystems	A heterogeneous system collects and combines data from multiple sources.	• Automation • Autonomy
(2) Towards dynamic interfaces	A dynamic interface continually updates and optimizes the information it presents.	• Optimization • Accuracy

7 Conclusion

In this paper, we explore the user interface and the ecosystem dimension of IoT systems. We develop a model that captures these dimensions and we evaluate the model in five case companies. Based on our findings, we conclude that *(1)* companies transition towards heterogeneous ecosystems to increase system automation and autonomy, *(2)* companies transition towards dynamic user interfaces to improve system accuracy and optimization, and *(3)* companies foresee future IoT systems as increasingly autonomous systems for which the desire for user interaction will decrease over time.

References

1. Fenn, J., Raskino, M.: Mastering the Hype cycle: How to Choose the Right Innovation at the Right Time. Harvard Business Press, Boston (2008)
2. Gartner's 2015 Hype Cycle for Emerging Technologies Identifies the Computing Innovations that Organizations Should Monitor. http://www.gartner.com/newsroom/id/3114217
3. Levy, H.: What's New in Gartner's Hype Cycle for Emerging Technologies (2015). http://www.gartner.com/smarterwithgartner/whats-new-in-gartners-hype-cycle-for-emerging-technologies-2015/
4. Yonezawa, T., Galache, J.A., Gurgen, L., Matranga, I., Maeomichi, H., Shibuya, T.: A citizen-centric approach towards global-scale smart city platform. In: 2015 International Conference on Recent Advances in Internet of Things (RIoT), pp. 1–6 (2015)

5. De Silva, L.C., Morikawa, C., Petra, I.M.: State of the art of smart homes. Eng. Appl. Artif. Intell. **25**, 1313–1321 (2012)
6. Kovatcheva, E., Nikolov, R., Madjarova, M., Chikalanov, A.: Internet of things for wellbeing – pilot case of a smart health cardio belt. In: Roa Romero, L.M. (ed.) XIII Mediterranean Conference on Medical and Biological Engineering and Computing 2013. IFMBE Proceedings, vol. 41, pp. 1221–1224. Springer, Heidelberg (2014)
7. Miorandi, D., Sicari, S., De Pellegrini, F., Chlamtac, I.: Internet of things: vision, applications and research challenges. Ad Hoc Netw. **10**, 1497–1516 (2012)
8. Gubbi, J., Buyya, R., Marusic, S., Palaniswami, M.: Internet of things (IoT): a vision, architectural elements, and future directions. Future Gener. Comput. Syst. **29**, 1645–1660 (2013)
9. Chen, G., Huang, J., Cheng, B., Chen, J.: A social network based approach for IoT device management and service composition. In: 2015 IEEE World Congress on Services (SERVICES), pp. 1–8 (2015)
10. VentureScanner: The State of Internet of Things in Six Visuals. https://medium.com/@VentureScanner/the-state-of-internet-of-things-in-six-visuals-a4b9cda3324c#.qu0y4pk2k
11. Kranz, M., Holleis, P., Schmidt, A.: Embedded interaction: interacting with the internet of things. IEEE Internet Comput. **14**, 46–53 (2010)
12. Rukzio, E., Leichtenstern, K., Callaghan, V., Holleis, P., Schmidt, A., Chin, J.: An experimental comparison of physical mobile interaction techniques: touching, pointing and scanning. In: Dourish, P., Friday, A. (eds.) UbiComp 2006. LNCS, vol. 4206, pp. 87–104. Springer, Heidelberg (2006)
13. Rowland, C., Goodman, E., Charlier, M., Light, A., Lui, A.: Designing Connected Products: UX for the Consumer Internet of Things. O'Reilly Media Inc., Sebastopol (2015)
14. Yau, S.S., Buduru, A.B.: intelligent planning for developing mobile IoT applications using cloud systems. In: 2014 IEEE International Conference on Mobile Services (MS), pp. 55–62 (2014)
15. Evans, D.: The Internet of Things: How the next evolution of the internet is changing everything. CISCO White Paper, vol. 1, p. 14 (2011)
16. Leminen, S., Westerlund, M., Nyström, A.-G.: Living labs as open-innovation networks. Technol. Innov. Manag. Rev. **2**, 6–11 (2012)
17. Hunter, J.: The Hierarchy of IoT "Thing" Needs. http://social.techcrunch.com/2015/09/05/the-hierarchy-of-iot-thing-needs/
18. Liu, Y., Zhou, G.: Key technologies and applications of internet of things. In: 2012 Fifth International Conference on Intelligent Computation Technology and Automation (ICICTA), pp. 197–200 (2012)
19. Dubé, L., Paré, G.: Rigor in information systems positivist case research: current practices, trends, and recommendations. MIS Q. **27**, 597–636 (2003)
20. Yin, R.K.: Case Study Research: Design and Methods. Sage Publications, Los Angeles (2009)

How Do Software Startups Pivot? Empirical Results from a Multiple Case Study

Sohaib Shahid Bajwa[1,3(✉)], Xiaofeng Wang[1,3], Anh Nguyen Duc[2,3], and Pekka Abrahamsson[2,3]

[1] Free University of Bozen-Bolzano, Piazza Domenicani 3, 39100 Bolzano, Italy
bajwa@inf.unibz.it
[2] Norwegian University of Science and Technology, 7491 Trondheim, Norway
[3] Software Startups Research Network, Trondheim, Norway
http://www.unibz.it,
http://softwarestartups.org

Abstract. In order to handle intense time pressure and survive in dynamic market, software startups have to make crucial decisions constantly on whether to change directions or stay on chosen courses, or in the terms of Lean Startup, to pivot or to persevere. The existing research and knowledge on software startup pivots are very limited. In this study, we focused on understanding the pivoting processes of software startups, and identified the triggering factors and pivot types. To achieve this, we employed a multiple case study approach, and analyzed the data obtained from four software startups. The initial findings show that different software startups make different types of pivots related to business and technology during their product development life cycle. The pivots are triggered by various factors including negative customer feedback.

Keywords: Software startup · Lean startup · Pivot · Validated learning

1 Introduction

Many people know Twitter as arguably the most famous microblogging platform. Much less are aware that it was a podcast service provider back in its startup phase in 2005 [8]. Similarly, Instagram back in its early days was a social check-in application called Burbn, combining features of a photo share app (Foursquare) and a game (Mafiawars) [7]. As the examples show, very few software startups get their products or business right immediately, and most do not end up with what they had initially started.

This is because software startups intend to produce cutting edge products and grow fast under the condition of extreme technology and business uncertainty. In order to obtain a sustainable business model, software startups change their direction relentlessly, or make a *pivot* in Lean Startup approach [1]. Ries [1] defines *pivot* as a strategic change, designed to test a fundamental hypothesis about a product, business model or engine of growth. Pivot is often considered the outcome of validated learning, another key concept of the Lean Startup to test a business hypothesis and measure the result. Software startups often neglect the validated learning process and avoid pivot when needed, which is one of the reasons behind many startup failures [2]. Pivot is

A. Maglyas and A.-L. Lamprecht (Eds.): ICSOB 2016, LNBIP 240, pp. 169–176, 2016.
DOI: 10.1007/978-3-319-40515-5_14

considered vital for software startups to survive, grow, and eventually obtain a suitable business model.

Due to the nascent nature of software startup research, previous empirical studies specially focusing on pivot are scarce. To the best of our knowledge, no study has been conducted exploring different types of pivots and identifying different triggering factors. This study attempts to fill this knowledge gap, examining pivots in software startups during different product development stages, from concept to mature product. The main objective of our study is to provide a better understanding of pivots happening in software startups. To this end, the main research question asked in the study is: *How do software startups pivot during different product development stages*?

The rest of this paper is organized as follows. In Sect. 2, background and related work is presented. Section 3 describes the empirical research approach. The findings are presented in detail in Sect. 4 and further discussed in Sect. 5. The paper is summarized in Sect. 6 outlining the future research.

2 Background and Related Work

Pivot is a core concept of Lean Startup [1], a startup methodology that focuses on the Build-Measure-Learn (BML) loop with three steps: turn idea into product, measure its effect, and learn from the result. This learning is referred to as validated learning [1]. Each hypothesis regarding the business model is tested, and a decision is made accordingly on whether to pivot or persevere. Pivot is not about introducing just any change, even though the two terms are often used as synonyms. Pivot is a special kind of change designed to test and validate the assumptions a startup has about its product, business model, and the engine of growth [1]. Ries presents ten different types of pivots that can happen in a startup [1], listed in Table 1.

Only few studies touch upon the topic of startup pivot [2–4, 9, 10]. By providing evidence of two real world software startup failures, Giardino et al. [2] concluded that neglecting the learning process and avoiding pivot can become the reasons of software startup failure. Bosch et al. [9] offer an alternative to pivot or persevere. They present a software development model for early stage software startups. But the study is not primarily focused on investigating pivot in software startups. Another study related to pivot was conducted by Van der Van and Bosch [4], which gives a broader overview on pivots in software startups. It compares the similarities and differences between pivot decisions and software architecture decisions. The study considers a pivot as a business decision only, and is not primarily focused on how software startups pivot during their life cycles.

The work closely related to this study was from Terho et al. [3], in which the authors explain how pivots can change business hypotheses in a lean canvas model. They have identified some pivot types, e.g. zoom-out, customer segment, and platform pivots. However, there is a lack of evidence of how they were identified and how the link between pivot types and lean canvas was built.

Based on the observed knowledge gap, we focused our study on understanding pivots in software startups by identifying their types and examining the factors

Table 1. Pivot types [1]

Zoom-in	A single feature of a product becomes the whole product itself.
Zoom-out	The whole product becomes a single feature of a much larger product, mainly because the original product is insufficient to address customer needs.
Customer segment	While trying to solve the right problem, a startup discovers a different segment of customers than originally anticipated.
Customer need	A startup realizes the problem they try to solve is not very important for the customers, and discovers other related problems that are more important.
Platform pivot	An application is turned into its supporting platform or vice versa.
Business Architecture	A startup switches its business architecture e.g. aiming for low volume, high margin, instead of focusing on mass market.
Value Capture	Changing the way/method to capture value (monetize) for a startup.
Engine of Growth	A startup makes significant changes in its growth strategy to seek rapid and more profitable growth.
Channel Pivot	A startup has identified a more effective way to reach its customers than its previous one.
Technology Pivot	A startup delivers the same solution by using completely different technology.

triggering them. As Nguyen-Duc et al. [10] argue, different types of pivots might happen in different phases of a startup's lifecycle. Therefore we adopted a product development perspective on the phases of a startup's lifecycle. A startup goes through different product development stages during their life cycles, which are: concept, in development, working prototype, functional product with limited users, functional product with high growth, and mature product [6]. The product development stages allow us to obtain a contextualized understanding of pivots in software startups.

3 Research Approach

Given the exploratory nature of our study and the "how" research question, we employed a multiple qualitative case study approach [11]. The selected four cases were software-based startups. Each was covering a different product development stage at the time of our study (Table 2). All pivoted during their product development.

The main data collection method was interviews. We conducted semi-structured interviews with open-ended questions. Each interview lasted from 30 min to one hour, and was transcribed for further analysis. All of the interviewees were the founders, were involved in the decision making process and knew the journey of their startups from the inception till today.

The data analysis followed the multiple-case analysis suggested by Yin [11]. Within-case analysis was conducted firstly. Then in the cross-case comparison, the identified pivots and different triggering factors causing pivots across cases were compared and contrasted.

Table 2. Profiles of the software startups

Software startup	Business domain	Founded	# of Founders	Current product dev. stage	Country
Dicy	Video service	2014	2	Working prototype	Italy
DocMine	Software as a service	2015	3	Functional product with limited users	Austria
Hooka	Event Ticketing system	2011	2	Functional product with high growth	Norway
Easy Learning	Game based Learning	2006	2	Mature Product	Norway

4 Results

Case 1: Dicy. Dicy is a software-based startup that provides video service specially designed for other startups to create their promotion videos. It started as an online community platform in 2014, where entrepreneurs could meet, share their ideas and also ask for different resources according to their needs. In July 2014, when their online platform already had limited users, they identified a different need of customers, and pivoted from online community platform towards providing video service facilities for startups.

The main factor causing this customer need pivot was feedback obtained from the customers, according to the co-founder of Dicy we interviewed: *"We realized that most of the startups, especially software startups, don't really want to talk about their ideas because of people stealing their ideas."* The co-founder explained the rationale behind conducting this pivot: *"We decided if we want to help startups in this communication, we need to find a different solution, in order to approach to investors in an easy and comfortable way."* The outcome of this pivot was positive, as the co-founder stated: *"During the trial stage, we could see that the concept was kind of approved. We see that this demand exists."*

When asked about the realization of being flexible and allowing pivot, the co-founder suggested: *"You would realize something is not coming up. And you need change. That's very important. You should allow this kind of change. You need to be flexible. You need to try out what are you capable of doing and what it takes to."*

Case 2: DocMine. The original idea of DocMine when it started was to develop better encryption software. They made their first significant change when they pivoted towards providing a unified API to access different social media sources, such as Facebook and Twitter. The founder commented on the reason behind this pivoting: *"In Sweden, another company is also working on this and developing better than us. So we shifted and stopped working on this idea."* When describing the reason of not competing with their competitors, the founder described: *"You have to react very fast in this IT world. If you have idea, you have to react fast and take your product into market* *quickly especially if there is another one."* Consequently DocMine conducted different brainstorming and mind mapping sessions within the team to discover the new direction of their startup.

Meanwhile, there has been significant change in the DocMine founding team. Before the pivot described above, one of the co-founders left the team and worked for Audi. While working on the new social media API idea and the working prototype of the new product was developed, the left co-founder requested to rejoin the team. At that time DocMine already hired one person due to this co-founder's leaving. However DocMine decided to take back their co-founder. The founder explained the rationale behind this decision: *"We decided to take him [back], not only because of performance, but because we knew him. So when you are working together, you know who is he, how he thinks, I think it's very important for startup to have perfect group dynamic."*

In August 2015, DocMine discovered from the feedback of their customers that their solution seemed to be more interesting for developers rather than the private markets and different companies they initially conceived. Even though at that time the new product was already functional with limited users, they shifted their focus to the developers, therefore pivoted in terms of customer segment.

Case 3: Hooka. Hooka provides a ticketing system for different events focusing on small companies in a user friendly way. The main focus is on small companies who cannot afford expensive solutions to organize events. Their initial service, however, was completely different: selling magnetic cubes. The business did not get much traction and they made a complete pivot in 2011.

It is followed by another pivot related to customer segment in the concept stage of the ticketing system idea. The initial focus of the idea was to develop a bidding system for bar and nightclub seats. The founder described the situation before pivoting: *"We started to do some research and found out that discos and clubs would not want a product. They manage things fine as it was."* Due to this negative feedback from the potential customers, they pivoted towards providing a ticket validation system for small companies who organize events.

At the same time, they also made significant change in their product from providing a simple SMS-based application towards developing a complete ticket validation system. This is an example of zoom-out (product) pivot.

A team pivot was made when the prototype did not work. The founder described: *"They (developers) use Google to search for the code. They are 'copy-paste' programmers. They are not skilled enough basically. They made a prototype that barely held together... I need to hire the professionals. We did not find any previous work useful and we scrapped everything."* As a result Hooka changed the whole development team, and hired new professionals who could develop.

Case 4: EasyLearning. EasyLearning is a game-based learning platform to be used in the classrooms (or in any other learning environment) in which a teacher asks a quiz and students answer using their mobile devices. Initially it started with developing quiz for Sony Phones or PC's, but later pivoted to developing quiz for iPhone and Android. The main factor causing this pivot was the emergence of the smartphone, as the co-founder explained: *"At that time, Android and iPhone was not available. It is a major change. So after maybe in 2008 or 2009 we got smartphones and tablets with proper web browsers then we could make a web-based client to make it a lot easier for development and we make the whole platform from scratch."*

Although this technology pivot solved their problem of involving a maximum number of students simultaneously, it had consequences. The co-founder recalled: *"The major issue is, due to the early web technology, due to slow, large latency, we did not implement web socket or something like that. The client was just pulling the server, the performance is horrible because client keep pulling the server all the time."*

In order to solve these issues, in the version 3.0, they threw away everything and started from scratch. The CEO explained: *"The main different is nice user interface, java based server with graphic engine. Web based client as before, but we have editor to create quiz which was not possible before."*

Table 3 provides a summary of the pivot types and triggering factors found in the four studied software startup companies.

Table 3. Summary of pivots in software startups

Case name	Pivot type	Triggering factor	At which product dev. stage pivot happened
Dicy	Customer need	Negative customer feedback	Functional product with limited users
DocMine	Complete	Failing to compete with competitors	Functional product with limited users
	Team	Founder's decision	Working prototype
	Customer segment	Negative customer feedback	Functional product with limited users
Hooka	Complete	Negative customer feedback	Functional product with limited users
	Customer segment	Negative customer feedback	Concept
	Product Zoom-out	Negative customer feedback	Concept
	Team	Missing team competence	Working prototype
Easy Learning	Technology	Emergence of smartphone	Working prototype
	Technology	Technology limitation	Functional product with high growth

5 Discussion

Software startups often lie in the soil of extreme uncertainty, and do not know their customers in advance. Although they are solving a problem, their initially perceived customers may not be interested in that problem. Startups try their ideas and learn from their failure, and pivot towards the real needs and right segments of the customers. As shown in the cases of Dicy, DocMine and Hooka, they all experienced customer need or segment pivots. Learning from their initial failures, they identified the right problems or customer segments and pivoted towards the new directions. In the cases of DocMine and Hooka, some pivots were so profound that almost all aspects of the startups were changed, product, targeted market and business model, only the original entrepreneurial team remained the same. We termed this type of pivot *complete pivot.* This is an addition to the pivot types listed in Table 1 [1].

Building an entrepreneurial team is one of the key challenges faced by many software startups [5]. As a response to this challenge, the entrepreneurial teams go through significant changes in team composition. This kind of pivot is termed as team pivot. It is another addition to Table 1. The change can be related to key members (e.g. co-founder) or having a new development team completely. Both Hooka and DocMine experienced team pivots. A lack of competency needed can be one factor causing software startup teams to pivot, as exhibited in the Hooka case. In contrast, DocMine evidences the team pivots as consequences of their founders' decision.

Our study also indicates the potential links between pivots. It happened in all but Dicy case that one pivot caused another pivot, therefore an evidence of what Terho et al. [3] call the "domino" effect. For example, after Hooka decided to make customer segment pivot, they soon realized that their original solution was only a feature of a much larger solution and therefore performed a product zoom-out pivot. Future studies need to be conducted in order to investigate the effect of different types of pivots, and the relationship among them.

The validity threats of our study are hereby discussed. One validity threat is related to the generalizability of the results. As our study is exploratory in nature, qualitative case study is a suitable approach to understand how software startups pivot in real world. More case studies and further quantitative studies need to be conducted e.g. survey, in order to make the result more generalizable. Another validity threat is related to the interviewees and their knowledge about their startups' history. It is mitigated to a large extent by interviewing the founders who generally have the best knowledge of their startup processes.

6 Conclusions

Software startups are developing cutting-edge software products significantly contributing to the world economy. However, in order to achieve success, most of the software startups need to learn and pivot continuously. This paper provides a deeper contextual understanding of how software startups pivot, employing a multiple qualitative case study approach.

The findings of the study show that software startups make different pivots in early product development stages. Customer segment and technology pivots are common. The pivots can be triggered by different factors. Negative feedback from customers is the major factor causing pivots.

We call for further investigation on the consequences and relationship among different pivots. Further quantitative studies (e.g. survey) need to be conducted to obtain quantitative validation and to generalize the results.

Acknowledgement. We are thankful to Pertti Seppänen from University of Oulu, Finland for his help and support in conducting this study.

References

1. Ries, E.: The Lean Startup: How Today's Entrepreneurs Use Continuous Innovation to Create Radically Successful Businesses. Crown Business, New York (2011)
2. Giardino, C., Wang, X., Abrahamsson, P.: Why early-stage software startups fail: a behavioral framework. In: Lassenius, C., Smolander, K. (eds.) ICSOB 2014. LNBIP, vol. 182, pp. 27–41. Springer, Heidelberg (2014)
3. Terho, H., Suonsyrjä, S., Karisalo, A., Mikkonen, T.: Ways to cross the rubicon: pivoting in software startups. In: Abrahamsson, P., Corral, L., Oivo, M., Russo, B. (eds.) PROFES 2015. LNCS, vol. 9459, pp. 555–568. Springer, Heidelberg (2015). doi:10.1007/978-3-319-26844-6_41
4. Van der Van, J.S., Bosch, J.: Pivots and architectural decisions: two sides of the same medal? What architecture research and lean startup can learn from each other. In: Proceedings of Eight International Conference on Software Engineering Advances (ICSEA 2013), Venice, Italy, pp. 310–317 (2013)
5. Giardino, C., Bajwa, S.S., Wang, X., Abrahamsson, P.: Key challenges in early-stage software startups. In: Lassenius, C., Dingsøyr, T., Paasivaara, M., Abásolo, M.J. (eds.) XP 2015. LNBIP, vol. 212, pp. 52–63. Springer, Heidelberg (2015). doi:10.1007/978-3-319-18612-2_5
6. Blank, S.: The Four Steps to the Epiphany, 1st edn. CafePress, San Mateo (2005)
7. Nazar, J.: 14 Fanous business pivots (2013). http://www.forbes.com/sites/jasonnazar/2013/10/08/14famous-business-pivots/. Accessed on 03 Feb 2016
8. Carlson, N.: The real history of Twitter. Business Insider (2011). http://businessinsider.com/how-twitter-was-founded-2011-4/. Accessed on 03 Feb 2016
9. Bosch, J., Holmström Olsson, H., Björk, J., Ljungblad, J.: The Early stage software startup development model: a framework for operationalizing lean principles in software startups. In: Fitzgerald, B., Conboy, K., Power, K., Valerdi, R., Morgan, L., Stol, K.-J. (eds.) LESS 2013. LNBIP, vol. 167, pp. 1–15. Springer, Heidelberg (2013)
10. Nguyen-Duc, A., Seppänen, P., Abrahamsson, P.: Hunter-gatherer cycle: a conceptual model of the evolution of software startups. In: Proceedings of the 2015 International Conference on Software and System Process (ICSSP 2015), NY, USA, pp. 199–203 (2015)
11. Yin, R.: Case Study Research: Design and Methods. SAGE Publications, Thousand Oaks (2003)

Mobile Gamification Principles Applied to Social Engagement

Short Paper of Industry Experience

Ethan Hadar(✉)

Communities Informatics, Zefat Academic College, Zefat, Israel
ethan.hadar@gmail.com

Abstract. Gamification in consumer mobile applications involves unique usability interaction and gestures, environmental setting, and consumers' short attention span. In addition, privacy concerns introduce constraints to the gamified social activities particularly due to usage of social sharing. This paper presents mobile gamification principles applied at GAMIFO PaaS, a gamification-based social engagement cloud platform, and suggests requirements for constructing a flexible gamification toolset tuned for mobile applications. A case study is discussed with regard to the impact of location detection, Gyro and alerting, as well as gamification adjustment for mobile setting, such as the separation of allocated and redeemed events and timing of consumers' attention. During the field experiments over 40 marketing campaigns were investigated, in which sales conversion ratio varied from 5 % to 50 %.

Keywords: Gamification · Social engagement · Mobile application

1 Introduction

Gamification in the business context is considered as applying games methods to non-game setting in order to increase users engagement and motivate actions [2]. Many software business applications such as Support, Sales, and HR management tools, utilize incentives and rewards as part of their challenge to engage and incentivize employees to increase their productivity [4, 7, 10]. In the consumer and social networks space, gamification supports individuals' activities such as recognition of a contributor in Trip Advisor [1], or expectation setting for task completion in LinkedIn. Some systems also implement team gamification principles that incentivize collaboration or competition amongst several users [9].

In the consumer mobile applications domain additional challenges are introduced, due to unique usability interaction and gestures, environmental setting, and consumers' short attention span [5, 14, 15]. Retina size and information overload limit complex engagement scenarios. Usage of text and voice communication, alongside sensors of location and motion, enrich the mobile device usability and situational awareness, thus can contribute to social engagement opportunities [5].

Privacy risks and their effect on gamified social activities are intensified particularly due to usage of the social sharing capabilities of the mobile operation system [8, 11].

A. Maglyas and A.-L. Lamprecht (Eds.): ICSOB 2016, LNBIP 240, pp. 177–183, 2016.
DOI: 10.1007/978-3-319-40515-5_15

The ease of creating apps that receive and transmit data via social sharing may damage the effect of the intended social engagement acceptance of the application by exposing users to privacy risks. Developers should carefully control the format, timing, and content of the sharing action, adjusting the communication to the right social network channel.

In this paper we present mobile gamification principles applied in GAMIFO PaaS, a gamification-based social engagement platform, and propose a set of requirements for constructing a flexible gamification toolset tuned for mobile applications. We pay particular attention to privacy concerns in the context of social sharing and peer collaborations at the focal point of the business design. An industrial case study addressing the defined set of requirements is described and discussed.

2 Gamification Requirements for Mobile Social Engagement

The goals of some of the mobile applications business owners include monetization of the users community with targeted advertisements [6], such as the Facebook model, or improving business process conversion stages towards a business goal, such as the Amazon e-commerce model [12]. Monetization improvement is based on increasing the number of active users and multiplying the conversion ratio with a larger set of users, thus generating more user traffic towards the promoted website. Conversion rate increase technologies are tuned to maximize the probability of a single user to complete the process steps and engage with additional business processes [12, 13].

Targeting individuals [12] can be enhanced by a social proactive engagement that addresses the bi-directional influence of peers for improving cohort ratio of a business process [3, 14]. Trusted peers' passive recommendations or active pressure for performing an action have proved to be valuable in retail [3]. Common examples for such activities are recommendation sections in Hospitality or e-commerce, or e-mail automating for incentivizing and rewarding quality referrals [13].

Yet, incentivizing quality prospects requires that the influencer would be comfortable with the content and selected channel, such as e-mail, WhatsApp, Facebook, texting, and other social sharing and invite methods [8, 14].

Considering the factors and background presented above, and based on our experience, we recommend that a mobile application gamification technology should provide:

- **Adjustable content according to social channel capability**. Users expect readymade content, yet that is adjustable for communicating with a referred party. The readymade content should be adjustable to the social media channel via the social sharing capability of the mobile apps. Examples are text message length adjustment as required by Twitter, image resolution as limited by WhatsApp, and content automated imaged as required by Facebook.
- **Variable reward and social connectivity notification capability**. The assigned reward needs to be in proportion with the business value and divided between the influencer and the target referred lead. In addition, the allocated reward budget may be distributed not only between these parties, but also with consideration of the

process stages. Incentives may be allocated when commencing the engagement process, during and after the business goal is achieved by each party. Consider purchasing an item in an e-commerce system. The first user may purchase an item, and then influence another user. Upon providing a lead information to the e-commerce site, the influencer may receive a reward. When the influenced party accepts the invitation to purchase, the influencer may receive another reward. When the influenced party purchases the goods, the influencer may receive yet additional reward. The same stages and rewards may apply to the influenced party upon opening the influencer message, and when conducting the purchase. In order to expedite the success probability of the supporting referral system, a mobile application can propose readymade content, adjusted and tuned to the most likely to be used social network channel for influencing the prospect lead. In addition, the action should be accompanied by a gamified value of the reward according to the business value, business step and likelihood of success.

- **Rewards allocation, flexible timing and non-stable mobile network connectivity**. Reward allocation can occur immediately upon an engagement action by an influencer, or following the completion of the task by an influenced party. An example may be receiving a cash reward for each referred customer, whether the customer has purchased the goods or not, or per a successful purchase of the referred party. Reward allocation can be conducted directly via the mobile application rich client, assuring rapid response for improved user experience, as it does not require network connectivity. However, reward allocation following a completion of a requested task requires server-side follow-up of the business outcome. Consequently, a non-completed activity should trigger a reminder to the influencer to re-connect with the influenced party in order to ensure business process progress and completion. Such reconnection requires additional reward allocation and incentives. Namely, the rewards' structure can be a monolithic one, or a breadcrumb gradual incentive leading to task completion.
- **Rewards redeeming management with gamified push-notification**. Allocation and redeeming of rewards are different. Allocation manages the potential usage of rewards and the business future commitment. Redeeming is the substitution of the allocated rewards voucher or token with goods, funds, or other business value transactions as defined by the business and its consumer, impacting inventory and profit. Businesses consider allocation of rewards as a future debt and business exposure. Allocated rewards that were not redeemed should decrease risks and obligations. Examples are expired loyally club points for aviation companies, particularly points that should have been transferred to a third party, such as done by Star Alliance travel affiliation. In mobile application design, adding a timer and countdown to an allocated reward, and informing its status to the user by a push-notification service, will assist in controlling such risks.
- **Reward usage reminder using geo-location.** In addition to the timer expiration of a reward, regular geo-location based services [13] can inform a user on an unredeemed reward that is relevant to the transient location. Once allocated, a reward can be self-aware of the physical environment and according to geo-location proximity, trigger a notification to the user. Proactive notifications can increase consumers' traffic to physical stores, without spamming since the contextual

opportunity of a geographic proximity will be considered more appealing. Redeeming fulfillment of an allocated reward is meant to increase customer satisfaction. Just consider how many times you forgot to use a coupon that you placed in your physical or digital wallet.

- **Geo and Gyro mobile engagement capability**. Usage of idle business time may increase the probability for a user to engage and influence others. Geo location and Gyro activity detection can indicate if a user is riding a train, or at home, sitting on a couch. Mobile device sensors and applied analytics can support the detection of the user situational condition. The mobile application can notify the user of an option to influence others or conduct a task when the user's attention is more focused and relevant [11]. The timing of receiving a notification message is crucial for the probability of reply according to the user attention span. As such, profiling the consumer behavior and correlating it with location and activity of the mobile device, will increase the probability of conversion or task completion.

3 The Case Study

Gamifo created a set of gamification technologies that employed all the above principles and more. The gamification purpose was to support the promotion of hospitality, restaurants, clothing and other retail small and medium businesses products and services, while detecting micro-influencers. The technology set was comprised of a cloud platform, NetSales, and a consumer mobile application, TaPrize (Fig. 1).

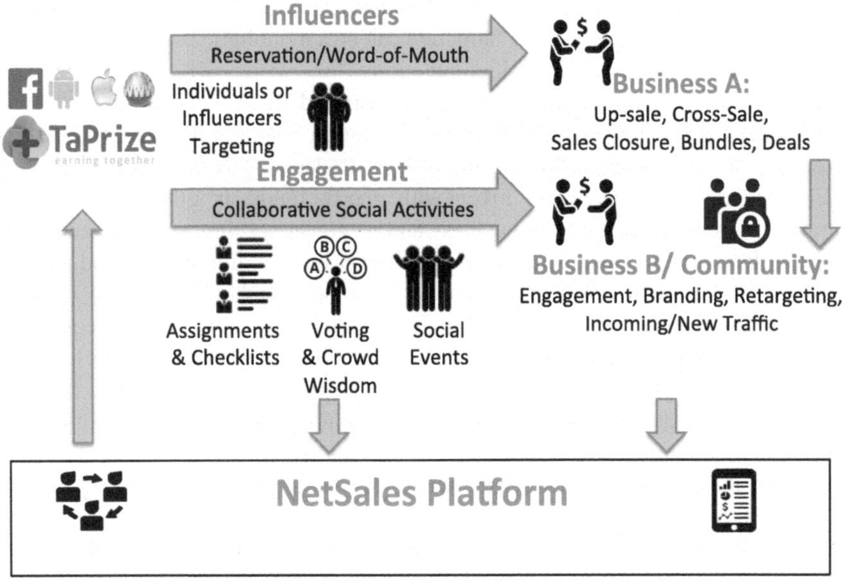

Fig. 1. A case study that exemplifies a gamified marketing campaign and social engagement technology, implemented at Gamifo LTD.

NetSales enables retailers to configure gamification parameters for their marketing campaigns. More than 4300 different types of social gamified activities can be constructed by the NetSales platform, such as managing joint assignments, voting on favorite items or product brand, answering questionnaires for contributing crowd wisdom, setting an auction, and scheduling appointments. NetSales enabled rapid creation of social engagement activities to support marketing campaigns over multiple consumers' social and mobile outlets.

TaPrize enables consumers to be exposed to campaigns, engage with other users, and manage their personal allocated and redeemed rewards. TaPrize Social Engagement mobile application is a word-of-mouth technology that assists people to collaborate around their social activities. Although constructed for mobile consumption primarily, the HTML5-based application can also be used as embedded technology within Facebook pages, brand websites and e-commerce sites, while maintaining the mobile usability aspects.

The digital marketing manager can create increasing customer engagement with the brand or products, and improve timing of targeted advertisements while adjusting the social engagement activities to their business. In the case study, more than 40 marketing campaigns were investigated. Conversion rates varied from 5 % to 50 %. In some cases, when the engagement process and incentives were changed for combining both pre and post rewards for a certain business process, the conversion rate increased from 8 % to 32 % in average. Collaboration between businesses enabled allocation of rewards by one business and redeeming by another, redirecting consumers' traffic between the businesses. An example is purchasing a vacation at a hotel and receiving a free ticket to a tourist attraction that is valid for a year after the vacation. NetSales ensures transactions integrity by funding a losing product, which is the incentive reward such as the free ticket above, or commission for increasing sale of another product (up-sale).

Figure 1 depicts the conceptual business flow of the technology as follows:

- **Campaign Curation**. Curated marketing campaigns in performed on NetSales, controlling multiple parameters. An example is controlling participant number in a purchasing group campaign. In case of multiple participants, incentive could be allocated monolithically or proportional to the participants' number as done with prorated purchasing groups. Another example is the reward timing as detailed above, ranging from a first exposure event, through the breadcrumb actions while preforming a word-of-mouth task. A third example is privacy sensitivity of proactive reminders by push-notification technology. Over-usage may cause consumers to block the retailer, whereas under-usage may reduce conversation rates.
- **Campaign Publishing**. The curated campaign is published to the consumers via the TaPrize technology set on their mobile applications and on the retailer Facebook page or e-commerce site, yet while maintaining a mobile application UI layout for usability. Namely, ensuring inception towards mobile application even when interacted on a desktop screen.
- **Social Engagement Adjustments of Word-of-Mouth**. Consumers can interact with a proposed business deal, receive allocated rewards, delegate to a friend, influence a friend and propagate the campaign with the social sharing options of a

mobile app and redeem a reward. Content adjustment to the social channel capabilities, method of redeeming and verification is automatically adjusted.
- **Collaborative Social Activities**. Consumers can also interact with their friends on a non-commercial setting such as forming groups for going out to dinner or a movie. Such social bonding activities, which are similar to WhatsApp groups, are rewarded with discounts from the sponsoring retailer. Accordingly, the retailer can improve the business branding and detect future retargeting audience.
- **Sales Increase**. New users receive notification and incentives from their trusted friends and family, namely, their tribal-influencers. Retailers can leverage such incoming traffic for up-sale, cross-sale, and expedite sales' closure. Notifications on allocated yet not redeemed rewards are monitored for increasing conversion rate, as well as proximity sensitivity for increasing the probability of an opportunistic sale.
- **Influencers Analytics**. Extracted from the influencers' invitation flow and type of content, as well as the mobile device's Geo-Location during interactions, the system can deduce what topics are relevant to which user based on their preferences and attention span.

4 Conclusions

This paper discussed an industrial experience for enhancing gamification by using mobile devices' unique properties. In particular, location detection services (GPS, Wi-Fi and cellular grid), movement services (Gyro), and alerting services (push-notification).

In addition, while combining these mobile services into a gamified business process, the fundamentals gamified parameters where also adjusted, such as:

- Separation of allocated and redeemed events.
- Motivating individuals to complete tasks for their own benefit, versus motivating influencers to engage in a word-of-mouth activity.
- Timing of consumers' attention to a gamified marketing campaign and rewards based on location and activity.
- Increasing users' confidence levels with the gamified business process, based on a first exposure created by a trusted tribal-influencer.

A case study of a startup company called Gamifo was examined, and relevant mobile attributes where discussed according to their implementation in Gamifo's cloud platform-as-a-service and a mobile hybrid application. The business results of employing the requirements with the above technology yielded better conversion rates. A future direction of the technology is to create a self-service gamification platform, in which the most successful conversion campaigns would be pre-packaged for ease of use and scalability.

References

1. Anderson, A., Huttenlocher, D., Kleinberg, J., Leskovec, J.: Steering user behavior with badges. In: Proceedings of the 22nd International Conference on World Wide Web, Rio de Janeiro, Brazil, pp. 95–106 (2013)

2. Bittner, J.V., Shipper, J.: Motivational effects and age differences of gamification in product advertising. J. Consum. Market. **31**(5), 391–400 (2014)
3. Blohm, I., Leimeister, J.M.: Gamification. Bus. Inf. Syst. Eng. **5**(4), 275–278 (2013)
4. Bohyun, K.: Understanding Gamification. ALA TechSource, Chicago (2015). Library Technology Reports, vol. 51(2)
5. Crowley, D.N., Breslin, J.G., Corcoran, P., Young, K.: Gamification of citizen sensing through mobile social reporting. In: IEEE International Games Innovation Conference (IGIC), pp. 1–5 (2012)
6. Fields, T.: Mobile & Social Game Design: Monetization Methods and Mechanics. CRC Press, Boca Raton (2014)
7. Gamification Market by Deployment, Application, Size: Worldwide Market Forecasts and Analysis for 2013–2018, Markets and Markets (2015). http://www.marketsandmarkets.com/PressReleases/gamification.asp
8. Hamari, J., Koivisto, J.: 'Working out for likes': an empirical study on social influence in exercise gamification. Comput. Hum. Behav. **50**, 333–347 (2015)
9. Hamari, J., Koivisto, J., Sarsh, H.: Does gamification work? A literature review of empirical studies on gamification. In: 47th Hawaii International Conference on System Sciences, pp. 6–9. IEEE, Hawaii, January 2014
10. Herzig, P., Ameling, M., Schill, A.: A generic platform for enterprise gamification. In: Joint Working IEEE/IFIP Conference on Software Architecture (WICSA) and European Conference on Software Architecture (ECSA), 20 August 2012, pp. 219–223. IEEE (2012)
11. Keller, J.M.: Using the ARCS motivational process in computer-based instruction and distance education. New Dir. Teach. Learn. **78**, 37–47 (1999)
12. Saleh, K., Shukairy, A.: Conversion Optimization: The Art and Science of Converting Prospects to Customers. O'Reilly Media Inc., Sebastopol (2010)
13. Sales Force.com.: 2015 State of Marketing, SalesForce Marketing Cloud (2015). https://secure.sfdcstatic.com/assets/pdf/datasheets/mc_2015stateofmarketing.pdf
14. Van Der Heijden, H., Verhhagen, T., Creemers, M.: Understanding online purchase intentions: contributions from technology and trust perspectives. Eur. J. Inf. Syst. **12**(1), 41–48 (2003)
15. Zichermann, G., Cunningham, C.: Gamification by Design: Implementing Game Mechanics in Web and Mobile Apps. O'Reilly Media, Sebastopol (2011)

Author Index

The manufacturer's authorised representative in the EU is Springer Nature Customer Service Centre GmbH, Europaplatz 3, 69115 Heidelberg, Germany. If you have any concerns regarding our products, please contact ProductSafety@springernature.com

Printed and bound by CPI Group (UK) Ltd, Croydon, CR0 4YY
30/09/2026
02225653-0018